Building Arduino Projects for the Internet of Things: Experiments with Real-World Applications

Adeel Javed
Lake Zurich, Illinois, USA

ISBN-13 (pbk): 978-1-4842-1939-3   ISBN-13 (electronic): 978-1-4842-1940-9
DOI 10.1007/978-1-4842-1940-9

Library of Congress Control Number: 2016943433

Managing Director: Welmoed Spahr
Lead Editor: Jonathan Gennick
Development Editor: James Markham
Technical Reviewer: Jeff Tang
Editorial Board: Steve Anglin, Pramila Balen, Louise Corrigan, James DeWolf,
    Jonathan Gennick, Robert Hutchinson, Celestin Suresh John, Nikhil Karkal,
    James Markham, Susan McDermott, Matthew Moodie, Douglas Pundick,
    Ben Renow-Clarke, Gwenan Spearing
Coordinating Editor: Melissa Maldonado
Copy Editor: Kezia Endsley
Compositor: SPi Global
Indexer: SPi Global
Artist: SPi Global

Distributed to the book trade worldwide by Springer Science+Business Media New York, 233 Spring Street, 6th Floor, New York, NY 10013. Phone 1-800-SPRINGER, fax (201) 348-4505, e-mail orders-ny@springer-sbm.com, or visit www.springer.com. Apress Media, LLC is a California LLC and the sole member (owner) is Springer Science + Business Media Finance Inc (SSBM Finance Inc). SSBM Finance Inc is a **Delaware** corporation.

For information on translations, please e-mail rights@apress.com, or visit www.apress.com.

Apress and friends of ED books may be purchased in bulk for academic, corporate, or promotional use. eBook versions and licenses are also available for most titles. For more information, reference our Special Bulk Sales–eBook Licensing web page at www.apress.com/bulk-sales.

Any source code or other supplementary materials referenced by the author in this text is available to readers at www.apress.com. For detailed information about how to locate your book's source code, go to www.apress.com/source-code/.

Printed on acid-free paper

To my wife Naila, for supporting me throughout the process.

Contents at a Glance

Contents

About the Author

Adeel Javed is a Solutions Architect with over 11 years of software development, design, and systems-architect experience in enterprise-wide business process management (BPM) and service-oriented architecture (SOA) solutions. He helps organizations from diverse global-industry domains with process improvements and implementation initiatives. Adeel Javed regularly writes about BPM, SOA, IoT, cloud, and all things process-oriented on his blog, ProcessRamblings.com, as well as for other major industry sites such as BPMLeader.com, BPTrends.com, and IBM developerWorks.

In his time off, Adeel is an avid—and process-driven—Arduino enthusiast and device developer.

About the Technical Reviewer

Jeff Tang worked on enterprise and web app development for many years before reinventing himself to focus on building great iOS and Android apps. He had Apple-featured, top-selling iOS apps with millions of users and was recognized by Google as a Top Android Market Developer. He's the author of the *Beginning Google Glass Development* book published by Apress in 2014. His current passion is in IoT and AI and he actually received his master's degree in AI.

Preface

Analysts are forecasting that by the year 2020 there will be more than 50 billion connected things (devices) and the total revenue from the Internet of things (IoT) will easily surpass $1.5 trillion.

The numbers look phenomenal, but what exactly is IoT? Is it simply things connected to the Internet? Why do connected things matter?

IoT is much more than things connected to the Internet. IoT is about making dumb things smarter by giving them the ability to sense, communicate, and respond. We have five senses—we can see, hear, taste, smell, and touch. Similarly if you add these sensors to things they can do the same as well. For example, using a camera things can see, using a sound detector things can hear, and using a speaker things can talk. There are so many other sensors that things can use to do so much more than us. By connecting these things to the Internet, they can communicate with us, with other things, and the next frontier where they can use artificial intelligence to think as well. There are numerous applications of IoT, but here are a couple of examples to further understand how IoT is being used to improve our lives:

- A wristband with the ability to monitor your vitals. If it finds anything out of the ordinary, it can alert you and your doctor immediately.

- A security system that monitors the premises of your house for any intrusions and alerts you and any security agencies.

What This Book Covers

This book is based on my personal experience of getting started with IoT. It is divided into two logical sections. The first one teaches the basics of building IoT applications and the second section follows a project-based approach. At the end of each chapter you will have a working prototype of an IoT application.

Part 1: Building Blocks

Chapters 1-3 cover the building blocks of IoT:

- Chapter 1, "Arduino Basics," introduces the Arduino prototyping platform, which is used throughout the book.

- Chapter 2, "Internet Connectivity," discusses the different options available for connecting things to the Internet.

- Chapter 3, "Communication Protocols," teaches you what communication protocols are and which ones are available for IoT.

Part 2: Prototypes

Chapters 4-12 use the information covered in Part 1 to build prototypes of IoT applications.

- Chapter 4, "Complex Flows: Node-RED," introduces Node-RED, which is a visual designer that helps reduce the amount of code required for IoT applications.

- Chapter 5, "IoT Patterns: Realtime Clients," talks about components required for building IoT applications that provide data to users in real time and shows you how to build an intrusion detection system as an example.

- Chapter 6, "IoT Patterns: Remote Control," discusses components of IoT applications that can remotely control things, such as a lighting control system.

- Chapter 7, "IoT Patterns: On-Demand Clients," shows you different components involved in building an on-demand IoT application. You'll build a smarter parking system in this chapter.

- Chapter 8, "IoT Patterns: Web Apps," teaches you scenarios where web clients are preferred and uses a temperature monitoring system as an example.

- Chapter 9, "IoT Patterns: Location-Aware Devices," discusses importance of location-aware devices. You'll develop a livestock tracking system as an example.

- Chapter 10, "IoT Patterns: Machine to Human," talks about scenarios where human response is needed; you'll build a waste management system as an example.

- Chapter 11, "IoT Patterns: Machine to Machine," discusses a pattern of IoT that is going to be very popular as things get smarter. The example is an energy conservation system.

- Chapter 12, "IoT Platforms," wraps up the book by introducing you to IoT platforms that help expedite entry into IoT. The example in this chapter builds a soil moisture control system.

What You Need for This Book

IoT applications require hardware and software and can span different technologies, so this book uses quite a few technologies. However, we have tried to keep them as simple and minimal as possible.

Required Hardware

Read the complete instructions provided in each chapter because, based on your device, you may or may not need additional components.

- Arduino Uno or Arduino Yún
- Ethernet shield
- WiFi (wireless) shield
- Breadboard
- Jumper cables (male-male, male-female)
- Light sensor
- Motion sensor (HC-SR501)
- LED
- 220Ω resistor
- Proximity sensor (Ultrasonic Rangemeter HC-SR04)
- Temperature sensor (TMP36)
- GPS module (NEO6MV2)
- Soil moisture sensor

Software

- Arduino IDE
- Node-RED
- MQTT broker (book uses free and publicly available broker from Eclipse Foundation)
- Android Studio
- Xcode/Swift
- PHP server
- MySQL server
- Text editor
- Effektif BPM (cloud-based, free account required)
- Xively (cloud-based, free account required)
- Zapier (cloud-based, free account required)

To further help you, we have also created a web site at `http://codifythings.com` dedicated to the book. The web site contains variations and enhancements to prototypes developed in this book along with additional prototypes.

Who This Book Is For

This book is for hobbyists and professionals who want to enter the world of IoT.

The material in this book requires some prior knowledge of Arduino or similar devices and programming experience. We have used basic hardware components and provided step-by-step instructions for building circuits. We kept the code simple, readable, and minimal to help newbies understand concepts and develop useable prototypes. Throughout the book, the code is consistent and, wherever needed, is explained in detail.

PART 1

Building Blocks

CHAPTER 1

■ ■ ■

Arduino Basics

Arduino is an open-source platform that's composed of very simple and easy-to-use hardware and software. In a nutshell your Arduino can read sensor data and control components such as lights, motors, thermostats, and garage doors. It has mainly been developed for prototyping purposes, so it is a great fit for this IoT beginner's book.

Learning Objectives

At the end of this chapter, you will be able to:

- Use Arduino hardware

- Use the Arduino IDE

- Write, upload, and execute basic Arduino programs

Hardware Requirements

Arduino comes in various models (also known as *boards*). Each board has different specifications. If your board does not come built-in with the features you are looking for, then you always have an option to add a shield that supports required features. In the Arduino world, a shield is very similar to a board, but it only supports specific functionality such as the ability to connect to a WiFi network or the ability to control servo motors. A shield acts as an add-on; that is, it is physically attached to the top of an Arduino board. Once attached, the Arduino board becomes capable of handling shield features as well.

Figure 1-1 shows a diagram of Arduino Uno, while Figure 1-2 shows a diagram of an Ethernet shield.

Electronic supplementary material The online version of this chapter (doi:10.1007/978-1-4842-1940-9_1) contains supplementary material, which is available to authorized users.

© Adeel Javed 2016
A. Javed, *Building Arduino Projects for the Internet of Things*,
DOI 10.1007/978-1-4842-1940-9_1

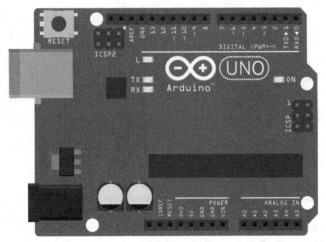

Figure 1-1. *Arduino Uno*

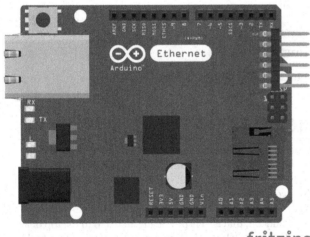

Figure 1-2. *Ethernet shield*

The following list summarizes some of the important parts of the board that have been used in projects throughout the book.

■ **Note**   Parts will vary based on the Arduino board you choose.

- **Digital pins:** In total there are 14 digital pins on Arduino Uno. Digital pins can be both INPUT and OUTPUT, but their state can only be HIGH or LOW. HIGH means there is current while LOW means no current. An example of digital pin usage is turning an LED light on or off. To turn it on, the digital pin should be set to HIGH and to turn it off the digital pin should be set to LOW.

- **Analog pins:** Arduino Uno supports six analog pins, A0 through A5. Unlike digital pins, the readings of analog pins can range from 0 to 1023. A good example of a sensor that provides analog readings is a soil moisture sensor. The range helps identify how much moisture is left in the soil.

- **USB connector:** A USB connector lets you connect Arduino to the computer, power the board, upload code, and receive logs on a serial monitor.

- **Battery power:** IoT applications that need to be placed in remote locations will need their own power source. You can use the battery power connector to power the board.

This book uses Arduino Uno for all projects. Arduino Uno is categorized as an entry-level board most suited for beginners. Even though the book uses Arduino Uno, you are not required to use it; you can choose any of the Arduino boards to complete projects in this book. Since this book is about the Internet of things, Internet connectivity is an important requirement. Whichever Arduino board you decide to use, just make sure that it supports Internet connectivity in some form. The Arduino board should either come with a built-in Internet connectivity option or you should have the required Internet connectivity shield.

■ **Note** Arduino Uno does not come with built-in Internet connectivity support, so in the book both Ethernet and WiFi shields have been used. On the other hand, a more advanced model of Arduino called *Yún* does support built-in Ethernet and WiFi connectivity. Chapter 2 discusses Internet connectivity in more detail.

Software Requirements

Arduino provides a C-like language for programming Arduino boards. You will be using the Arduino IDE for writing code and uploading it to an Arduino board. You can install the latest version of Arduino IDE from https://www.arduino.cc/en/Main/Software.

Once Arduino IDE has been installed on your machine, open it and, as shown in Figure 1-3, it will load with default code.

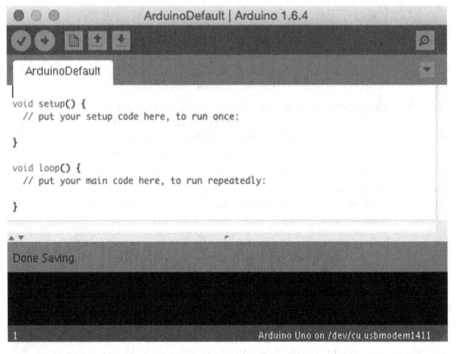

Figure 1-3. Default view of Arduino IDE

There are three components of Arduino IDE that are referenced in every chapter of this book.

- Toolbar
- Status window
- Serial Monitor window

Toolbar

The toolbar on top of the IDE, as shown in Figure 1-4, provides easy access to frequently used options.

Figure 1-4. Arduino IDE toolbar

- **Verify/Compile:** This is the first button from the left (the tick mark). Click this button to verify and compile your code for correctness. You can view the results in the Status window at the bottom.

- **Upload:** This is the second button from left (right-pointing arrow). If your Arduino board is connected to your machine that is running the Arduino IDE, this will upload the code on the Arduino board. You can view the deployment results in the Status window at the bottom.

- **New/Open/Save:** The next three buttons, as their names suggest, let you open a new code window, open an existing code file, or save the currently open code. Arduino code files have an *.ino extension.

- **Serial/Monitor:** The last button on the right lets you open the Serial Monitor window.

Status Window

When you verify the code or upload it to a board, the Status window shown in Figure 1-5 lists all the results. Any errors that occur during code verification or uploading will be shown in the Status window.

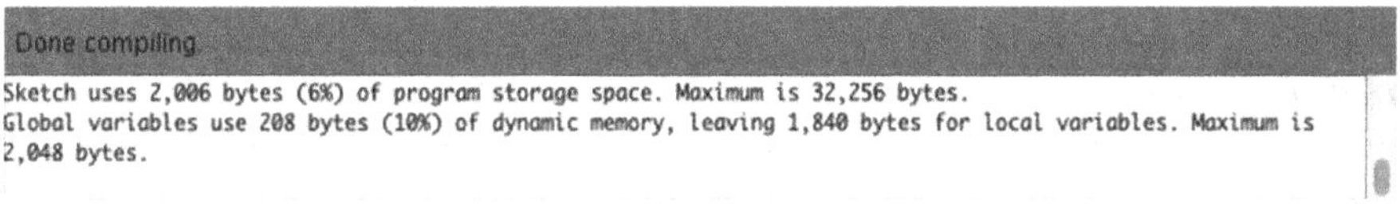

```
Done compiling.

Sketch uses 2,006 bytes (6%) of program storage space. Maximum is 32,256 bytes.
Global variables use 208 bytes (10%) of dynamic memory, leaving 1,840 bytes for local variables. Maximum is
2,048 bytes.
```

Figure 1-5. *Arduino IDE Status window*

Serial Monitor Window

The Serial Monitor window shown in Figure 1-6 prints all log messages generated by the Serial.print() and Serial.println() functions in the code. In order to print any messages on the Serial Monitor window, you first need to initialize the message in the code (discussed later).

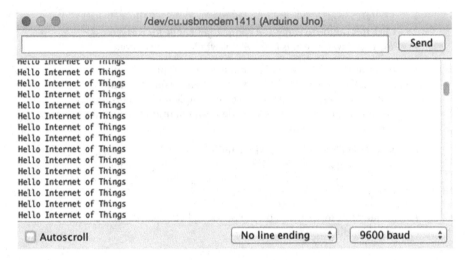

Figure 1-6. Log messages on the Serial Monitor window

Arduino Programming Language Reference

The Arduino programming language has quite a few constructs. However, this chapter provides the basics that have been used throughout the projects in this book; see Table 1-1.

Table 1-1. Language Reference

Code Construct	Description
int	Integer values, such as 123
float	Decimal values, such as 1.15
char[]	String values, such as "Arduino"
HIGH	Digital pin with current
LOW	Digital pin with no current
INPUT	Pin can only be read
OUTPUT	Pin can only be set
A0 – A7	Constants for analog pins; varies by board
0 – 13	Value for digital pins; varies by board
analogRead()	Returns analog pin value (0 – 1023)
analogWrite(...)	Sets analog pin value
digitalRead()	Returns digital pin value (HIGH or LOW)

(continued)

Table 1-1. (*continued*)

Code Construct	Description
digitalWrite(...)	Sets digital pin value (HIGH or LOW)
Serial.begin()	Initializes serial monitor
Serial.print()	Logs message on serial monitor
Serial.println()	Logs message on serial monitor with new line
delay(ms)	Adds a wait in processing
setup()	Standard Arduino function called once
loop()	Standard Arduino function called repeatedly
if	Checks for a true/false condition
if ... else	Checks for a true/false condition; if false goes to else
//	Single-line comment
/* */	Multiline comment
#define	Defines a constant
#include	Includes an external library

You can explore the complete language at https://www.arduino.cc/en/Reference. The Arduino IDE provides a very simple and clean interface to write code. Normally you would structure your code in three parts:

- **External libraries:** Includes all required libraries. A library is a fully developed and tested piece of code that you can include and use in your code. For instance, if you wanted to communicate over the Internet using an Ethernet connection, instead of writing all of that code from scratch, you could simply import and include the Ethernet library using #include <Ethernet.h>.

- **Constants and variables:** Defines all constants and variables that will be used to read and manipulate data. Constants do not change, so you can, for instance, use them for port numbers on the board. Variables can change, so they can be used for reading sensor data.

- **Functions:** Provides implementation of all custom and standard functions. A function encapsulates a specific functionality. It is recommended to put your code in functions, especially when you are looking to reuse that piece of code. Functions help avoid code duplication.

Listing 1-1 provides an example of code that is structured according to points discussed previously.

Listing 1-1. Recommended Code Structure

```
/*
 * External Libraries
 */

#include <SPI.h>

/*
 * Constants & Variables
 */

char message[] = "Hello Internet of Things"; // Single line comment

/*
 * Custom & Standard Functions
 */

void printMessage()
{
    Serial.println(message);
}

void setup()
{
  // Initialize serial port
  Serial.begin(9600);
}

void loop()
{
  printMessage();
  delay(5000);
}
```

Listing 1-1 consists of three functions. It has two standard Arduino functions, called setup() and loop(), which are automatically called by Arduino once the code is uploaded. They therefore must be present for the code to run. The third is a custom function called printMessage() that simply prints a message to the Serial Monitor window shown in Figure 1-6.

The setup() function is called only once. Initializations are done in this function including serial monitor initialization using code Serial.begin(9600). The loop() function, as the name suggests, runs in a continuous loop. Any post-initialization processing such as reading sensor data can be done in this function. The loop() function calls printMessage() function and then waits 5,000 milliseconds before repeating.

Arduino Code Execution

Start your Arduino IDE and either type the code provided in Listing 1-1 or download it from book's site and open it. Click on the Verify button to compile and check the code.

Next, using the USB cable that came with your Arduino, connect your Arduino to the computer that is running Arduino IDE.

Once Arduino is connected to your computer, as shown in Figure 1-7, click on Tools ➤ Board and select Arduino Uno (or whichever board you are using). This informs Arduino IDE about the board where the code will be uploaded.

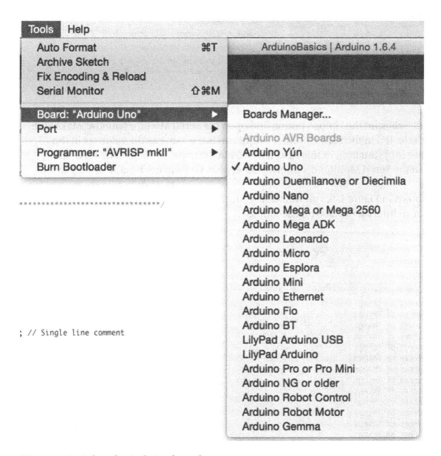

Figure 1-7. *Select the Arduino board*

You will also need to select what port to use for code upload. As shown in Figure 1-8 from Tools ➤ Port, select the USB port that connects Arduino to your computer.

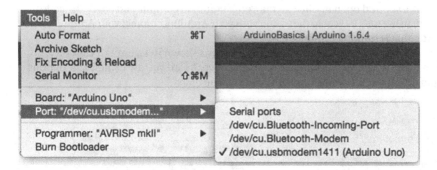

Figure 1-8. *Select the Arduino port*

Finally, click on the Upload button and open the Serial Monitor window. Make sure the value selected in the Serial Monitor dropdown is the same as the value set in the Serial.begin() function. In this case, it is 9600 in the code, so 9600 baud needs to be selected in the Serial Monitor dropdown. Otherwise, you will not be able to see the log messages.

As shown in Figure 1-9, you will start seeing log messages in the Serial Monitor window at an interval of 5,000 milliseconds.

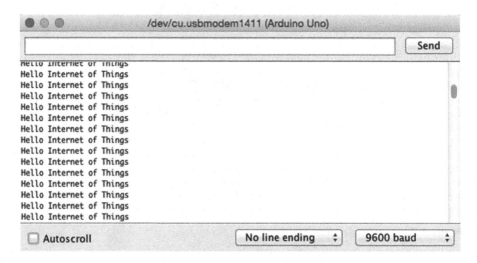

Figure 1-9. *Log messages from the code in the Serial Monitor window*

Summary

In this chapter you learned the basics of Arduino hardware and software. You also learned the common code constructs of the Arduino programming language, which will be used throughout this book.

This chapter in no way is a complete reference of Arduino; it only provides the basics required to complete all the projects in this book. To learn more about Arduino, visit the official web site at `https://www.arduino.cc`.

CHAPTER 2

■ ■ ■

Internet Connectivity

All IoT devices require a mechanism to send or receive data. There are numerous options available for connecting devices to the Internet, including wired and wireless options, Bluetooth, cellular networks, and many more. The option you choose depends on various factors, such as:

- Scale and size of the network where the application will run

- Amount of data that needs to be processed and transferred

- Physical location of the device

Table 2-1 lists some of the Internet connectivity options with an example of where they have been used.

Table 2-1. *Internet Connectivity Options for IoT Devices*

Option	Example
Wired (Ethernet)	Food storage temperature monitoring
Wireless (WiFi)	Soil moisture sensor
Bluetooth	Key tracker
Cellular data	Wildlife tracker
RFID (Radio Frequency Identification)	Inventory management

Learning Objectives

At the end of this chapter, you will be able to:

- Attach an Ethernet shield to Arduino and write Ethernet connectivity code

- Attach a WiFi shield to Arduino and write WiFi connectivity code

- Set up Arduino Yún to connect to WiFi

© Adeel Javed 2016
A. Javed, *Building Arduino Projects for the Internet of Things*,
DOI 10.1007/978-1-4842-1940-9_2

Arduino Uno Wired Connectivity (Ethernet)

In this section, you are going to attach an Ethernet shield to your Arduino Uno and write code to connect it to the Internet using Ethernet.

■ **Note** If you are using a model of Arduino that comes with built-in Ethernet capabilities such as Arduino Yún, then you do not need a separate Ethernet shield. Arduino Yún Internet connectivity setup is discussed later in this chapter.

Hardware Required

Figure 2-1 provides a list of all hardware components required for connecting Arduino Uno to the Internet using an Ethernet shield.

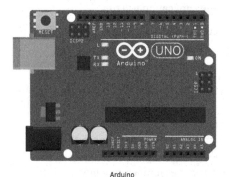
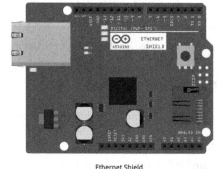

Arduino   Ethernet Shield

fritzing

Figure 2-1. *Hardware required for wired Internet connectivity*

Software Required

In order to write the Internet connectivity code, you need following software:

- Arduino IDE 1.6.4 or later version

Circuit

In this section, you are going to build the circuit required for Internet connectivity using Ethernet.

1. Make sure your Arduino is not connected to a power source, such as a computer via USB or a battery.

2.   Attach the Ethernet shield to the top of Arduino. All the pins
      should align.

3.   Connect an Ethernet cable from Arduino to the LAN (Local
      Area Network) port of your router. The router should already
      be connected to the Internet.

Once the Ethernet shield has been attached to Arduino, it should look similar to
Figure 2-2.

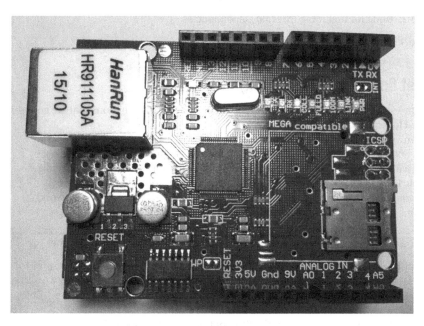

Figure 2-2. *Ethernet shield attached to the top of Arduino Uno*

Code (Arduino)

Now that your Arduino is physically connected to Ethernet, you are going to write the
code that will allow your Arduino to send and receive data over the Internet.

Start Arduino IDE and type the code provided here or download it from the book's
site and open it. All the code goes into a single source file (*.ino), but in order to make it
easy to understand and reuse, it is divided into three sections.

- External libraries

- Internet connectivity (Ethernet)

- Standard functions

External Libraries

First section of the code as provided in Listing 2-1 includes all external libraries required to run the code. Since you are connecting to the Internet using Ethernet, the main dependency of code is on <Ethernet.h>. Your Arduino IDE should already have the Ethernet library installed, but for any reason it is missing, you can download it from:

- <Ethernet.h>: https://github.com/arduino/Arduino/tree/master/libraries/Ethernet

Listing 2-1. Code for Including External Dependencies

```
#include <Ethernet.h>
```

Internet Connectivity (Ethernet)

The second section of the code defines variables, constants, and functions that are going to be used for connecting to the Internet.

As provided in Listing 2-2, first you need to define the MAC address in the mac[] variable. For newer Ethernet shields, the MAC address might be printed on a sticker.

You will also need to set a static IP address of Arduino for cases where it fails to get a dynamic IP from DHCP (Dynamic Host Configuration Protocol). Make sure the IP address you use is free, i.e., not currently in use by some other device on the network.

Define the EthernetClient variable that will be used for connectivity.

Listing 2-2. Constants and Variables for Connecting to the Internet Using Ethernet

```
byte mac[] = { 0xDE, 0xAD, 0xBE, 0xEF, 0xFE, 0xED };
IPAddress staticIP(10, 0, 0, 20);
EthernetClient client;
```

Listing 2-3 provides the code for the Ethernet connectivity setup. The connectToInternet() function first attempts to connect to Ethernet with DHCP. If DHCP fails to assign a dynamic IP address to Arduino, it will attempt connection to Ethernet with the static IP you defined.

Listing 2-3. Code for Connecting to the Internet Using Ethernet

```
void connectToInternet()
{
  // Attempt to connect to Ethernet with DHCP
  if (Ethernet.begin(mac) == 0)
  {
    Serial.print("[ERROR] Failed to Configure Ethernet using DHCP");
```

```
  // DHCP failed, attempt to connect to Ethernet with static IP
  Ethernet.begin(mac, staticIP);
}

// Delay to let Ethernet shield initialize

delay(1000);

// Connection successful
Serial.println("[INFO] Connection Successful");
Serial.print("");
printConnectionInformation();
Serial.println("------------------------------------------------");
Serial.println("");
}
```

Once Arduino has successfully connected to the Internet, the Ethernet printConnectionInformation() function, provided in Listing 2-4, is called. This function prints connection information such as IP address, subnet mask, gateway, and DNS to the Serial Monitor window.

Listing 2-4. Function to Display Connection Information

```
void printConnectionInformation()
{
  // Print Connection Information
  Serial.print("[INFO] IP Address: ");
  Serial.println(Ethernet.localIP());
  Serial.print("[INFO] Subnet Mask: ");
  Serial.println(Ethernet.subnetMask());
  Serial.print("[INFO] Gateway: ");
  Serial.println(Ethernet.gatewayIP());
  Serial.print("[INFO] DNS: ");
  Serial.println(Ethernet.dnsServerIP());
}
```

Standard Functions

Finally, the code in this third and last section is provided in Listing 2-5. It implements Arduino's standard setup() and loop() functions. For this project, you are simply connecting Arduino to the Internet with no processing thereafter, so the loop() function will remain empty.

Listing 2-5. Code for Standard Arduino Functions

```
void setup()
{
  // Initialize serial port
  Serial.begin(9600);

  // Connect Arduino to internet
  connectToInternet();
}

void loop()
{
  // Do nothing
}
```

Your Arduino code is complete.

Final Product

To test the application, verify and upload the code to Arduino as discussed in Chapter 1. Once the code has been uploaded, open the Serial Monitor window. You will start seeing log messages as shown in Figure 2-3.

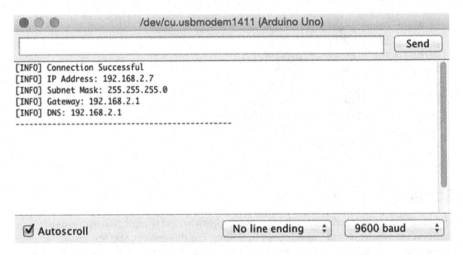

Figure 2-3. Log messages from Arduino

Arduino Uno Wireless Connectivity (WiFi)

In this section, you are going to attach a Wireless shield to your Arduino Uno and write code to connect it to the Internet using WiFi.

■ **Note** If you are using a model of Arduino that comes with built-in wireless capabilities such as Arduino Yún, then you do not need a separate Wireless shield. Arduino Yún Internet connectivity setup is discussed later in this chapter.

Hardware Required

Figure 2-4 provides a list of all hardware components required for connecting Arduino Uno to the Internet using a Wireless shield.

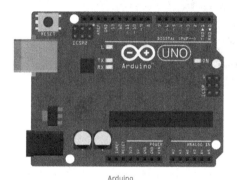
Arduino

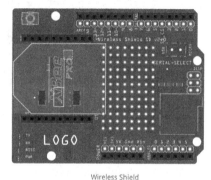
Wireless Shield

fritzing

Figure 2-4. *Hardware required for wireless Internet connectivity*

Software Required

In order to write the Internet connectivity code, you will need following software:

- Arduino IDE 1.6.4 or later version

Circuit

In this section you are going to build the circuit required for Internet connectivity using WiFi.

1. Make sure your Arduino is not connected to a power source, such as a computer via USB or a battery.

2. Attach the WiFi shield (a.k.a., wireless shield) to the top of your Arduino. All the pins should align.

21

Once the wireless shield has been attached to Arduino, it should look similar to Figure 2-5.

Figure 2-5. *WiFi shield attached to the top of Arduino Uno*

Code (Arduino)

Now that your Arduino is capable of connecting to a wireless network, you are going to write the code that will allow your Arduino to send and receive data over the Internet.

Start your Arduino IDE and type the following code or download it from book's site and open it. All the code goes into a single source file (`*.ino`), but in order to make it easy to understand and reuse, it has been divided into three sections.

- External libraries

- Internet connectivity (wireless)

- Standard functions

External Libraries

The first section of the code, as provided in Listing 2-6, includes all external libraries required to run the code. Since you are connecting to the Internet wirelessly, the main dependency of code is on `<WiFi.h>`. Your Arduino IDE should already have WiFi library installed, but for any reason it is missing, you can download it from:

- `<WiFi.h>`: `https://github.com/arduino/Arduino/tree/master/libraries/WiFi`

Listing 2-6. External Libraries

```
#include <SPI.h>
#include <WiFi.h>
```

Internet Connectivity (Wireless)

The second section of the code defines variables, constants, and functions that are going to be used for connecting to the Internet.

To connect Arduino to your wireless router, set the ssid and password (pass) of your wireless network, as provided in Listing 2-7. Also create a WiFiClient variable that will be used for Internet connectivity.

Listing 2-7. Constants and Variables for Connecting to the Internet Using WiFi

```
char ssid[] = "YOUR_SSID";
char pass[] = "YOUR_PASSWORD";

int keyIndex = 0;
int status = WL_IDLE_STATUS;

WiFiClient client;
```

Listing 2-8 provides code for wireless connectivity setup. The connectToInternet() function first checks if the WiFi shield is attached. Next, the code keeps attempting to connect to the wireless network. The loop and the function end once Arduino successfully connects to the wireless network.

Listing 2-8. Code for Connecting to the Internet Using WiFi

```
void connectToInternet()
{
  status = WiFi.status();

  // Check for the presence of the shield
  if (status == WL_NO_SHIELD)
  {
    Serial.println("[ERROR] WiFi Shield Not Present");
    // Do nothing
    while (true);
  }

  // Attempt to connect to WPA/WPA2 Wifi network
  while ( status != WL_CONNECTED)
  {
    Serial.print("[INFO] Attempting Connection - WPA SSID: ");
    Serial.println(ssid);

    status = WiFi.begin(ssid, pass);
  }
```

```
// Connection successful
Serial.print("[INFO] Connection Successful");
Serial.print("");
printConnectionInformation();
Serial.println("-----------------------------------------------");
Serial.println("");
}
```

Once Arduino has successfully connected to the wireless network, the printConnectionInformation() function provided in Listing 2-9 is called. It prints the SSID, the router's MAC address, the Signal Strength (RSSI), Arduino's IP address, and Arduino's MAC address, all on the Serial Monitor window.

Listing 2-9. Function to Display Connection Information

```
void printConnectionInformation()
{
  // Print Network SSID
  Serial.print("[INFO] SSID: ");
  Serial.println(WiFi.SSID());

  // Print Router's MAC address
  byte bssid[6];
  WiFi.BSSID(bssid);
  Serial.print("[INFO] BSSID: ");
  Serial.print(bssid[5], HEX);
  Serial.print(":");
  Serial.print(bssid[4], HEX);
  Serial.print(":");
  Serial.print(bssid[3], HEX);
  Serial.print(":");
  Serial.print(bssid[2], HEX);
  Serial.print(":");
  Serial.print(bssid[1], HEX);
  Serial.print(":");
  Serial.println(bssid[0], HEX);

  // Print received signal strength
  long rssi = WiFi.RSSI();
  Serial.print("[INFO] Signal Strength (RSSI): ");
  Serial.println(rssi);

  // Print encryption type
  byte encryption = WiFi.encryptionType();
  Serial.print("[INFO] Encryption Type: ");
  Serial.println(encryption, HEX);
```

```
  // Print WiFi Shield's IP address
  IPAddress ip = WiFi.localIP();
  Serial.print("[INFO] IP Address: ");
  Serial.println(ip);

  // Print MAC address
  byte mac[6];
  WiFi.macAddress(mac);
  Serial.print("[INFO] MAC Address: ");
  Serial.print(mac[5], HEX);
  Serial.print(":");
  Serial.print(mac[4], HEX);
  Serial.print(":");
  Serial.print(mac[3], HEX);
  Serial.print(":");
  Serial.print(mac[2], HEX);
  Serial.print(":");
  Serial.print(mac[1], HEX);
  Serial.print(":");
  Serial.println(mac[0], HEX);
}
```

Standard Functions

Finally, the code in the third and last section, as provided in Listing 2-10, implements Arduino's standard setup() and loop() functions. For this project, all you are doing is connecting Arduino to the Internet and there is no processing thereafter, so the loop() function will remain empty.

Listing 2-10. Code for Standard Arduino Functions

```
void setup()
{
  // Initialize serial port
  Serial.begin(9600);

  // Connect Arduino to Internet
  connectToInternet();
}

void loop()
{
  // Do nothing
}
```

Your Arduino code is now complete.

Final Product

To test the application, verify and upload the code to Arduino as discussed in Chapter 1. Once the code has been uploaded, open the Serial Monitor window. You will start seeing log messages as shown in Figure 2-6.

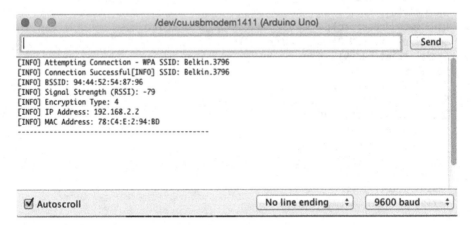

Figure 2-6. *Log messages from Arduino*

Arduino Yún Wireless Connectivity (WiFi)

Yún is a more advanced model of Arduino that has been developed for the Internet of things. For beginners, Arduino Yún may be a little complex as compared to Arduino Uno, but it comes with built-in Ethernet and wireless capabilities so you do not need to buy additional shields.

As mentioned in Chapter 1, this book uses Arduino Uno throughout. This section is only provided as a reference for readers who already have an Arduino Yún and still want to follow the real-life prototypes developed in this book. Even though Arduino Yún is not referenced in rest of the book, the code download contains Arduino Yún-compatible code as well.

Hardware Required

You do not need any additional hardware to connect Arduino Yún to the Internet, so Figure 2-7 only includes a diagram of Arduino Yún.

Figure 2-7. *Arduino Yún*

Software Required

In order to write the Internet connectivity code you will need following software:

- Arduino IDE 1.6.4 or later version

Wireless Setup

Unlike Arduino Uno, where you need to attach a wireless or Ethernet shield, Arduino Yún comes with a built-in Ethernet and wireless connectivity capability. Arduino Yún acts as a hotspot by directly connecting to your wired or wireless network. So, you do not need to write the Internet connectivity code; instead, you just need to set up your Arduino Yún to connect to your network. This section discusses the wireless setup for Arduino Yún.

1. Connect Arduino Yún to your computer with a Micro USB cable.

2. Arduino Yún acts as a hotspot as well, so from your computer's WiFi, search for Arduino Yún. Depending on where you purchased your Arduino Yún, it might appear as ArduinoYunXXXXXXXXXXXX or LininoXXXXXXXXXXXX in your computer's available WiFi connections. As shown in Figure 2-8, connect to Arduino Yún wirelessly.

Figure 2-8. *Select Arduino Yún from wireless networks*

3. Once it's connected, open a web browser on your computer and enter `http://arduino.local` (if this does not work then enter the default IP `http://192.168.240.1`). As shown in Figure 2-9, a login screen for your Arduino Yún should open.

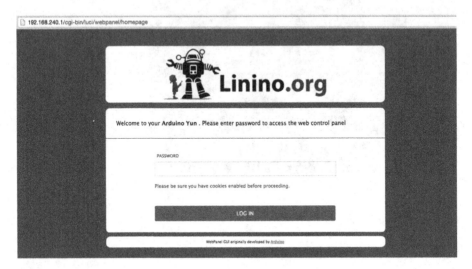

Figure 2-9. Arduino Yún login screen

4. If this is the first time you are accessing your Arduino Yún, then enter the default password `arduino` (if this does not work, try `doghunter`; otherwise check the manufacturer's documentation). Click the Log In button as shown in Figure 2-10.

Figure 2-10. Enter the password and log in

5. Upon successful login you will be redirected to the configuration page of your Arduino Yún, as shown in Figure 2-11. Click on the Configure button.

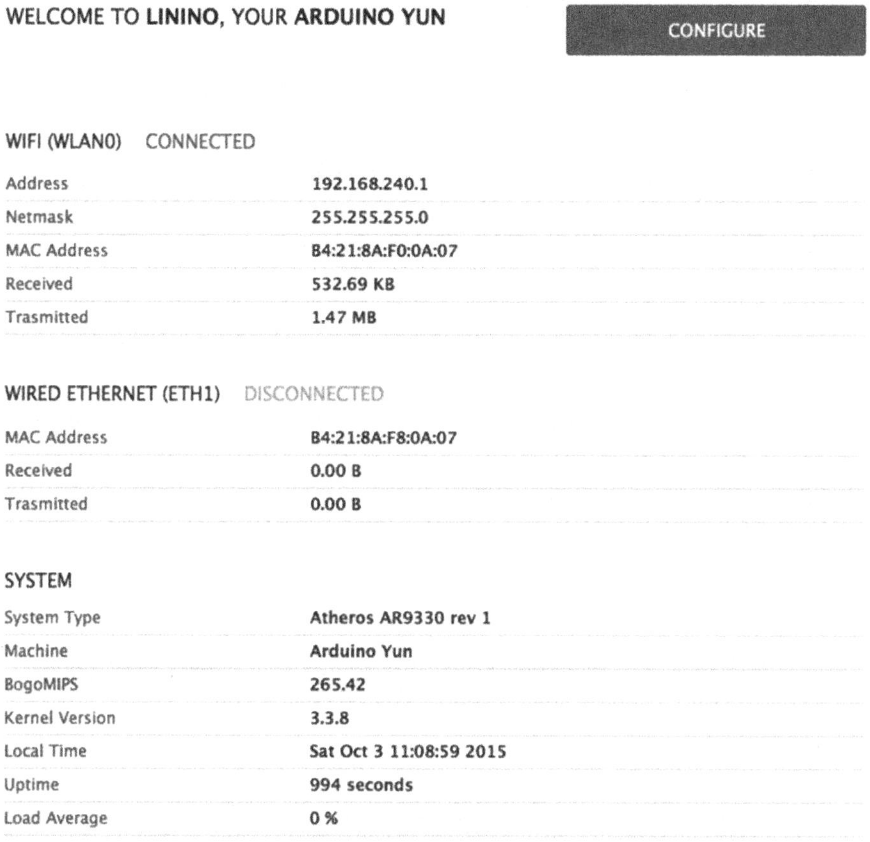

WELCOME TO **LININO**, YOUR **ARDUINO YUN**

CONFIGURE

WIFI (WLAN0)   CONNECTED

Address	192.168.240.1
Netmask	255.255.255.0
MAC Address	B4:21:8A:F0:0A:07
Received	532.69 KB
Trasmitted	1.47 MB

WIRED ETHERNET (ETH1)   DISCONNECTED

MAC Address	B4:21:8A:F8:0A:07
Received	0.00 B
Trasmitted	0.00 B

SYSTEM

System Type	Atheros AR9330 rev 1
Machine	Arduino Yun
BogoMIPS	265.42
Kernel Version	3.3.8
Local Time	Sat Oct 3 11:08:59 2015
Uptime	994 seconds
Load Average	0 %

Figure 2-11. *Arduino Yún default configuration*

6. As shown in Figure 2-12, you can change the Board Name, Password, and Timezone of your Arduino Yún. Under the Wireless Parameters section, select the wireless network you commonly use from the Detected Wireless Networks list. Select the security type and enter network Password. Once you are done, click the Configure & Restart button.

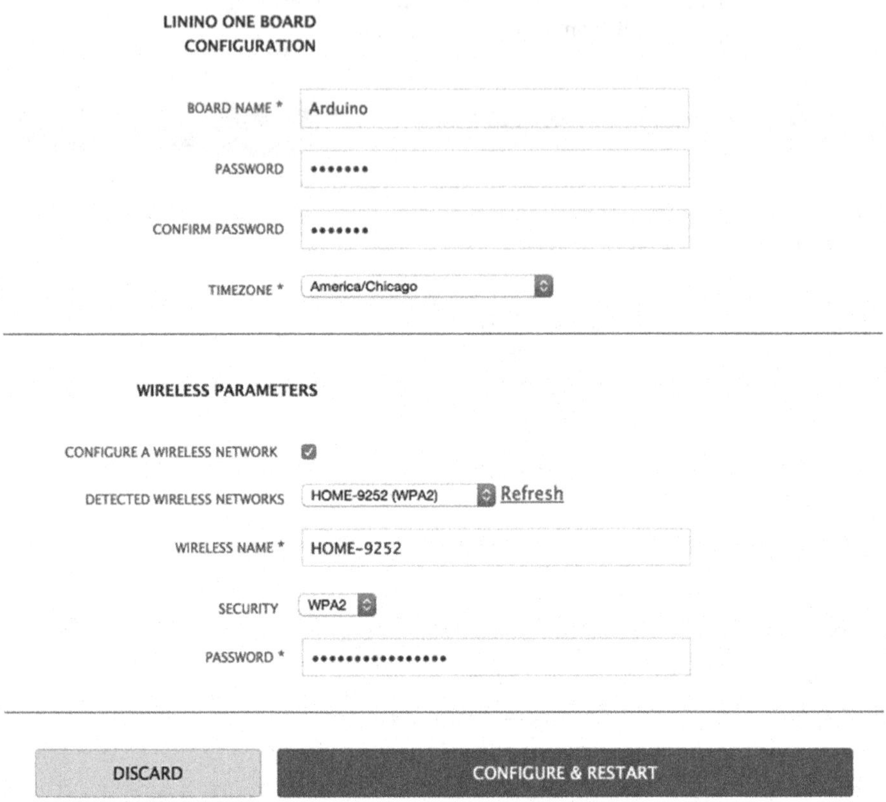

**LININO ONE BOARD
CONFIGURATION**

BOARD NAME *   Arduino

PASSWORD   •••••••

CONFIRM PASSWORD   •••••••

TIMEZONE *   America/Chicago

WIRELESS PARAMETERS

CONFIGURE A WIRELESS NETWORK   ☑

DETECTED WIRELESS NETWORKS   HOME-9252 (WPA2)   Refresh

WIRELESS NAME *   HOME-9252

SECURITY   WPA2

PASSWORD *   ••••••••••••••••

DISCARD   CONFIGURE & RESTART

Figure 2-12. *Arduino Yún wireless configuration*

7.   Arduino Yún will restart with updated settings, as shown in
     Figure 2-13.

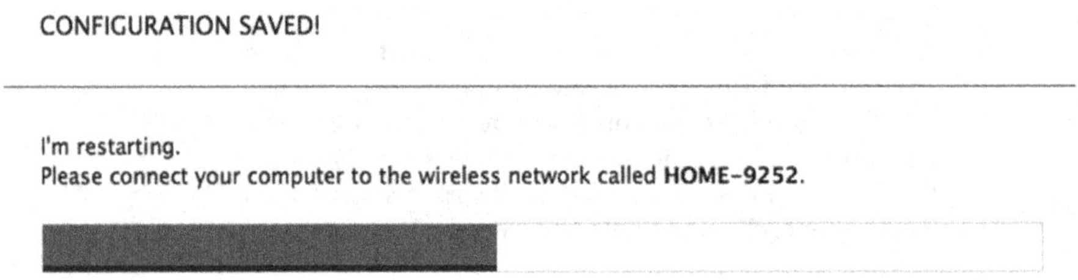

CONFIGURATION SAVED!

I'm restarting.
Please connect your computer to the wireless network called **HOME-9252**.

Figure 2-13. *Arduino Yún restarting*

8. As shown in Figure 2-14, during restart Arduino Yún will display a message for you to connect to the commonly used wireless network. Once restarted, you will be able to access your Arduino Yún using an IP assigned by your wireless router. If you are unable to find the assigned IP, follow rest of the steps and upload the code provided in a later section that prints connection information.

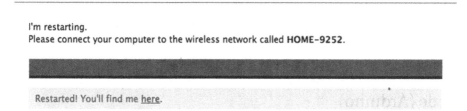

CONFIGURATION SAVED!

I'm restarting.
Please connect your computer to the wireless network called **HOME-9252**.

Restarted! You'll find me here.

Figure 2-14. *Arduino Yún restart complete*

9. Open Arduino IDE while Arduino Yún is still connected via Micro USB to your computer. As shown in Figure 2-15 from Tools ➤ Board, select Arduino Yún.

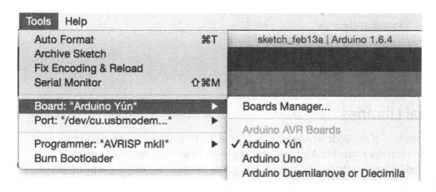

Figure 2-15. *Select the Arduino Yún board*

10. As shown in Figure 2-16, from Tools ➤ Port, select the port that says Arduino Yún.

Figure 2-16. *Select the Arduino Yún port*

Code (Arduino)

Now that your Arduino Yún is connected to a wireless network, you are going to write the code that will allow your Arduino to send and receive data over the Internet. Since Arduino Yún is already connected to the Internet, this is where the code will vary slightly. Instead of adding code to connect, you will simply use the library <Bridge.h> to use the wireless connection.

Start your Arduino IDE and either type the following code or download it from our site and open it. All the code goes into a single source file (*.ino), but in order to make it easy to understand and reuse it has been divided into three sections.

- External libraries

- Internet connectivity (Wireless)

- Read sensor data

External Libraries

The first section of the code as provided in Listing 2-11 includes all external libraries required to run the code. For Arduino Yún, <Bridge.h> lets you access the already established Internet connection. You are also going to use <Process.h> to print the connection information. Your Arduino IDE has both these libraries installed.

Listing 2-11. External Libraries

```
#include <Bridge.h>
#include <Process.h>
```

Internet Connectivity (Wireless)

The second section of the code, which is provided in Listing 2-12, defines the functions that are going to be used for displaying connection information.

Since Arduino is already connected to the wireless network, the printConnectionInformation() function is called. It prints the wireless connection information.

Listing 2-12. Function to Display Connection Information

```
void printConnectionInformation()
{
  // Initialize a new process
  Process wifiCheck;

  // Run Command

  wifiCheck.runShellCommand("/usr/bin/pretty-wifi-info.lua");

  // Print Connection Information
  while (wifiCheck.available() > 0)
  {
    char c = wifiCheck.read();
    Serial.print(c);
  }

  Serial.println("---------------------------------------------");
  Serial.println("");
}
```

Standard Functions

Finally, the code in third and last section, provided in Listing 2-13, implements Arduino's standard setup() and loop() functions. For this project, all you are doing is printing the Internet connection information and there is no processing thereafter, so the loop() function will remain empty.

One main difference in this code versus the Arduino Uno code is that you need to initialize the bridge using Bridge.begin(). This basically lets you access the Arduino Yún Internet connection.

Listing 2-13. Code for Standard Arduino Functions

```
void setup()
{
  // Initialize serial port
  Serial.begin(9600);

  // Do nothing until serial monitor is opened
  while (!Serial);
```

```
// Contact the Linux processor
Bridge.begin();

// Connect Arduino to Internet
printConnectionInformation();
}

void loop()
{
  // Do nothing
}
```

Your Arduino code is now complete.

Final Product

To test the application, verify and upload the code to Arduino, as discussed in Chapter 1. Once the code has been uploaded, open the Serial Monitor window. You will start seeing log messages as shown in Figure 2-17.

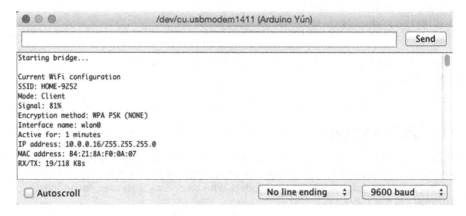

Figure 2-17. Log messages from Arduino

Summary

In this chapter you developed code to connect Arduino Uno to the Internet using both Ethernet shield and WiFi shield. You also looked at the wireless setup for Arduino Yún and the code needed to access the Internet connection.

For any of your future projects that require Internet connectivity using Ethernet or WiFi, you can use the code provided in this chapter as a base and then add your own code to it.

■ ■ ■

CHAPTER 3

Communication Protocols

In Chapter 2, you connected Arduino to the Internet using Ethernet and WiFi respectively. This chapter looks at two protocols used for sending and receiving data. A *protocol* is an agreed-upon structured format that is used for network communication. It defines what should be sent and received and what actions should be taken.

Learning Objectives

At the end of this chapter, you will be able to:

- Understand the basics of the HTTP protocol

- Send an HTTP request to the server

- Understand the basics of the MQTT protocol

- Publish and subscribe to an MQTT broker

HTTP

The web uses Hyper Text Transfer Protocol (HTTP) as its underlying protocol. HTTP supports multiple methods of data transmission, but in this project you are going to write code for the two more popular methods, GET and POST. The GET and POST methods do the same job and their code is very similar, but there is a slight variation in their request formats. GET has a limit on how much data it can transmit compared to POST, which has no such limitations. POST is also considered safer compared to GET. Based on your requirements, you can decide which one works better for you. Figure 3-1 shows a high-level interaction between a device and an HTTP server.

© Adeel Javed 2016
A. Javed, *Building Arduino Projects for the Internet of Things*,
DOI 10.1007/978-1-4842-1940-9_3

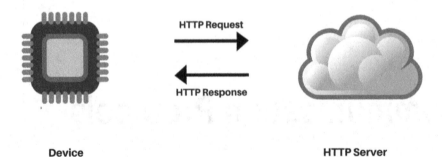

Device   **HTTP Server**

Figure 3-1. Hyper Text Transfer Protocol (HTTP)

■ **Note** For hardware and software requirements and circuit instructions, refer to the "Arduino Uno Wireless Connectivity (WiFi)" section in Chapter 2.

Code (Arduino)

Next you are going to write the code for connecting Arduino to the Internet using WiFi and sending test data to a server using HTTP.

Start Arduino IDE and type the following code or download it from book's site and open it. All the code goes into a single source file (`*.ino`) in the same sequence as provided here, but in order to make it easy to understand and reuse, it has been divided into four sections.

- External libraries
- Internet connectivity (wireless)
- Data publish (HTTP)
- Standard functions

External Libraries

The first section of the code includes all external libraries required to run the code. Code in this section is the same as Listing 2-6.

Internet Connectivity (Wireless)

The second section of the code defines variables, constants, and functions that are going to be used for connecting to the Internet. Use the code from Listings 2-7, 2-8, and 2-9 (Chapter 2) here.

Data Publish

The third section of the code defines variables, constants, and functions that are going to be used for sending data to the server using HTTP.

As provided in Listing 3-1, you first define the address and port of server that Arduino will connect to and send data. For the purposes of this project, you can publish it to www.httpbin.org, which is an openly available test server that simply echoes all the request information along with some additional information. In future projects, you will use servers that process the request data.

Listing 3-1. Variables to Define the HTTP Server

```
char server[] = {"www.httpbin.org"};
int port = 80;
```

The doHttpGet() function provided in Listing 3-2 encapsulates all the details of preparing the request for the GET method, connecting to the server and sending request.

Attempt to connect to the server using client.connect(server, port) in an IF condition. If the connection is successful, then prepare the request.

In a request that uses the GET method, data is sent as part of the URL in a name/value pair format, for example, http://www.httpbin.org/get?temperatureSensor=85&metric=F. The example shows that two parameters will be sent, the first is the temperatureSensor with a value of 85 and the second is metric with a value of F.

Finally, transmit the HTTP request to the server using the client.println() method. This method will send the commands to the server over the network and then receive any response from the server.

Listing 3-2. HTTP GET Request

```
void doHttpGet()
{
  // Prepare data or parameters that need to be posted to server
  String requestData = "requestVar=test";

  // Check if a connection to server:port was made
  if (client.connect(server, port))
  {
    Serial.println("[INFO] Server Connected - HTTP GET Started");

    // Make HTTP GET request
    client.println("GET /get?" + requestData + " HTTP/1.1");
    client.println("Host: " + String(server));
    client.println("Connection: close");
    client.println();
    Serial.println("[INFO] HTTP GET Completed");
  }
```

```
else
{
    Serial.println("[ERROR] Connection Failed");
}

Serial.println("-------------------------------------------------");
}
```

This code is for sending an HTTP GET request, but as mentioned earlier, it has a length limitation, so if you want to avoid this limitation then use HTTP POST instead.

The doHttpPost () function provided in Listing 3-3 encapsulates all the details of preparing request for the POST method, connecting to the server, and sending the request.

Attempt to connect to the server using client.connect(server, port) in an IF condition. So far, the code is similar to the HTTP GET request. If the connection is successful, then prepare the request.

In a request that uses the POST method, data is also sent in name/value pair format, but it is part of the request. As you can see in Listing 3-3, sending an HTTP POST request requires additional header information.

Finally, transmit the HTTP request to the server using the client.println() method. This method will send the commands to the server over the network and then receive any response from the server.

Listing 3-3. HTTP POST Request

```
void doHttpPost()
{
    // Prepare data or parameters that need to be posted to server
    String requestData = "requestData={\"requestVar:test\"}";

    // Check if a connection to server:port was made
    if (client.connect(server, port))
    {
        Serial.println("[INFO] Server Connected - HTTP POST Started");

        // Make HTTP POST request
        client.println("POST /post HTTP/1.1");
        client.println("Host: " + String(server));
        client.println("User-Agent: Arduino/1.0");
        client.println("Connection: close");
        client.println("Content-Type: application/x-www-form-urlencoded;");
        client.print("Content-Length: ");
        client.println(requestData.length());
        client.println();
        client.println(requestData);

        Serial.println("[INFO] HTTP POST Completed");
    }
```

```
  else
  {
    // Connection to server:port failed
    Serial.println("[ERROR] Connection Failed");
  }

  Serial.println("----------------------------------------------");
}
```

That is pretty much it for publishing data from your Arduino to a server.

Standard Functions

The code in the fourth and final section implements Arduino's standard setup() and
loop() functions.

As Listing 3-4 shows, the setup() function initializes the serial port, connects to
Internet, and then makes either the HTTP GET request by calling doHttpGet() or the
HTTP POST request by calling the doHttpPost() function.

Listing 3-4. Code for Standard Arduino Functions—setup()

```
void setup()
{
  // Initialize serial port
  Serial.begin(9600);

  // Connect Arduino to internet
  connectToInternet();

  // Make HTTP GET request
  doHttpGet();
}
```

Since in this project you are not doing any server-side processing with the data that
is being sent from sensor, you will add code to read response from the server to loop()
function. The test server that you are using simply echoes all the request information in
the response, so you are just going to read the response and print it to the Serial Monitor
window.

As provided in Listing 3-5, check if there are any bytes available to be read from
WiFiClient, read all the available bytes, and print them to the Serial Monitor window.
Once all the bytes have been read and printed, stop the client.

Listing 3-5. Code for Standard Arduino Functions—loop()

```
void loop()
{
  if (client.available())
  {
    Serial.println("[INFO] HTTP Response");
  }

  // Read available incoming bytes from the server and print
  while (client.available())
  {
    char c = client.read();
    Serial.write(c);
  }

  // If the server:port has disconnected, then stop the client
  if (!client.connected())
  {
    Serial.println();
    Serial.println("[INFO] Disconnecting From Server");
    client.stop();
  }
}
```

Your Arduino code is complete.

Final Product

To test the application, verify and upload the code as discussed in Chapter 1. Once the code has been uploaded, open the Serial Monitor window. You will start seeing log messages similar to ones shown in Figure 3-2 for HTTP GET and in Figure 3-3 for HTTP POST.

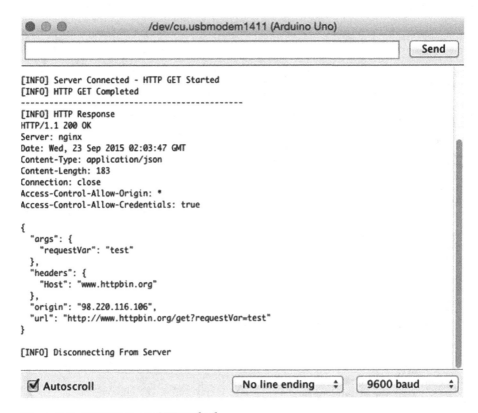

Figure 3-2. *HTTP request: GET method*

Figure 3-3. *HTTP request: POST method*

MQTT

MQTT is a lightweight machine-to-machine protocol. It follows the publisher-subscriber model, whereby a publisher publishes data to a server (a.k.a., a broker) and subscribers receive the data. Publishers and subscribers do not know each other; they connect to the broker, which makes this communication asynchronous. The broker notifies all subscribers that relevant data has been published using the concept of topics. A topic is similar to a newsfeed, in that you subscribe to certain topics you want to receive news about. Publishers and subscribers could be sensors, machines, and mobile apps. Figure 3-4 provides a high-level overview of the MQTT protocol.

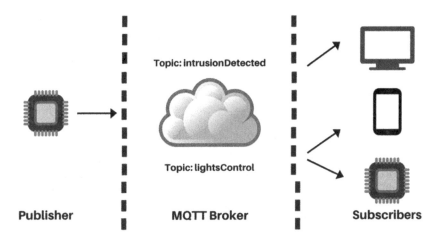

Figure 3-4. *The MQTT protocol*

Understanding MQTT is important for building IoT applications, so let's take a look at a few scenarios that will help you understand MQTT.

Intrusion Detection System

A simple version of an intrusion detection system is shown in Figure 3-5. It will consist of three components—the motion sensors that detect intrusions and publish data, a mobile app that receives this data and alerts the app user, and the component, which is a topic on an MQTT broker.

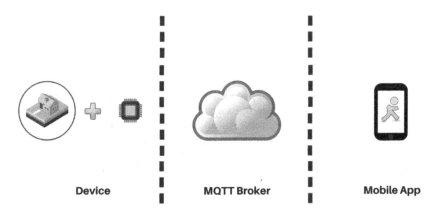

Figure 3-5. *Components of the intrusion detection system*

43

The sensor will act as a publisher and publish a new message to the `codifythings/ intrusionDetected` topic on the MQTT broker as soon as an intrusion is detected. The MQTT broker will add this message to the topic. The mobile app will be a subscriber of the `codifythings/intrusionDetected` topic. Whenever a new message is published to the topic, it will get notified. This will result in the mobile app creating a notification for the app user. You will build this system in Chapter 6.

Remote Lighting Control

Another great usage of MQTT is developing mobile apps that act as remote controls for various types of devices, such as a lighting control app. As shown in Figure 3-6, a remote control app will also consist of three components, but compared to the previous example the order of first two components is reversed. That means the first component is a mobile app that lets the user switch the lights on or off, the second component is a device connected to lights, and the third component is a topic on an MQTT broker.

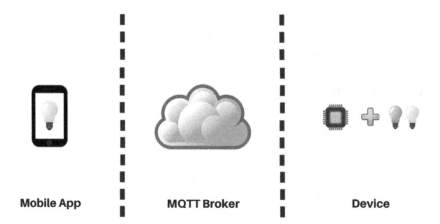

Mobile App   **MQTT Broker**   **Device**

Figure 3-6. *Components of the remote lighting control*

Mobile app users interact with the app to turn the lights on or off, whatever selection is made the mobile app will publish a new message to the `codifythings/lightsControl` topic on the MQTT broker. The MQTT broker will add this message to the topic. The device that is connected to the physical lights will be a subscriber of the `codifythings/ lightsControl` topic. Whenever a new message is published to the topic it will get notified; the device as a result will turn the lights on or off. You will build this remote control in Chapter 8.

■ **Note** For hardware and software requirements and circuit instructions, refer to the "Arduino Uno Wireless Connectivity (WiFi)" section in Chapter 2.

Code (Arduino)

Next you are going to write the code for connecting Arduino to the Internet using WiFi and publishing it to a server using MQTT.

Start your Arduino IDE and type the following code or download it from book's site and open it. All the code goes into a single source file (*.ino) in the same sequence as provided here, but in order to make it easy to understand and reuse, it has been divided into four sections.

- External libraries

- Internet connectivity (wireless)

- Data publish (MQTT)

- Data subscribe (MQTT)

External Libraries

The first section of code is provided in Listing 3-6. It includes all the external libraries required to run the code. This sketch has two main dependencies. For Internet connectivity, you need to include <WiFi.h> (assuming you are using WiFi shield) and, for MQTT broker communication, you need to include <PubSubClient.h>. You can install the <PubSubClient.h> library from:

- <PubSubClient.h>:https://github.com/knolleary/
  pubsubclient/releases/tag/v2.3

Listing 3-6. External Libraries

```
#include <SPI.h>
#include <WiFi.h>
#include <PubSubClient.h>
```

Internet Connectivity (Wireless)

The second section of the code defines variables, constants, and functions that are going to be used for connecting to the Internet. Use the code from Listings 2-7, 2-8, and Listing 2-9 from Chapter 2 here.

Data Publish/Subscribe MQTT

The third section of the code defines variables, constants, and functions that are going to be used for publishing and subscribing to an MQTT broker. The code publishes and subscribes to same topic.

Define the address and port (default is 1883) of the MQTT broker that you want Arduino to connect to, as shown in Listing 3-7. The topic variable defines which topic on the broker data will be published and subscribed. If you do not have an MQTT broker installed on your machine, you can use the openly available MQTT broker from Eclipse Foundation (iot.eclipse.org) or Mosquitto (test.mosquitto.org).

Listing 3-7. MQTT Setup

```
// IP address of the MQTT broker
char server[] = {"iot.eclipse.org"};
int port = 1883
char topic[] = {"codifythings/testMessage"};
```

As shown in Listing 3-8, initialize the MQTT client. The callback() function encapsulates all the details of receiving payload from broker.

Listing 3-8. MQTT Initialization and Callback Function

```
PubSubClient pubSubClient(server, 1883, callback, client);

void callback(char* topic, byte* payload, unsigned int length)
{
  // Print payload
  String payloadContent = String((char *)payload);
  Serial.println("[INFO] Payload: " + payloadContent);
}
```

Standard Functions

Finally, the code in this last section is provided in Listing 3-9. It implements Arduino's standard setup() and loop() functions.

In the setup() function, the code initializes the serial port and connects to the Internet. If the MQTT broker is connected, it will subscribe to the codifythings/testMessage topic. Once successfully subscribed, the code publishes a new message to the codifythings/testMessage topic. The code subscribes to same topic to which it is publishing. Therefore, as soon as a message is published, the callback() function will be called. The loop() function simply waits for new messages from the MQTT broker.

Listing 3-9. Code for Standard Arduino Functions

```
void setup()
{
  // Initialize serial port
  Serial.begin(9600);

  // Connect Arduino to internet
  connectToInternet();
```

```
//Connect MQTT Broker
Serial.println("[INFO] Connecting to MQTT Broker");
if (pubSubClient.connect("arduinoClient"))
{
  Serial.println("[INFO] Connection to MQTT Broker Successful");

  pubSubClient.subscribe(topic);
  Serial.println("[INFO] Successfully Subscribed to MQTT Topic ");

  Serial.println("[INFO] Publishing to MQTT Broker");
  pubSubClient.publish(topic, "Test Message");
}
else
{
  Serial.println("[INFO] Connection to MQTT Broker Failed");
}
}

void loop()
{
  // Wait for messages from MQTT broker
  pubSubClient.loop();
}
```

Your Arduino code is complete.

Final Product

To test the application, verify and upload the code as discussed in Chapter 1. Once the code has been deployed, open the Serial Monitor window. You will start seeing log messages from Arduino as shown in Figure 3-7.

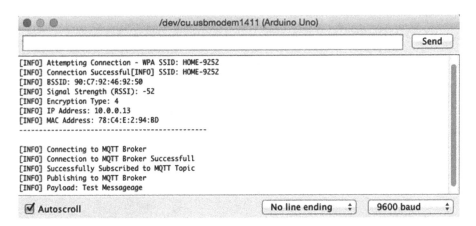

Figure 3-7. MQTT: Publish/subscribe log messages

Summary

In this chapter, you learned about HTTP and MQTT, two very important, popular, and lightweight communication protocols used in IoT applications. These protocols are device agnostic, so they can be used for communication with any type of device or server. You will use both these protocols extensively in the next chapters.

PART 2

Prototypes

CHAPTER 4

■ ■ ■

Complex Flows: Node-RED

Now that you understand the basics of Arduino, including the different connectivity options available and the communication protocols, you are going to use that knowledge to prototype IoT applications.

This chapter starts with a hypothetical scenario. Imagine that you are responsible for monitoring noise levels around an animal sanctuary. Whenever noise levels cross a certain threshold, you are required to send an SMS to the supervisor and log noise information in a database for future trends analysis. Let's look at what will it take to implement this IoT application:

- Connect a sound sensor to Arduino

- Write code that sends an HTTP request to a server whenever noise levels exceed a threshold

- Create a service on a server that receives HTTP requests

- Write a service to send an SMS to the supervisor

- Write a service to store sensor data in a database

Looking at these tasks, you can see that a lot of code needs to be developed to create this application. Most IoT applications require implementation of tasks such as HTTP request/response, MQTT publish/subscribe, e-mails, SMS, tweets, and storing/loading data. Engineers at IBM faced this same issue. Every time they had to create a new prototype they were required to code the flow and tasks from scratch, even though they were repetitive. So, they developed Node-RED, which is an excellent drag-and-drop toolkit of reusable code that does these tasks and many more.

Node-RED is an event-processing engine that helps IoT developers avoid reinventing the wheel. You still need to write code but the amount of code required is significantly reduced. Figure 4-1 shows the Node-RED development environment.

© Adeel Javed 2016
A. Javed, *Building Arduino Projects for the Internet of Things*,
DOI 10.1007/978-1-4842-1940-9_4

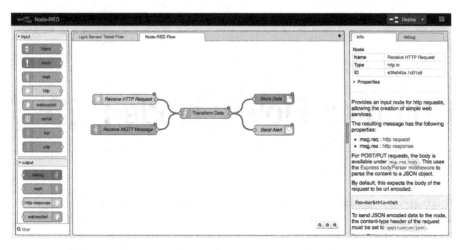

Figure 4-1. *Node-RED development environment*

As you can see, a Node-RED flow is made of nodes. Each node encapsulates a reusable piece of code that performs a certain task. To create a flow, you simply drag nodes from palette on the left and drop them on your flow designer. You can find a lot of nodes pre-built and openly available for use. A flow starts after receiving an input. There are quite a few standard input sources available, such as HTTP, MQTT, and TCP. A flow ends with an output task such as a HTTP response, an MQTT publish, a tweet, etc. A flow is not limited to one input/output node; it can start or end with multiple nodes. Nodes in between input and output usually transform or manipulate data, for example, converting an HTTP request into an e-mail body.

You are going to build a simple project in order to get more acquainted with Node-RED. The idea of this project is to tweet whenever it is sunny outside. Figure 4-2 displays all the components that will be used to design this system. The first component is an Arduino device with a light sensor attached to it. The second component is a Node-RED flow that is started by Arduino. The final component is Twitter, as your Node-RED flow will tweet a message whenever a certain threshold is crossed.

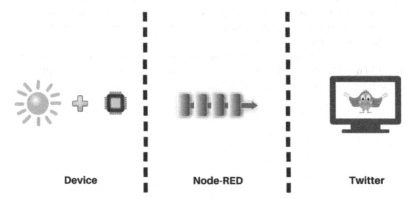

Figure 4-2. *Components of the light sensor tweet system*

Learning Objectives

At the end of this chapter, you will be able to:

- Read light sensor data from Arduino

- Build a Node-RED flow that receives an HTTP request and tweets a message

- Send sensor data in an HTTP request to start a Node-RED flow

Hardware Required

Figure 4-3 provides a list of all hardware components required for building the light sensor tweet system.

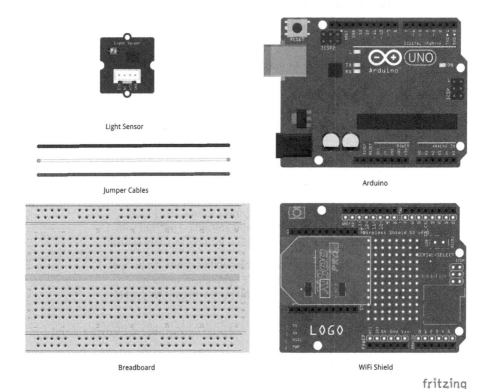

Figure 4-3. *Hardware required for light sensor tweet system*

Software Required

In order to develop the light sensor tweet system, you need following software:

- Arduino IDE 1.6.4 or later version
- Node-RED 0.13.2 or later version

Circuit

In this section you are going to build the circuit required for the light sensor tweet system. This circuit uses an analog light intensity sensor, which returns values between 0 and 1023. Higher values mean higher intensity of light.

1. Make sure your Arduino is not connected to a power source, such as a computer via a USB or a battery.

2. Attach a WiFi shield to the top of Arduino. All the pins should align.

3. Using jumper cables, connect the power (5V) and ground (GND) ports on Arduino to the power (+) and ground (-) ports on the breadboard.

■ **Tip**   It is a good practice to use red jumper cables for power (+/VNC/5V/3.3V) and black jumper cables for ground (-/GND).

---

4. Now that your breadboard has a power source, use jumper cables to connect the power (+) and ground (-) ports of your breadboard to the power and ground ports of the light sensor.

5. To read the light sensor values, you need to connect a jumper cable from the analog read port of light sensor to the A0 (analog) port of your Arduino. Your code will use this port to read the light's intensity value.

   Your circuit is now complete and it should look similar to Figures 4-4 and 4-5.

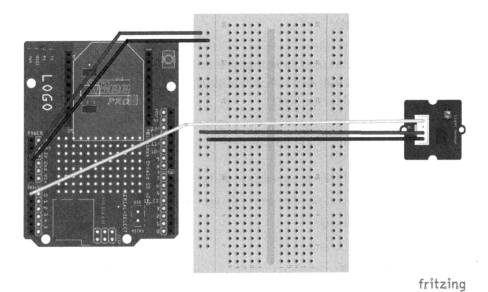

fritzing

Figure 4-4. *Circuit diagram of the light sensor tweet system*

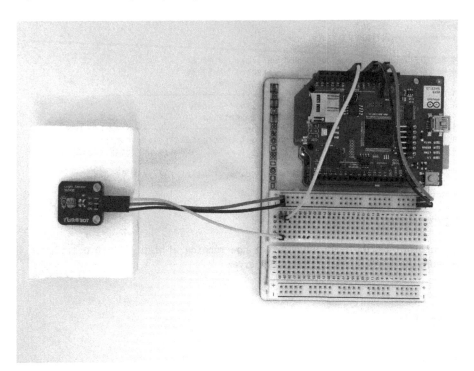

Figure 4-5. *Actual circuit of the light sensor tweet system*

Node-RED Flow

■ **Note** This book does not cover the installation of the Node-RED server. You can find installation instructions at Node-RED's official web site (http://nodered.org/docs/getting-started/installation.html).

In this section you are going to develop a flow in Node-RED that will perform the following tasks:

- Receive an HTTP request sent from the light sensor

- Prepare a tweet using data sent by the light sensor

- Tweet the message

- Send an HTTP response

Start your Node-RED server using the node-red command in a terminal window. Figure 4-6 shows the log messages you will see once the Node-RED server starts.

```
Adeels-MacBook-Air:~ adeeljaved$ node-red

Welcome to Node-RED
===================

4 Oct 17:25:28 - [info] Node-RED version: v0.10.6
4 Oct 17:25:28 - [info] Node.js  version: v0.10.36
4 Oct 17:25:28 - [info] Loading palette nodes
4 Oct 17:25:29 - [warn] ------------------------------------------
4 Oct 17:25:29 - [warn] Failed to register 4 node types
4 Oct 17:25:29 - [warn] Run with -v for details
4 Oct 17:25:29 - [warn] ------------------------------------------
4 Oct 17:25:29 - [info] User Directory : /Users/adeeljaved/.node-red
4 Oct 17:25:29 - [info] Flows file     : /Users/adeeljaved/.node-red/flows_Adeel
s-MacBook-Air.local.json
4 Oct 17:25:30 - [info] Server now running at http://127.0.0.1:1880/
4 Oct 17:25:30 - [info] Starting flows
4 Oct 17:25:30 - [info] Started flows
```

Figure 4-6. *Startup logs of Node-RED*

In Figure 4-6, the log message Server now running at http://127.0.0.1:1880 contains the exact URL of the Node-RED server.

■ **Note**   The Node-RED server URL in logs `http://127.0.0.1:1880` is the IP of your local computer and cannot be accessed by Arduino. You will need to replace the local IP `127.0.0.1` with the network IP of your machine. The IP of the Node-RED server used in this book was `10.0.0.6`, so the URL you will see is `http://10.0.0.6:1880`.

Enter the Node-RED server URL in a browser to access the designer. The designer opens up with an empty flow tab called Flow 1. Figure 4-7 shows the default view of the Node-RED designer.

Figure 4-7. *Default view of the Node-RED designer*

On the left side of designer, as shown in Figure 4-7, is a palette with all available nodes. Nodes are grouped into various categories, such as input, output, function, etc. Figure 4-8 shows the list of input nodes that comes with default installation of Node-RED, and Figure 4-9 shows the list of output nodes in the default installation.

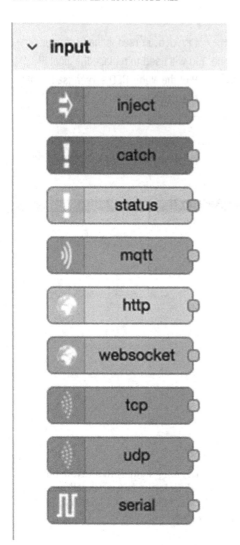

Figure 4-8. *Input nodes in the default installation of Node-RED*

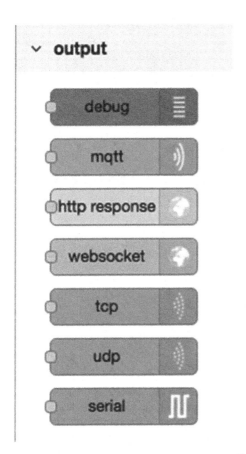

Figure 4-9. *Output nodes in the default installation of Node-RED*

On the right side of the designer, as shown in Figure 4-7, are the Info and Debug tabs. The Info tab displays documentation about the currently selected node in the Node palette or Flow tab. The Debug tab displays log messages and errors generated from the flow during execution.

Finally, the Deploy button on the top-right of the designer, as shown in Figure 4-7, lets you deploy and activate your flow changes to the server.

Now let's start creating the flow. If this is your first flow in Node-RED, you can use Flow 1 to create your flow. If you have already created some flows and want to create a new one, click on the plus (+) button on top-right side to add a new flow. Double-click the flow tab name to open the properties dialog box shown in Figure 4-10. Call the new flow Light Sensor Tweet Flow and then click OK to save your changes.

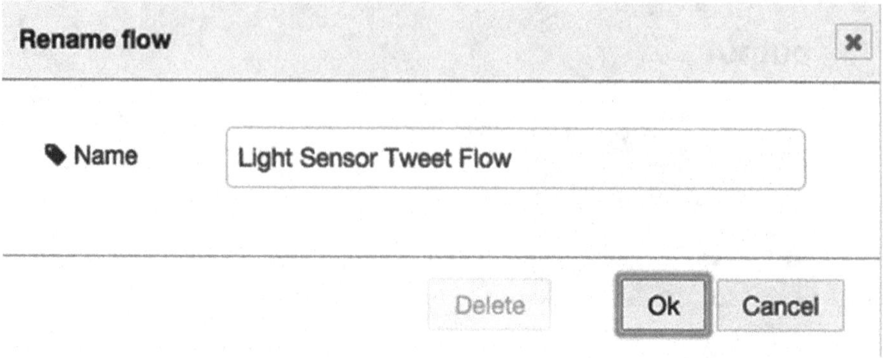

Rename flow   ✖

🏷 Name | Light Sensor Tweet Flow |

                                        Delete   **Ok**   Cancel

Figure 4-10. *Flow properties dialog box*

Drag and drop the http request input node from the palette in the Flow tab. Your flow should look similar to Figure 4-11.

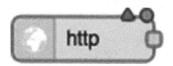

Figure 4-11. *HTTP request node*

Double-click the http node to open the properties dialog box, as shown in Figure 4-12. Set the method to GET, which specifies that the HTTP request will be sent by the client (in this case, the light sensor) using a GET method. As discussed in Chapter 3, the structure of the request varies based on the method you select. You saw the Arduino code for the GET and POST methods in Chapter 3.

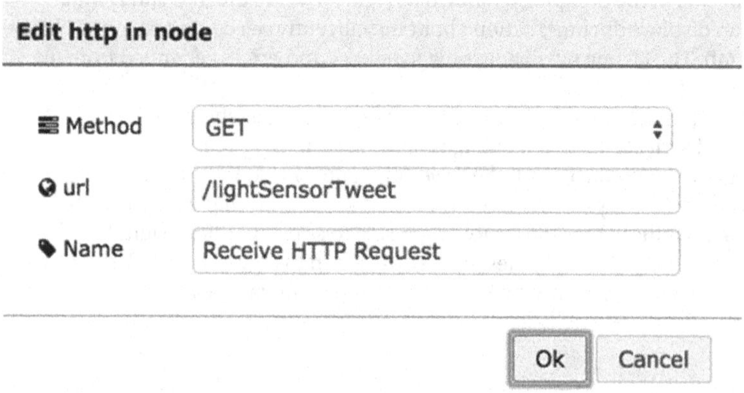

Edit http in node

≣ Method | GET   ⬍ |
◉ url | /lightSensorTweet |
🏷 Name | Receive HTTP Request |

                                            Ok   Cancel

Figure 4-12. *HTTP request node properties dialog box*

Set the URL property to /lightSensorTweet. This URL will be prepended by the Node-RED server and port. The Node-RED server used in this project is available at 10.0.0.6:1880, so Arduino will send data to 10.0.0.6:1880/lightSensorTweet.

Finally, each node can be given a custom name that describes the task it performs. Call this node Receive HTTP Request.

Click OK to make the updates.

Data coming from the device using HTTP is in string format, so you need to convert it into a number. Drag and drop a function node and place it in the Flow tab after the Receive HTTP Request node. A function node lets you write code to manipulate payload. Your flow should look similar to Figure 4-13 at this point.

Figure 4-13. Function node

Double-click the function node to open the properties dialog, as shown in Figure 4-14. Change the name to Convert to Number. Update the code inside function as provided in Listing 4-1. Click OK to save your changes. Connect your Receive HTTP Request and Convert to Number nodes.

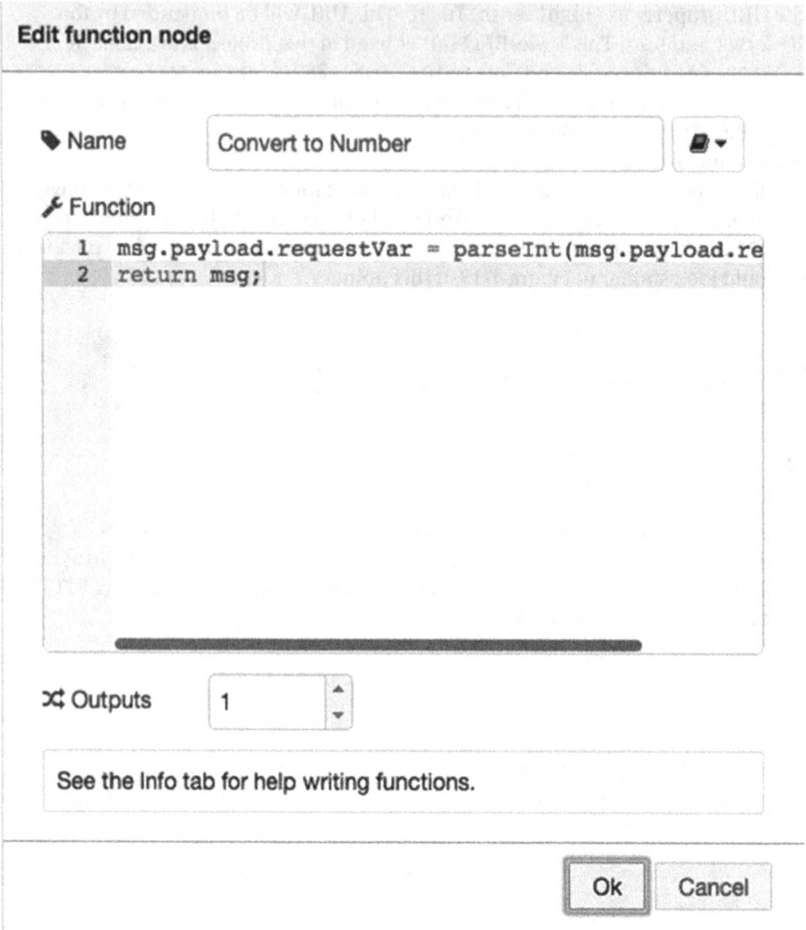

Edit function node

🏷 Name   Convert to Number   📄▾

🔧 Function

```
1   msg.payload.requestVar = parseInt(msg.payload.re
2   return msg;
```

⤨ Outputs   1   ▲▼

See the Info tab for help writing functions.

Ok   Cancel

Figure 4-14. *Function node properties dialog box*

Listing 4-1. Code for Converting a String to a Number

```
msg.payload.requestVar = parseInt(msg.payload.requestVar);
return msg;
```

At this point, your light sensor will send readings every few seconds whether it's sunny or not. So within the Node-RED flow, you need to add a rule to check if the sensor value has crossed a certain threshold and only tweet when that threshold has been crossed.

You can add this threshold check within Arduino code as well, but consider a real-life implementation of this same project. Instead of tweeting you can also use same logic to build an application that conserves energy by opening window blinds and turning lights inside the house off if it is sunny outside. If you hard-code such checks in Arduino code, then individual users might not be able to set their light preferences, because they cannot directly update the code. Taking such logic away from sensors will enable you to build something that can be customized by individual users.

Drag and drop a switch node from the function category and place it in the Flow tab after the Convert to Number node. Your flow should look similar to Figure 4-15 at this point.

Figure 4-15. *Switch node*

A switch node lets you follow a certain path in the flow based on a condition. Double-click the switch node to open its properties dialog box and set the conditions shown in Figure 4-16.

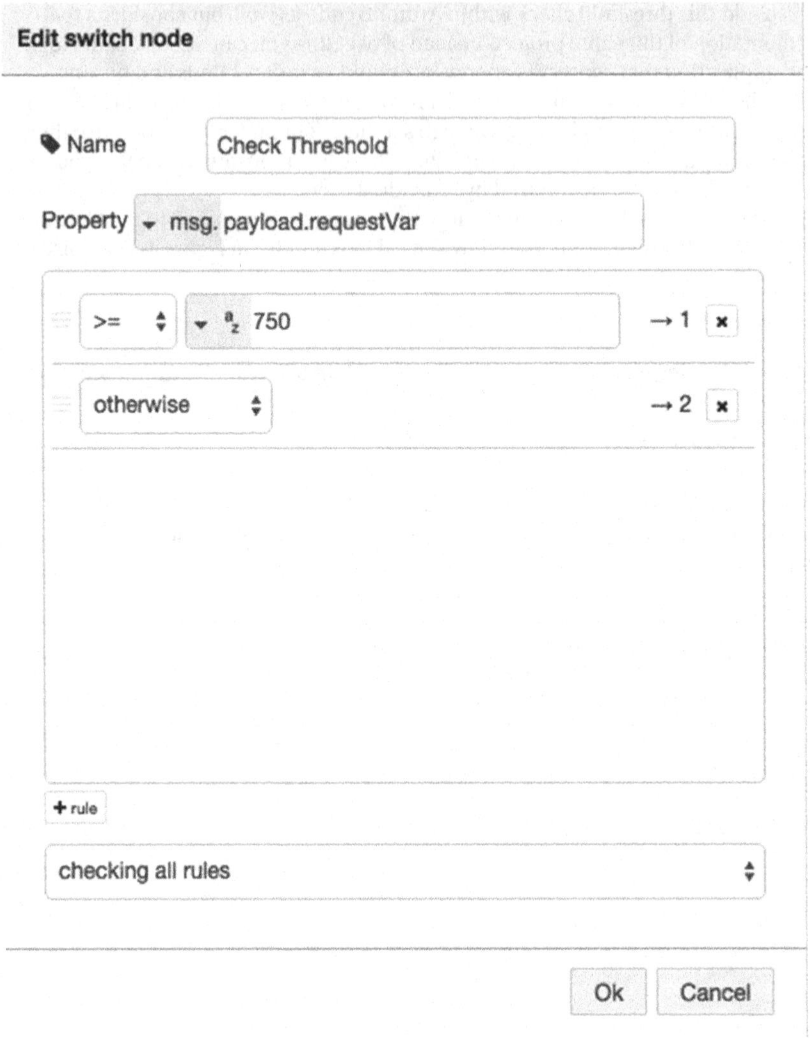

Edit switch node

🏷 Name   Check Threshold

Property ▾ msg. payload.requestVar

>= ⬍   ▾ ᵃ₂ 750   → 1 ✖

otherwise ⬍   → 2 ✖

➕ rule

checking all rules   ⬍

Ok   Cancel

Figure 4-16.   *Switch node properties dialog box*

Change the name to Check Threshold. By default, there will be only one path, so click on the + Rule button to add a new path. If the sensor value is greater than 750, it will follow path 1; otherwise, it will follow path 2. Path 2 will not check any conditions, so you can change it to otherwise from the dropdown.

Node-RED keeps all input information in msg.payload. You will be sending the sensor value in requestVar from Arduino, which is why the condition checks msg. payload.requestVar.

Connect your Convert to Number and Check Threshold nodes.

You are going to use the sensor value to create a tweet message. Drag and drop a function node on to the flow diagram. Place it after the Check Threshold node, as shown in Figure 4-17.

Receive HTTP Request
Convert to Number
Check Threshold

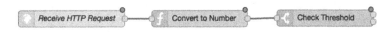

Figure 4-17. Function node

Double-click the function node to open the properties dialog box, as shown in Figure 4-18. Name it `Set Tweet Message`. Update the code inside the function node, as shown in Listing 4-2. Click OK to save your changes.

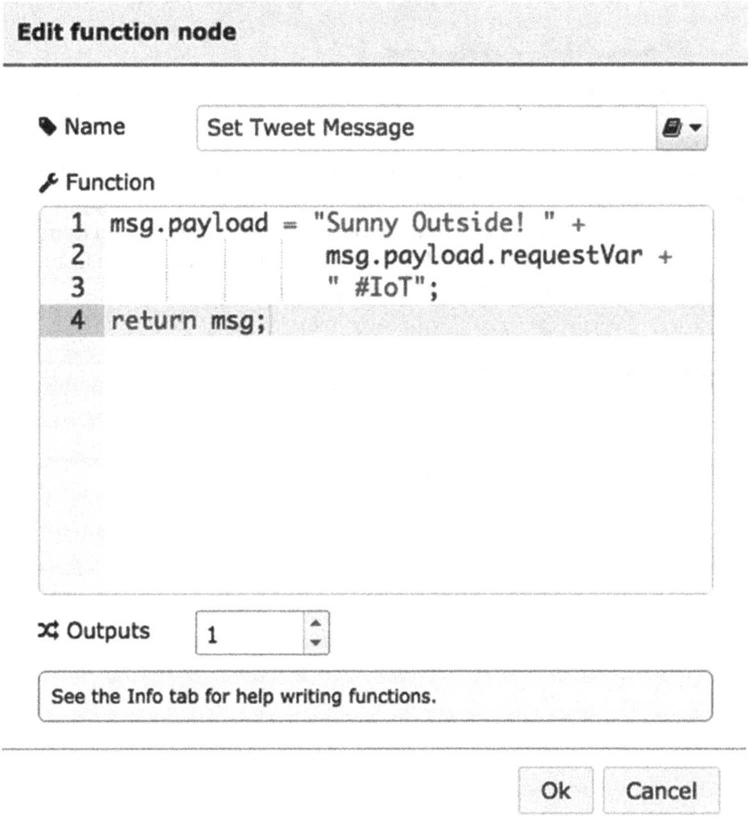

Edit function node
Name
Set Tweet Message
Function
msg.payload = "Sunny Outside! " +
msg.payload.requestVar +
" #IoT";
return msg;
Outputs
1
See the Info tab for help writing functions.
Ok
Cancel

Figure 4-18. Function node properties dialog box

Listing 4-2. Code for Creating the Tweet

```
msg.payload = "Sunny Outside! " + msg.payload.requestVar + " #IoT";
return msg;
```

Connect the Set Tweet Message node to the first path of the Check Threshold switch node. This connection will make sure that whenever a light sensor value crosses the threshold of 750, the flow follows path 1 that tweets.

Next, drag and drop a Tweet node on to the flow diagram after the Set Tweet Message node, as shown in Figure 4-19.

Figure 4-19. Tweet node

For Node-RED to be able to tweet, you need to configure your Twitter credentials. Double-click the twitter out node to open the properties dialog box shown in Figure 4-20. If you already have your Twitter credentials configured in Node-RED, select them from the Twitter dropdown. Otherwise, select the Add New Twitter-Credentials option from the dropdown and click on the Edit/Pencil icon to start the configuration steps.

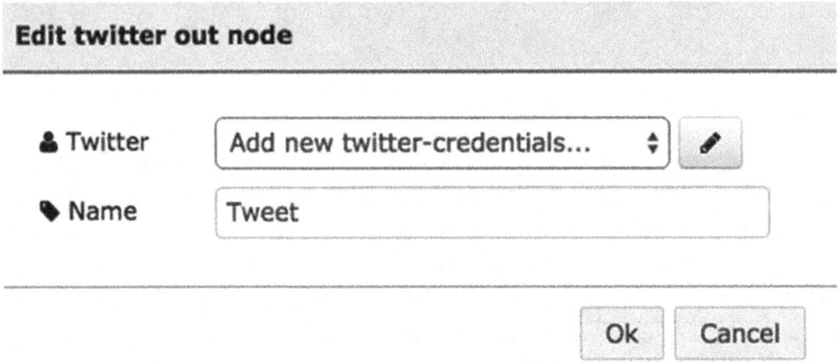

Edit twitter out node

♟ **Twitter** | Add new twitter-credentials... ⬍ | 🖊 |

🔖 **Name** | Tweet |

| | Ok | Cancel |

Figure 4-20. Add new Twitter credentials

Figure 4-21 shows the next dialog box that appears. Click on the Click Here to Authenticate with Twitter button.

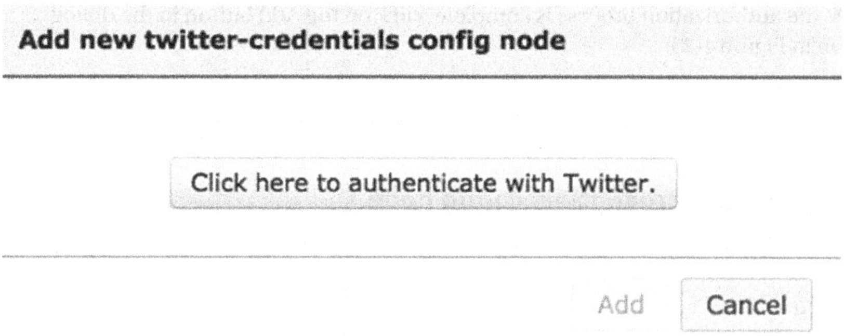

Add new twitter-credentials config node

Click here to authenticate with Twitter.

Add   Cancel

Figure 4-21. Authenticate the Twitter account

On the next screen, shown in Figure 4-22, enter your Twitter username and password and click the Authorize App button to grant Node-RED access to your Twitter account.

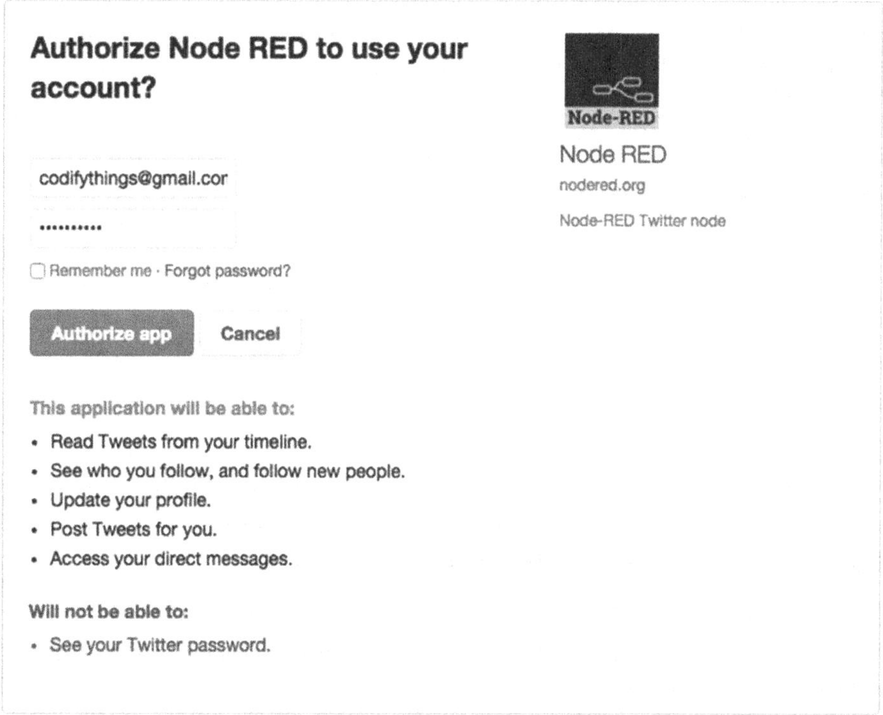

Authorize Node RED to use your account?

Node-RED
Node RED
nodered.org
Node-RED Twitter node

codifythings@gmail.cor

••••••••••

☐ Remember me · Forgot password?

Authorize app   Cancel

This application will be able to:
- Read Tweets from your timeline.
- See who you follow, and follow new people.
- Update your profile.
- Post Tweets for you.
- Access your direct messages.

Will not be able to:
- See your Twitter password.

Figure 4-22. Authorize Node-RED to use your Twitter account

Once the authorization process is complete, click on the Add button in the dialog box shown in Figure 4-23.

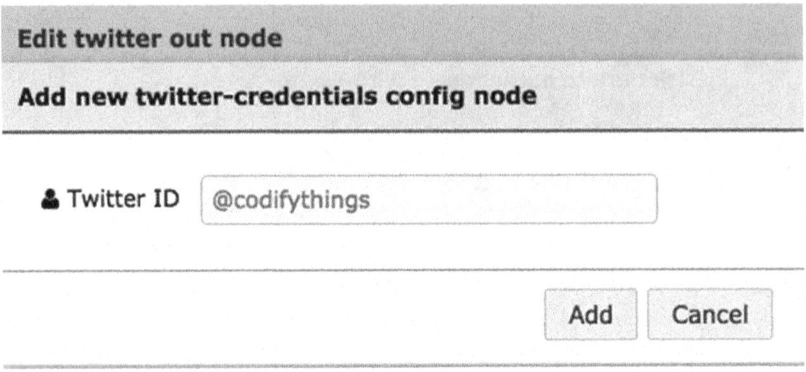

Edit twitter out node

Add new twitter-credentials config node

  & Twitter ID @codifythings

                                                     Add   **Cancel**

Figure 4-23. Add the authorized Twitter account to the flow

Figure 4-24 shows the dialog box that you will be presented with next; it's the same dialog box where you started the Twitter configuration process. Click OK to complete the Twitter configuration.

Edit twitter out node

  & Twitter   @codifythings

  ➤ Name   Tweet

                                                     Ok   **Cancel**

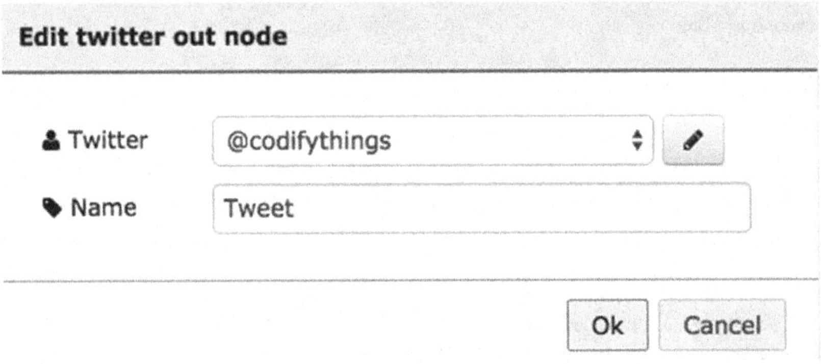

Figure 4-24. Select the authorized Twitter credentials

Connect the Tweet node to the Set Tweet Message node.

Finally, add an HTTP response node to your flow under the Twitter node. Your flow should look similar to Figure 4-25.

Figure 4-25. *HTTP response node*

The HTTP response node will simply send `msg.payload` back to the client in the JSON format. Change the name of this node to `Send HTTP Response`.

Connect the Send HTTP Response node to the second path of the Check Threshold switch node and also to the Set Tweet Message. Your final flow should look similar to Figure 4-26.

Figure 4-26. *Completed Node-RED flow*

Code (Arduino)

Next, you are going to write code for connecting Arduino to the Internet using WiFi, reading light sensor data, and sending it to the Node-RED server as an HTTP request.

Start your Arduino IDE and either type the code provided here or download it from book's site and open it. All the code goes into a single source file (*.ino), but in order to make it easy to understand and reuse, it has been divided into five sections.

- External libraries
- Internet connectivity (WiFi)
- Read sensor data
- HTTP (GET)
- Standard functions

External Libraries

The first section of the code, as provided in Listing 4-3, includes all the external libraries required to run the code. Since you are connecting to the Internet wirelessly, the main dependency of code is on <WiFi.h>.

Listing 4-3. Code for Including External Dependencies

```
#include <SPI.h>
#include <WiFi.h>
```

69

Internet Connectivity (Wireless)

The second section of the code defines variables, constants and functions that are going to be used for connecting to the Internet. Use the code from Listings 2-7, 2-8, and 2-9 (Chapter 2) here.

Read Sensor Data

The third section of the code is provided in Listing 4-4. It defines variables, constants, and functions that are going to be used for reading sensor data.

The readSensorData() function reads data from Analog Pin A0, and the result is between 0 and 1023. The greater the value returned, the brighter the light source. The light sensor value is assigned to the lightValue variable.

Listing 4-4. Code for the Reading Light Sensor Data

```
int lightValue;

void readSensorData()
{
  //Read Light Sensor Value
  lightValue = analogRead(A0);

  Serial.print("[INFO] Light Sensor Reading: ");
  Serial.println(lightValue);
}
```

Data Publish

The fourth section of the code is provided in Listing 4-5. It defines variables, constants, and functions that are going to be used for creating and sending an HTTP request to the server. This code is a slightly modified version of the HTTP GET that you developed in Chapter 3.

The main modification in this code is its ability to open and close a connection to the server repeatedly. Apart from that, make sure to change the server and port values to your Node-RED server's values. The other changes include passing a lightValue variable in the request and invoking the /lightSensorTweet URL.

Listing 4-5. Code for Starting the Node-RED Flow Using HTTP Request

```
//IP address of the HTTP server
char server[] = {"10.0.0.6"};
int port = 1880;

unsigned long lastConnectionTime s= 0;
const unsigned long postingInterval = 10L * 1000L;
```

```
void doHttpGet()
{
  // Read all incoming data (if any)
  while (client.available())
  {
    char c = client.read();
    Serial.write(c);
  }

  Serial.println();
  Serial.println("--------------------------------------------------");
  if (millis() - lastConnectionTime > postingInterval)
  {
    client.stop();

    //Read sensor data

    readSensorData();

    // Prepare data or parameters that need to be posted to server
    String requestData = "requestVar=" + String(lightValue);

    Serial.println("[INFO] Connecting to Server");

    // Check if a connection to server:port was made
    if (client.connect(server, port))
    {
      Serial.println("[INFO] Server Connected - HTTP GET Started");

      // Make HTTP GET request
      client.println("GET /lightSensorTweet?" + requestData + " HTTP/1.1");
      client.println("Host: " + String(server));
      client.println("Connection: close");
      client.println();

      lastConnectionTime = millis();

      Serial.println("[INFO] HTTP GET Completed");
    }
    else
    {
      // Connection to server:port failed
      Serial.println("[ERROR] Connection failed");
    }
  }
}
```

Standard Functions

Finally, the code in the fifth and last section is provided in Listing 4-6. It implements Arduino's standard setup() and loop() functions.

The setup() function initializes the serial port and connects to the Internet. While it's in the loop() function, it calls doHttpGet() at an interval of 5,000 milliseconds. The doHttpGet() function reads the sensor data and sends this sensor value to Node-RED in an HTTP request.

Listing 4-6. Code for the Standard Arduino Functions

```
void setup()
{
  // Initialize serial port
  Serial.begin(9600);

  // Connect Arduino to internet
  connectToInternet();
}

void loop()
{
  // Make HTTP GET request
  doHttpGet();

  delay(5000);

}
```

Your Arduino code is now complete.

Final Product

To test the application, make sure your Node-RED server is up and running with the flow deployed.

Also verify and upload the Arduino code, as discussed in Chapter 1. Once the code has been uploaded, open the Serial Monitor window. You will start seeing log messages similar to the ones shown in Figure 4-27.

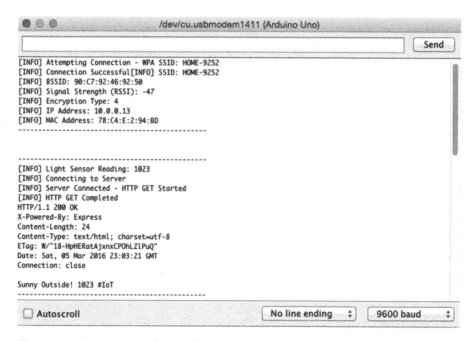

Figure 4-27. Log messages from the light sensor tweet system

Arduino will be continuously sending data to the server, so as soon as you put the sensor in bright light, the Node-RED flow condition will become true and a tweet will be sent. This is shown in Figure 4-28. There is no condition to send this once, so the application will keep sending tweets unless the sensor is moved away from bright light or turned off.

Figure 4-28. Tweet from the light sensor tweet system

Summary

In this chapter you learned about Node-RED and developed a simple flow that is initiated by Arduino. This flow publishes a tweet whenever a certain threshold value is crossed.

You can utilize hundreds of readily available nodes in Node-RED to expedite your IoT application development.

CHAPTER 5

IoT Patterns: Realtime Clients

An important pattern of IoT is the ability to sense data and make it available to users in realtime, such as with home monitoring solutions, perimeter security applications, and inventory alerts.

In this chapter, you are going to build an example of this pattern, an intrusion detection system. Figure 5-1 shows components of an intrusion detection system. The first component is an Arduino device that has a motion sensor attached to it. The second component is an MQTT broker. You will use the publish-subscribe model of MQTT for sending intrusion detection notifications in realtime (for details, see Chapter 3). The final component of your IoT application is an Android app that subscribes to the MQTT broker and shows an alert notification to users whenever Arduino detects an intrusion and publishes a message to the MQTT broker.

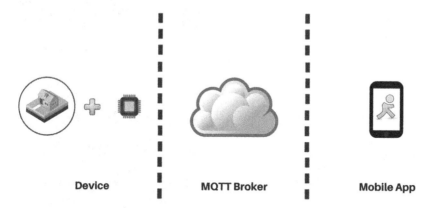

Device   MQTT Broker   Mobile App

Figure 5-1. Components of the intrusion detection system

© Adeel Javed 2016
A. Javed, *Building Arduino Projects for the Internet of Things*,
DOI 10.1007/978-1-4842-1940-9_5

Learning Objectives

At the end of this chapter, you will be able to:

- Read motion sensor data from Arduino

- Publish sensor data to an MQTT broker

- Build an Android app that subscribes to an MQTT broker

- Display a notification in the app whenever a new message is published to the MQTT broker

Hardware Required

Figure 5-2 provides a list of all hardware components required for building the intrusion detection system.

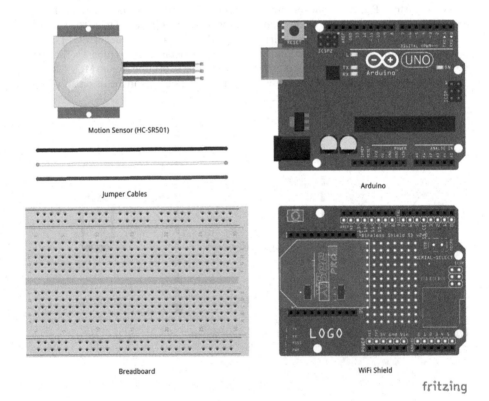

Figure 5-2. *Hardware required for the intrusion detection system*

Software Required

In order to develop the intrusion detection system, you need the following software:

- Arduino IDE 1.6.4 or later version

- Android Studio 1.5.1 or later

Circuit

In this section, you are going to build the circuit required for the intrusion detection system. This circuit uses an HC-SR501 motion sensor to detect intrusions.

1. Make sure your Arduino is not connected to a power source, such as to a computer via a USB or a battery.

2. Attach a WiFi shield to the top of Arduino. All the pins should align.

3. Use jumper cables to connect the power (5V) and ground (GND) ports on Arduino to the power (+) and ground (-) ports on the breadboard.

4. Now that your breadboard has a power source, use jumper cables to connect the power (+) and ground (-) ports of your breadboard to the power and ground ports of the motion sensor.

5. To read motion sensor values, you need to connect a jumper cable from signal port of the motion sensor (usually the middle port) to digital port 3 of your Arduino. You can use other digital ports as well, but if you do, make sure to change the Arduino code appropriately.

Your circuit is now complete and it should look similar to Figures 5-3 and 5-4.

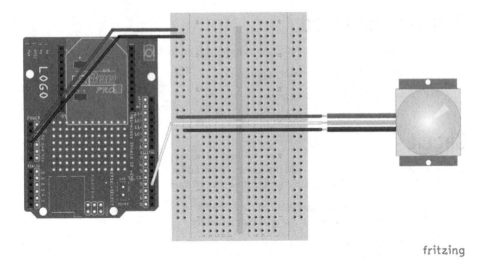

Figure 5-3. *Circuit diagram of the intrusion detection system*

Figure 5-4. *Actual circuit of the intrusion detection system*

Code (Arduino)

Next you are going to write code for connecting Arduino to the Internet using WiFi, reading motion sensor data, and publishing it to an MQTT broker.

Start your Arduino IDE and type the code provided here or download it from book's site and open it. All the code goes into a single source file (*.ino), but in order to make it easy to understand and reuse, it has been divided into five sections.

- External libraries
- Internet connectivity (WiFi)
- Read sensor data
- MQTT (publish)
- Standard functions

External Libraries

The first section of code is provided in Listing 5-1. It includes all external libraries required to run the code. This sketch has two main dependencies. For Internet connectivity, you need to include the <WiFi.h> (assuming you are using a WiFi shield) and for MQTT broker communication, you need to include <PubSubClient.h>.

Listing 5-1. Code for Including External Dependencies

```
#include <SPI.h>
#include <WiFi.h>
#include <PubSubClient.h>
```

Internet Connectivity (Wireless)

The second section of the code defines variables, constants, and functions that are going to be used for connecting to the Internet. Use the code from Listings 2-7, 2-8, and 2-9 (from Chapter 2) here.

Read Sensor Data

The third section of code is shown in Listing 5-2. It defines variables, constants, and functions that are going to be used for reading the sensor data.

Listing 5-2. Variables for Reading Motion Sensor Data

```
int calibrationTime = 30;
long unsigned int lowIn;
long unsigned int pause = 5000;
boolean lockLow = true;
boolean takeLowTime;
int pirPin = 3;
```

Listing 5-3 provides the code for the calibrateSensor() function, which waits for the motion sensor to calibrate properly. The sensor can take between 5 and 15 seconds to calibrate, so the code allows 30 seconds for sensor to calibrate. Once calibration is complete, the motion sensor is active and can start detection. If you do not give it enough time to calibrate, the motion sensor might return incorrect readings.

Listing 5-3. Function to Calibrate the Motion Sensor

```
void calibrateSensor()
{
  pinMode(pirPin, INPUT);
  digitalWrite(pirPin, LOW);

  Serial.println("[INFO] Calibrating Sensor ");

  for(int i = 0; i < calibrationTime; i++)
  {
    Serial.print(".");
    delay(1000);
  }

  Serial.println("");
  Serial.println("[INFO] Calibration Complete");
  Serial.println("[INFO] Sensor Active");
  delay(50);
}
```

The readSensorData() function in Listing 5-4 reads data from Digital Pin 3 and the result is either HIGH or LOW. HIGHmeans motion was detected and LOW means there was no motion or the motion stopped. The additional condition if(lockLow) is there to avoid publishing too many messages to the MQTT broker for the same motion.

Listing 5-4. Code for Reading Motion Sensor Data

```
void readSensorData()
{
  if(digitalRead(pirPin) == HIGH)
  {
    if(lockLow)
    {
      lockLow = false;
      Serial.print("[INFO] Activity Detected @ ");
      Serial.print(millis()/1000);
      Serial.print(" secs");
      Serial.println("");
```

```
    // Publish sensor data to MQTT broker
    publishSensorData();

    delay(50);

  }

  takeLowTime = true;
}

if(digitalRead(pirPin) == LOW)
{
  if(takeLowTime)
  {
    lowIn = millis();
    takeLowTime = false;
  }

  if(!lockLow && millis() - lowIn > pause)
  {
    lockLow = true;

    Serial.print("[INFO] Activity Ended @ ");      //output
    Serial.print((millis() - pause)/1000);
    Serial.print(" secs");
    Serial.println("");

    delay(50);
  }
 }
}
```

Data Publish

The fourth section of the code defines variables, constants, and functions that are going to be used for publishing the data to an MQTT broker.

This is the same code that you saw in Chapter 3. You do not need to make any changes for the code to work, but it is recommended that you customize some of the messages so that they do not get mixed up with someone else using the same values. All values that can be changed have been highlighted in bold in Listing 5-5. If you are using your own MQTT server, make sure to change the server and port values. The two recommended changes include value of the topic variable and the name of the client that you need to pass while connecting to the MQTT broker.

Listing 5-5. Code for Publishing an MQTT Message

```
// IP address of the MQTT broker
char server[] = {"iot.eclipse.org"};
int port = 1883;
char topic[] = {" codifythings/intrusiondetection"};

void callback(char* topic, byte* payload, unsigned int length)
{
  //Handle message arrived
}

PubSubClient pubSubClient(server, port, 0, client);

void publishSensorData()
{
  // Connect MQTT Broker
  Serial.println("[INFO] Connecting to MQTT Broker");

  if (pubSubClient.connect("arduinoIoTClient"))
  {
    Serial.println("[INFO] Connection to MQTT Broker Successful");
  }
  else
  {
    Serial.println("[INFO] Connection to MQTT Broker Failed");
  }

  // Publish to MQTT Topic
  if (pubSubClient.connected())
  {
    Serial.println("[INFO] Publishing to MQTT Broker"); .
    pubSubClient.publish(topic, "Intrusion Detected");
    Serial.println("[INFO] Publish to MQTT Broker Complete");
  }
  else
  {
    Serial.println("[ERROR] Publish to MQTT Broker Failed");
  }

  pubSubClient.disconnect();
}
```

Standard Functions

The code in the fifth and final section implements Arduino's standard setup() and loop() functions.

In the setup() function, you initialize the serial port, connect to the Internet, and calibrate the sensor for correct readings, as shown in Listing 5-6.

Listing 5-6. Code for Standard Arduino Function—setup()

```
void setup()
{
  // Initialize serial port
  Serial.begin(9600);

  // Connect Arduino to internet
  connectToInternet();

  // Calibrate motion sensor
  calibrateSensor();
}
```

In the loop() function, you only need to call the readSensorData() function, as shown in Listing 5-7.

Listing 5-7. Code for Standard Arduino Function—loop()

```
void loop()
{
  //Read sensor data
  readSensorData();
}
```

Your Arduino code is now complete.

Code (Android)

This section provides instructions for developing an Android app that will fulfill the following two requirements:

- Display a notification in realtime whenever motion is detected by the sensor

- Create a simple screen where app users can see when last motion was detected

Project Setup

In this section, you are going to create a new project in Android Studio to develop an app. Android Studio is the official IDE for Android platform development and can be downloaded from http://developer.android.com/sdk/index.html.

Start Android Studio and create a new Android Studio project.

If you are on the Quick Start screen, as shown in Figure 5-5, click on the Start a New Android Studio Project option to create a new project.

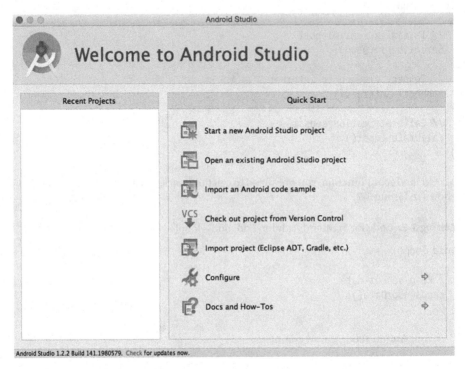

Figure 5-5. *Create new project from the Quick Start screen*

If you are already in Android Studio, as shown in Figure 5-6, choose File ➤ New ➤ New Project to create a new Android Studio project.

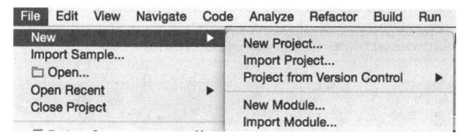

Figure 5-6. *Create new project from the Android Studio menu bar*

Figure 5-7 shows the new project configuration screen. Enter a name for the new project, for example, `Intrusion Detection System`. Enter your company or personal domain name. This will be used by Android Studio to define the package hierarchy of the Java code. Click Next.

Figure 5-7. *New project configuration*

■ **Note**   As a norm, package hierarchy is the domain name in reverse. Therefore, codifythings.com becomes com.codifythings.<packagename>.

For this project, you are only going to run your app on an Android phone or tablet, so select Phone and Tablet for the target platform, as shown in Figure 5-8.

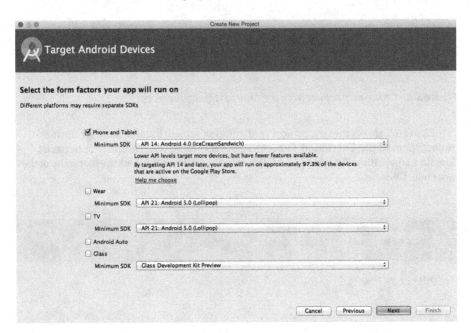

Figure 5-8. *Android device selection screen*

Your app requires a screen to display the time when the last intrusion was detected. To accomplish this, you need to create an activity. From the activity template selection screen, select Blank Activity; see Figure 5-9. Click Next.

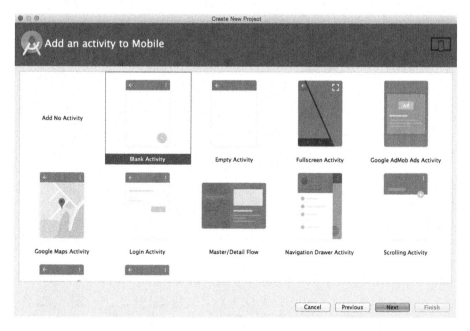

Figure 5-9. *Activity template selection screen*

Leave the default values for Activity Name, Layout Name, Title, and Menu Resource Name, as shown in Figure 5-10. The rest of the chapter will reference them with these same names.

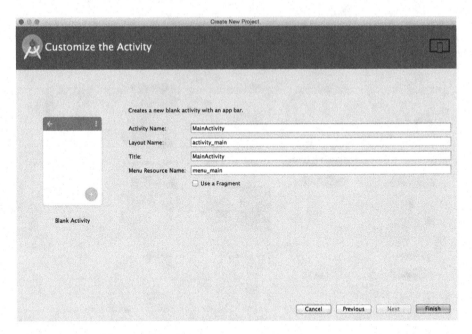

Figure 5-10. *Activity customization screen*

Click Finish. Android Studio will create quite a few folders and files, as shown in Figure 5-11. These are the most important ones:

- app > manifests > AndroidManifest.xml—A mandatory file required by the system that contains application information, such as required permissions, screens and services, etc. Most of the elements in this file are system-generated, but you can update it manually as well.

- app > java > *.* - package-hierarchy—Contains all Java code and unit tests.

- app > res > layout > *.xml—Contains layout XMLs for all screens. Determines how each screen will look, fonts, colors, position, etc. You can access any layout XML in Java using the auto-generated Java class R, such as R.layout.activity_main. To access an individual element in layout XML, you can use the syntax R.id.updated_field.

Figure 5-11. Default folders generated by Android Studio

Screen Layout

To start designing the screen layout, click on `activity_main.xml` in the App ➤ Res ➤ Layout folder. This will open the Main Activity screen. The default screen in Design view will look like Figure 5-12.

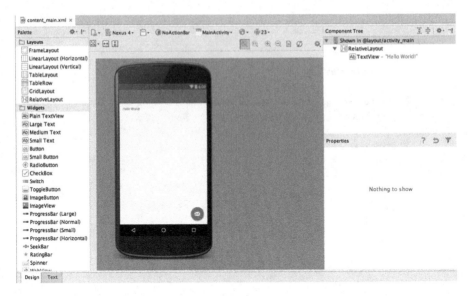

Figure 5-12. *Default development view of Android Studio*

There are two options to customize screen layout. You can either use the drag-and-drop feature in Design view or manually edit the XML file in Text view. We are going to directly edit the XML in Text view.

Switch to Text view and you will be able to see the screen layout in XML, as shown in Listing 5-8. This layout file acts as a container for other sub-layout files. As you can see in Listing 5-8, content_main is included in the `activity_main.xml` layout file.

Listing 5-8. Default Text View of activity_main.xml

```
< <?xml version="1.0" encoding="utf-8"?>
<android.support.design.widget.CoordinatorLayout xmlns:android="http://
schemas.android.com/apk/res/android"
    xmlns:app="http://schemas.android.com/apk/res-auto"
    xmlns:tools="http://schemas.android.com/tools"
    android:layout_width="match_parent"
    android:layout_height="match_parent"
    android:fitsSystemWindows="true"
    tools:context="com.codifythings.intrusiondetectionsystem.MainActivity">

    <android.support.design.widget.AppBarLayout
        android:layout_width="match_parent"
        android:layout_height="wrap_content"
        android:theme="@style/AppTheme.AppBarOverlay">

        <android.support.v7.widget.Toolbar
            android:id="@+id/toolbar"
            android:layout_width="match_parent"
```

```
            android:layout_height="?attr/actionBarSize"
            android:background="?attr/colorPrimary"
            app:popupTheme="@style/AppTheme.PopupOverlay" />

    </android.support.design.widget.AppBarLayout>

    <include layout="@layout/content_main" />

    <android.support.design.widget.FloatingActionButton
        android:id="@+id/fab"
        android:layout_width="wrap_content"
        android:layout_height="wrap_content"
        android:layout_gravity="bottom|end"
        android:layout_margin="@dimen/fab_margin"
        android:src="@android:drawable/ic_dialog_email" />

</android.support.design.widget.CoordinatorLayout>
```

The activity_main.xml file adds a toolbar and a floating action button on the view. None of these widgets is required in this app, so you will remove those two. After removing the toolbar and floating action button, activitiy_main.xml should look similar to Listing 5-9.

Listing 5-9. activity_main.xml Without the Toolbar and Floating Action Button

```
<?xml version="1.0" encoding="utf-8"?>
<android.support.design.widget.CoordinatorLayout xmlns:android="http://
schemas.android.com/apk/res/android"
    xmlns:app="http://schemas.android.com/apk/res-auto"
    xmlns:tools="http://schemas.android.com/tools"
    android:layout_width="match_parent"
    android:layout_height="match_parent"
    android:fitsSystemWindows="true"
    tools:context="com.codifythings.intrusiondetectionsystem.MainActivity">

    <include layout="@layout/content_main" />

</android.support.design.widget.CoordinatorLayout>
```

It is recommended to add custom content in the content_main.xml file. Listing 5-10 shows the default code of content_main.xml.

Listing 5-10. Default Text View of content_main.xml

```
<?xml version="1.0" encoding="utf-8"?>
<RelativeLayout xmlns:android="http://schemas.android.com/apk/res/android"
    xmlns:app="http://schemas.android.com/apk/res-auto"
    xmlns:tools="http://schemas.android.com/tools"
    android:layout_width="match_parent"
    android:layout_height="match_parent"
```

```
    android:paddingBottom="@dimen/activity_vertical_margin"
    android:paddingLeft="@dimen/activity_horizontal_margin"
    android:paddingRight="@dimen/activity_horizontal_margin"
    android:paddingTop="@dimen/activity_vertical_margin"
    app:layout_behavior="@string/appbar_scrolling_view_behavior"
    tools:context="com.codifythings.intrusiondetectionsystem.MainActivity"
    tools:showIn="@layout/activity_main">

    <TextView
        android:layout_width="wrap_content"
        android:layout_height="wrap_content"
        android:text="Hello World!" />
</RelativeLayout>
```

You are going to start by first removing the existing TextView element for Hello World shown in Listing 5-11.

Listing 5-11. Remove Default Element from content_main.xml

```
<TextView
        android:layout_width="wrap_content"
        android:layout_height="wrap_content"
        android:text="Hello World!" />
```

Next, add the ImageView element provided in Listing 5-12 to content_main.xml. This will display an intruder image.

Listing 5-12. Add an ImageView element to content_main.xml

```
<ImageView
        android:id="@+id/intrusion_icon"
        android:src="@drawable/intrusion_icon"
        android:layout_width="wrap_content"
        android:layout_height="wrap_content"
        android:layout_centerHorizontal="true"
        android:layout_centerVertical="true"
        />
```

The element references an image called intrusion_icon, so you need to paste an image named intrusion_icon.png to the App ➤ Res ➤ Drawable folder, as shown in Figure 5-13. You can upload your own image or download the one in the example from https://openclipart.org/detail/212125/walking.

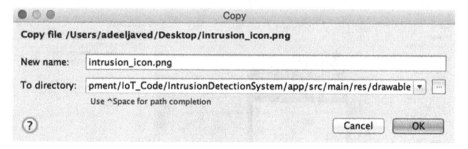

Figure 5-13. *Dialog box for adding an image to an app*

As provided in Listing 5-13, add a second element TextView. This will display the time when the last motion was detected.

Listing 5-13. Add a TextView Element to content_main.xml

```
<TextView
        android:id="@+id/updated_field"
        android:layout_width="wrap_content"
        android:layout_height="wrap_content"
        android:layout_centerHorizontal="true"
        android:layout_below="@+id/intrusion_icon"
        android:textAppearance="?android:attr/textAppearanceMedium"
        android:textSize="20sp"
        android:textColor="#000000"
        android:text="Intrusion Detected @ "
        />
```

Your app's screen layout is ready, and it should look similar to Figure 5-14.

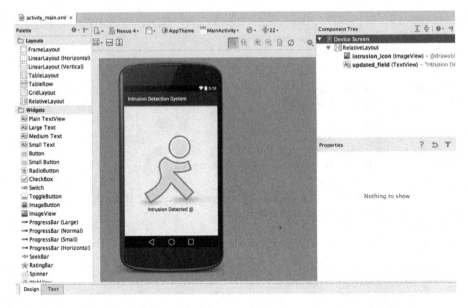

Figure 5-14. *Final screen layout of app*

Screen Logic

Next you are going to add logic to the screen that will make it dynamic and create a notification when a new message is received from the sensor.

Open the MainActivity.java file from the App ➤ Java ➤ com.codifythings. intrusiondetectionsystem package. By default, there will be three methods auto-generated by Android Studio, as shown in Listing 5-14.

Listing 5-14. Default Code for MainActivity.java

```java
public class MainActivity extends AppCompatActivity {
{
    @Override
    protected void onCreate(Bundle savedInstanceState) { ... }

    @Override
    public boolean onCreateOptionsMenu(Menu menu) { ... }

    @Override
    public boolean onOptionsItemSelected(MenuItem item) { ... }
}
```

For now you are going to add two new methods. The first method is provided in Listing 5-15. It's updateView(...) and will update the screen with new messages from the sensor.

Listing 5-15. Add the updateView(...) Method to MainActivity.java

```java
public void updateView(String sensorMessage) {
    try {
        SharedPreferences sharedPref = getSharedPreferences(
                "com.codifythings.motionsensorapp.PREFERENCE_FILE_KEY",
                Context.MODE_PRIVATE);

        if (sensorMessage == null || sensorMessage == "") {
            sensorMessage = sharedPref.getString("lastSensorMessage",
                    "No Activity Detected");
        }

        final String tempSensorMessage = sensorMessage;

        runOnUiThread(new Runnable() {
                    @Override
                    public void run() {

                        TextView updatedField = (TextView)
                                findViewById(R.id.updated_field);
                        updatedField.setText(tempSensorMessage);
                    }
                });

        SharedPreferences.Editor editor = sharedPref.edit();
        editor.putString("lastSensorMessage", sensorMessage);
        editor.commit();
    } catch (Exception ex) {
        Log.e(TAG, ex.getMessage());
    }
}
```

The second method is provided in Listing 5-16. It is createNotification(...) and will create a realtime notification on a phone or tablet to alert the users.

Listing 5-16. Add the createNotification(...) Method to MainActivity.java

```java
public void createNotification(String notificationTitle,
                               String notificationMessage) {
    NotificationCompat.Builder mBuilder =
            new NotificationCompat.Builder(getApplicationContext())
                .setSmallIcon(R.drawable.notification_template_icon_bg)
                    .setContentTitle(notificationTitle)
                    .setContentText(notificationMessage);
```

95

```
// Creates an explicit intent for an Activity in your app
Intent resultIntent = new Intent(getApplicationContext(),
        MainActivity.class);

// The stack builder object will contain an artificial back
// stack for the started Activity. This ensures that navigating
// backward from the Activity leads out of your application to the
// Home screen.
TaskStackBuilder stackBuilder =
        TaskStackBuilder.create(getApplicationContext());

// Adds the back stack for the Intent (but not the Intent itself)
stackBuilder.addParentStack(MainActivity.class);

// Adds the Intent that starts the Activity to the top of the stack
stackBuilder.addNextIntent(resultIntent);

PendingIntent resultPendingIntent =
        stackBuilder.getPendingIntent(0,
                PendingIntent.FLAG_UPDATE_CURRENT);

mBuilder.setContentIntent(resultPendingIntent);

NotificationManager mNotificationManager = (NotificationManager)

        getSystemService(Context.NOTIFICATION_SERVICE);

// mId allows you to update the notification later on.
mNotificationManager.notify(100, mBuilder.build());
}
```

MQTT Client

The final piece of your app is the MQTT client. It will connect to an MQTT server and subscribe to the codifythings/intrusiondetection topic.

In order to communicate with an MQTT broker, your app requires MQTT libraries. Therefore, download the following two libraries:

- MQTT client library: https://eclipse.org/paho/clients/java/

- Android service library: https://eclipse.org/paho/clients/android/

Once you have downloaded both JAR files, switch the view of Android Studio from Android to Project, as shown in Figure 5-15.

Figure 5-15. *Switch the perspective from Android to Project*

Expand IntrusionDetectionSystem ➤ App and paste both libraries into the `libs` folder. Figure 5-16 shows the `libs` folder where both libraries need to be pasted.

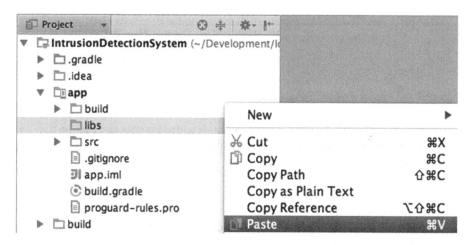

Figure 5-16. *Import library to resolve dependencies*

97

Figure 5-17 shows the dialog box that will be presented when you paste the MQTT library.

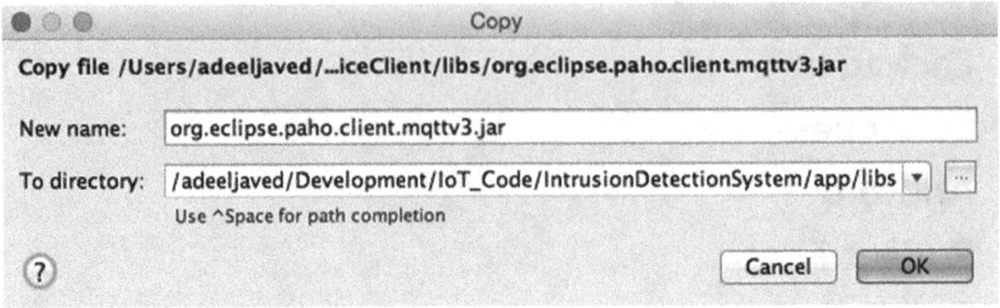

Figure 5-17. *Import MQTT library*

Figure 5-18 shows the dialog box that will be presented when you paste the Android Service library.

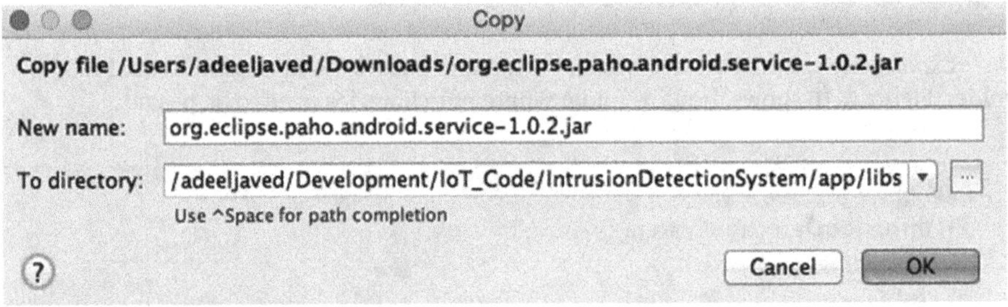

Figure 5-18. *Import Android Service library*

As shown in Figure 5-19, right-click on the newly added libraries and click on the Add As Library option. You can do this for both libraries individually or select both and then add them as libraries.

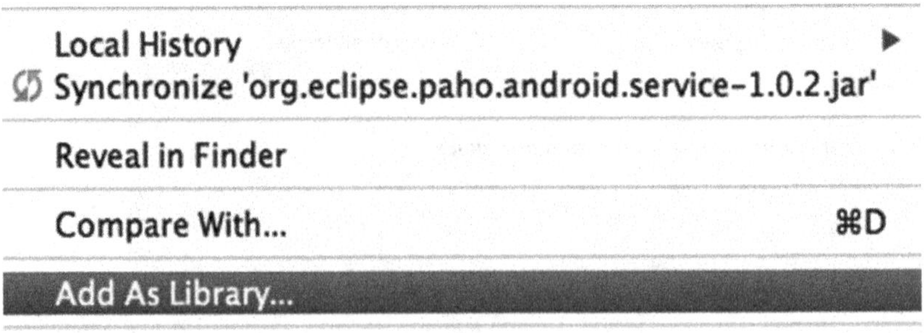

Figure 5-19. *Add the imported files as libraries*

As shown in Figure 5-20, select App from the Add to Module option. Click OK and switch back to the Android view.

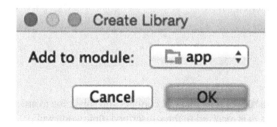

Figure 5-20. *Add libraries to app module*

Next you are going to write code to communicate with the MQTT broker. As shown in Figure 5-21, right-click on the top-level package (in the example, it is com.codifythings. intrusiondetectionsystem) and choose New ➤ Java Class.

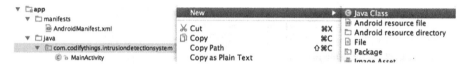

Figure 5-21. *Add a new class*

Enter MQTTClient in the Name field and click OK, as shown in Figure 5-22.

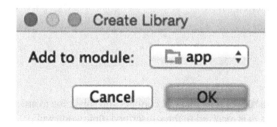

Figure 5-22. *Enter new class name*

Android Studio will generate an empty class file with the default code, as shown in Listing 5-17.

Listing 5-17. Default Code for MQTTClient.java

```
public class MQTTClient
{
    ...
}
```

Next you are going to add code to the MQTTClient that will connect and subscribe to an MQTT broker, and whenever a new message is received to the subscribed topic, code will update the app's user interface. Listing 5-18 provides the complete code for MQTTClient.

Listing 5-18. Complete Code of MQTTClient.java

```
package com.codifythings.intrusiondetectionsystem;

import android.util.Log;

import org.eclipse.paho.client.mqttv3.IMqttDeliveryToken;
import org.eclipse.paho.client.mqttv3.MqttCallback;
import org.eclipse.paho.client.mqttv3.MqttClient;
import org.eclipse.paho.client.mqttv3.MqttConnectOptions;
import org.eclipse.paho.client.mqttv3.MqttException;
import org.eclipse.paho.client.mqttv3.MqttMessage;
import org.eclipse.paho.client.mqttv3.persist.MemoryPersistence;

import java.text.DateFormat;
import java.util.Date;

public class MQTTClient {
    private static final String TAG = "MQTTClient";
    private String mqttBroker = "tcp://iot.eclipse.org:1883";
    private String mqttTopic = "codifythings/intrusiondetection";
    private String deviceId = "androidClient";

    // Variables to store reference to the user interface activity.
    private MainActivity activity = null;

    public MQTTClient(MainActivity activity) {
        this.activity = activity;
    }

    public void connectToMQTT() throws MqttException {
        // Request clean session in the connection options.
        Log.i(TAG, "Setting Connection Options");
        MqttConnectOptions options = new MqttConnectOptions();
        options.setCleanSession(true);
```

```java
    // Attempt a connection to MQTT broker using the values of
    // connection variables.
    Log.i(TAG, "Creating New Client");
    MqttClient client = new MqttClient(mqttBroker, deviceId, new
                                            MemoryPersistence());
    client.connect(options);

    // Set callback method name that will be invoked when a new message
    // is posted to topic, MqttEventCallback class is defined later in
    // the code.
    Log.i(TAG, "Subscribing to Topic");
    client.setCallback(new MqttEventCallback());

    // Subscribe to topic "codifythings/intrusiondetection", whenever a
    // new message is published to this topic
    // MqttEventCallback.messageArrived will be called.
    client.subscribe(mqttTopic, 0);
}
// Implementation of the MqttCallback.messageArrived method, which is
// invoked whenever a new message is published to the topic
// "codifythings/intrusiondetection".
private class MqttEventCallback implements MqttCallback {
    @Override
    public void connectionLost(Throwable arg0) {
        // Do nothing
    }

    @Override
    public void deliveryComplete(IMqttDeliveryToken arg0) {
        // Do nothing
    }

    @Override
    public void messageArrived(String topic, final MqttMessage msg)
                                                throws Exception {
        Log.i(TAG, "New Message Arrived from Topic - " + topic);

        try {
            // Append the payload message "Intrusion Detected"
            // with "@ Current Time".
            DateFormat df = DateFormat.getDateTimeInstance();
            String sensorMessage = new String(msg.getPayload()) + " @ "
                                        + df.format(new Date());

            // User is not going to be on the screen all the time,
            // so create a notification.
            activity.createNotification("Intrusion Detection System",
                                            sensorMessage);
```

```
                // Update the screen with newly received message.
                activity.updateView(sensorMessage);
            } catch (Exception ex) {
                Log.e(TAG, ex.getMessage());
            }
        }
    }
}
```

In Listing 5-18, variable TAG will be used while logging so that you can identify your app's messages in the log.

The mqttBroker, mqttTopic, and deviceId variables define the MQTT broker your app will connect to, the topic that your app is subscribing to, and the device ID that will show up on the server when your app successfully connects.

The activity variable is defined to store a reference of user interface activity so that you can directly make updates.

The code for connecting and subscribing to the MQTT broker goes in the connectToMQTT() method. Initialize a new MqttClient and connect it to the iot. eclipse.org:1883 server with a clean session. You need to execute your code whenever a new message is published to the codifythings/intrusiondetection queue, so first set the callback method by providing a new instance of MqttEventCallback and then subscribe to the topic codifythings/intrusiondetection.

Once you subscribe to a topic and set a callback method, the MQTT library will always call your MqttCallback.messageArrived method. So now you need to provide implementation that specifies what to do when a new message has arrived.

Your app has two requirements. It needs to create a new notification for users and to update the screen with the latest time the activity was detected. You have already implemented these two methods in the MainActivity class, so you are going to use the activity reference and call the createNotification and updateView methods.

Both the screen and MQTT client are now ready, but you have not yet added the code in the MainActivity class that actually starts the MQTTClient whenever the app is created. So update the onCreate() method of the MainActivity class to update the screen with an empty string and start the MQTTClient. Since you removed toolbar and floating action button from activity_main.xml, you will need to remove the reference in the onCreate method as well. The final code for MainActivity is provided in Listing 5-19, with the changes in the onCreate() method highlighted.

Listing 5-19. Complete Code of MainActivity.java

```java
package com.codifythings.intrusiondetectionsystem;

import android.app.NotificationManager;
import android.app.PendingIntent;
import android.app.TaskStackBuilder;
import android.content.Context;
import android.content.Intent;
import android.content.SharedPreferences;
import android.os.Bundle;
```

```java
import android.support.v4.app.NotificationCompat;
import android.support.v7.app.AppCompatActivity;
import android.util.Log;
import android.view.Menu;
import android.view.MenuItem;
import android.widget.TextView;

public class MainActivity extends AppCompatActivity {
    private static final String TAG = "MainActivity";

    @Override
    protected void onCreate(Bundle savedInstanceState) {
        super.onCreate(savedInstanceState);
        setContentView(R.layout.activity_main);

        updateView("");

        try
        {
            MQTTClient client = new MQTTClient(this);
            client.connectToMQTT();
        }
        catch(Exception ex)
        {
            Log.e(TAG, ex.getMessage());
        }
    }

    @Override
    public boolean onCreateOptionsMenu(Menu menu) {
        // Inflate the menu; this adds items to the action bar if it
        // is present.
        getMenuInflater().inflate(R.menu.menu_main, menu);
        return true;
    }

    @Override
    public boolean onOptionsItemSelected(MenuItem item) {
        // Handle action bar item clicks here. The action bar will
        // automatically handle clicks on the Home/Up button, so long
        // as you specify a parent activity in AndroidManifest.xml.
        int id = item.getItemId();

        //noinspection SimplifiableIfStatement
        if (id == R.id.action_settings) {
            return true;
        }
```

```
        return super.onOptionsItemSelected(item);

    }

    //Custom function that renders view
    public void updateView(String sensorMessage) {
        try {
            SharedPreferences sharedPref = getSharedPreferences(
                    "com.codifythings.motionsensorapp.PREFERENCE_FILE_KEY",
                    Context.MODE_PRIVATE);

            if (sensorMessage == null || sensorMessage == "") {
                sensorMessage = sharedPref.getString("lastSensorMessage",
                        "No Activity Detected");
            }

            final String tempSensorMessage = sensorMessage;

            runOnUiThread(new Runnable() {
                            @Override
                            public void run() {

                                    TextView updatedField = (TextView)
                                            findViewById(R.id.updated_field);
                                    updatedField.setText(tempSensorMessage);
                            }
                    });

            SharedPreferences.Editor editor = sharedPref.edit();
            editor.putString("lastSensorMessage", sensorMessage);
            editor.commit();
        } catch (Exception ex) {
            Log.e(TAG, ex.getMessage());
        }
    }

    public void createNotification(String notificationTitle,
                                    String notificationMessage) {
        NotificationCompat.Builder mBuilder =
                new NotificationCompat.Builder(getApplicationContext())
                    .setSmallIcon(R.drawable.notification_template_icon_bg)
                        .setContentTitle(notificationTitle)
                        .setContentText(notificationMessage);

        // Creates an explicit intent for an Activity in your app
        Intent resultIntent = new Intent(getApplicationContext(),
                MainActivity.class);
```

```
        // The stack builder object will contain an artificial back
        // stack for the started Activity. This ensures that navigating
        // backward from the Activity leads out of your application to the
        // Home screen.
        TaskStackBuilder stackBuilder =
                TaskStackBuilder.create(getApplicationContext());

        // Adds the back stack for the Intent (but not the Intent itself)
        stackBuilder.addParentStack(MainActivity.class);
        // Adds the Intent that starts the Activity to the top of the stack
        stackBuilder.addNextIntent(resultIntent);

        PendingIntent resultPendingIntent =
                stackBuilder.getPendingIntent(0,
                        PendingIntent.FLAG_UPDATE_CURRENT);

        mBuilder.setContentIntent(resultPendingIntent);

        NotificationManager mNotificationManager = (NotificationManager)

                getSystemService(Context.NOTIFICATION_SERVICE);

        // mId allows you to update the notification later on.
        mNotificationManager.notify(100, mBuilder.build());
    }
}
```

Finally, you need to update AndroidManifest.xml under the App ➤ Manifests folder. Your app uses MqttService in the backend, so you need to add a reference to the service. Your app also needs to access the Internet for connecting to the MQTT broker, so add the Internet permissions in AndroidManifest.xml as well. Listing 5-20 provides the code that needs to be added to AndroidManifest.xml.

Listing 5-20. Add App Permissions in AndroidManifest.xml

```
<!-- MQTT Service -->
<service android:name="org.eclipse.paho.android.service.MqttService" >
</service>

    <uses-permission android:name="android.permission.INTERNET" />
```

The Final Product

To test the application, verify and upload the Arduino code, as discussed in Chapter 1. Once the code has been uploaded, open the Serial Monitor window. You will start seeing log messages similar to ones shown in Figure 5-23.

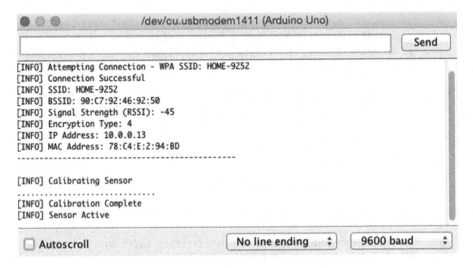

Figure 5-23. Log messages from the intrusion detection system

In Android Studio, deploy and run the app on your Android device by choosing Run ➤ Run 'App' from the menu bar, as shown in Figure 5-24.

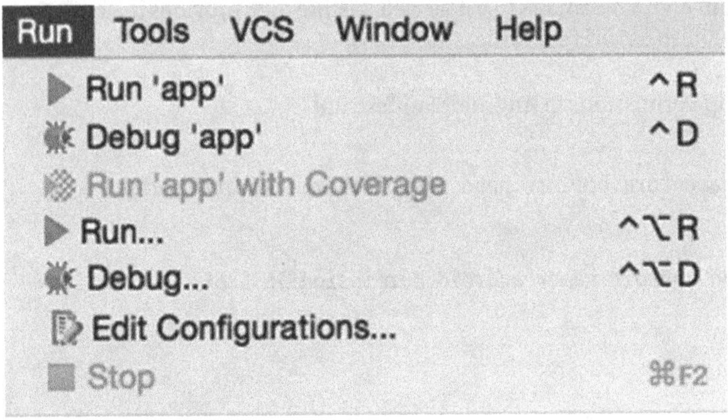

Figure 5-24. Deploy and run the app from Android Studio

If you have an Android device connected to your computer, Android Studio will prompt you to use your existing running device or launch a new emulator to run the app. As shown in Figure 5-25, select the emulator or device that you want to test your app on and click OK.

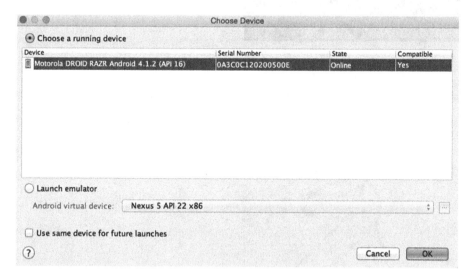

Figure 5-25. *Select the device to deploy and run app*

Open the device where your app was deployed. If your app is not already running, locate your app on the device and run it. Figure 5-26 shows the default view of your app.

Figure 5-26. *Default view of the Android app*

Make some movement in front of your motion sensor. As soon as the sensor detects the motion, a message will be published to the MQTT broker and your app will display a notification, as shown in Figure 5-27.

***Figure 5-27.** Intrusion notification from the Android app*

Click on the notification to open the app screen. It will display the last time an intrusion was detected, as shown in Figure 5-28.

Figure 5-28. *Intrusion details in Android app*

Summary

In this chapter, you learned about realtime clients, a very important pattern of IoT applications. You developed an intrusion detection system with an Android app as a client to illustrate this pattern.

The Android app is just one example and clients can be of many different types, including iOS, wearables, web-based apps, etc.

CHAPTER 6

■ ■ ■

IoT Patterns: Remote Control

Remote control is currently one of the most popular IoT patterns. Examples of this pattern can be found in IoT applications that let you remotely control things such as lights, thermostats, and garage doors using handheld devices or computers. It has mainly been used for home automation applications so far.

In this chapter, you are going to build a lighting control system. Figure 6-1 shows components of a lighting control system. The first component is an Android app that lets users control lights. It publishes messages to an MQTT broker whenever the user taps on the app screen. The second component is an MQTT broker, and the final component of this IoT application is an Arduino device that turns lights on or off based on messages received from the MQTT broker.

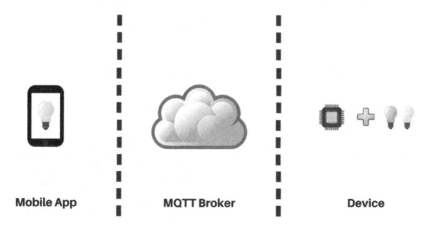

Mobile App   **MQTT Broker**   **Device**

Figure 6-1. *Components of the lighting control system*

© Adeel Javed 2016
A. Javed, *Building Arduino Projects for the Internet of Things*,
DOI 10.1007/978-1-4842-1940-9_6

Learning Objectives

At the end of this chapter, you will be able to:

- Write code to turn LEDs connected to Arduino on or off
- Subscribe Arduino to an MQTT broker
- Build an Android app that publishes to an MQTT broker

Hardware Required

Figure 6-2 provides a list of all hardware components required for building this lighting control system.

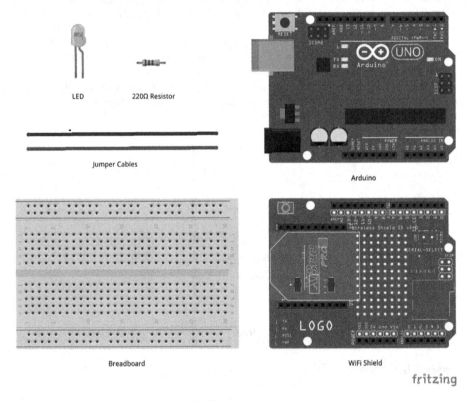

Figure 6-2. *Hardware required for this lighting control system*

Software Required

In order to develop this lighting control system, you need the following software:

- Arduino IDE 1.6.4 or later
- Android Studio 1.5.1 or later

Circuit

In this section, you are going to build the circuit required for the lighting control system.

1. Make sure your Arduino is not connected to a power source, such as to a computer via a USB or a battery.

2. Attach a WiFi shield to the top of the Arduino. All the pins should align.

3. Unlike previous circuits, you do not want to power your breadboard all the time, instead you want to control it. So use a jumper cable to connect digital port 3 of your Arduino to power (+) port on the breadboard. You will use this port to turn the LED on and off.

4. Use jumper cables to connect the ground (GND) port on Arduino to the ground (-) port on the breadboard.

5. Attach an LED to your breadboard.

6. Use the jumper cable to connect the power (+) port of the breadboard to the power (+) port of the LED.

7. Attach a 220Ω resistor between the ground (-) port of the breadboard and the ground (-) port of the LED.

Your circuit is now complete and should look similar to Figures 6-3 and 6-4.

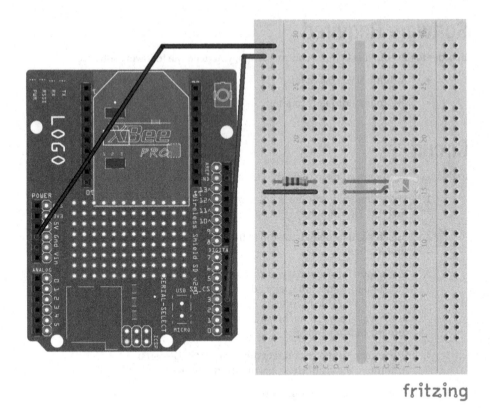

Figure 6-3. *Circuit diagram of the lighting control system*

Figure 6-4. Actual circuit of the lighting control system

Code (Android)

This section provides instructions for developing an Android app that will allow users to tap on the screen to turn the lights on and off.

Project Setup

In this section, you are going to create a new project in Android Studio to develop an app.

Start Android Studio and create a new Android Studio project.

If you are on the Quick Start screen, as shown in Figure 6-5, then click on Start a New Android Studio Project to create a new project.

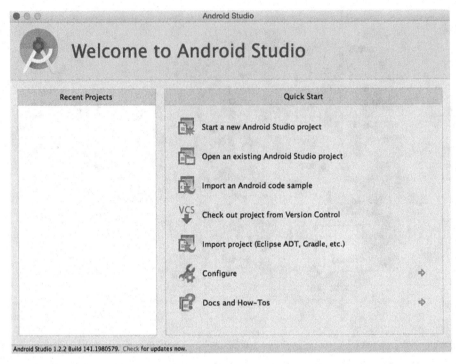

Figure 6-5. *Create a new project from the Quick Start screen*

If you are already in Android Studio, as shown in Figure 6-6, choose File ➤ New ➤ New Project to create a new Android Studio project.

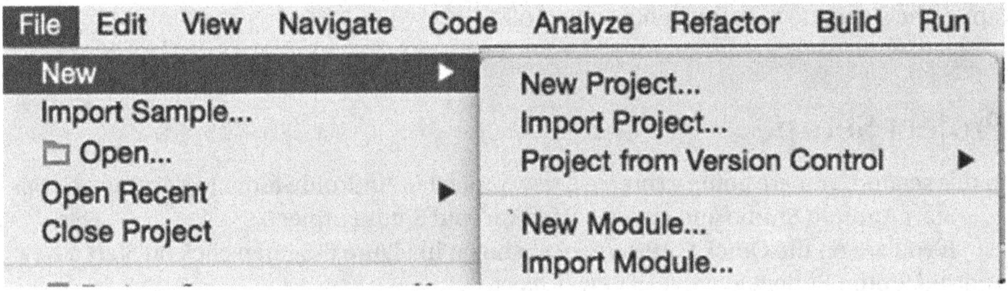

Figure 6-6. *Create new project from the Android Studio menu bar*

Figure 6-7 shows the new project configuration screen. Enter the name for the new project as Lighting Control System. Enter your company or personal domain name, as this will be used by Android Studio to define the package hierarchy of the Java code. Click Next.

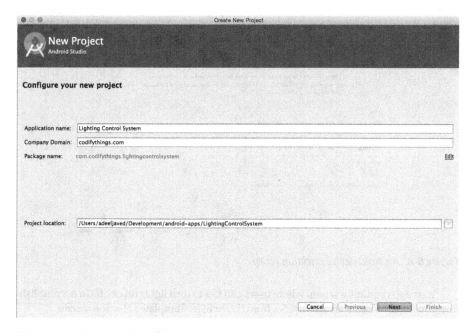

Figure 6-7. *New project configuration*

■ **Note** As a norm, package hierarchy is the domain name in reverse, so codifythings.com becomes com.codifythings.<packagename>.

For this project, you are only going to run your app on an Android phone or tablet. As shown in Figure 6-8, check Phone and Tablet as the target platform and click Next.

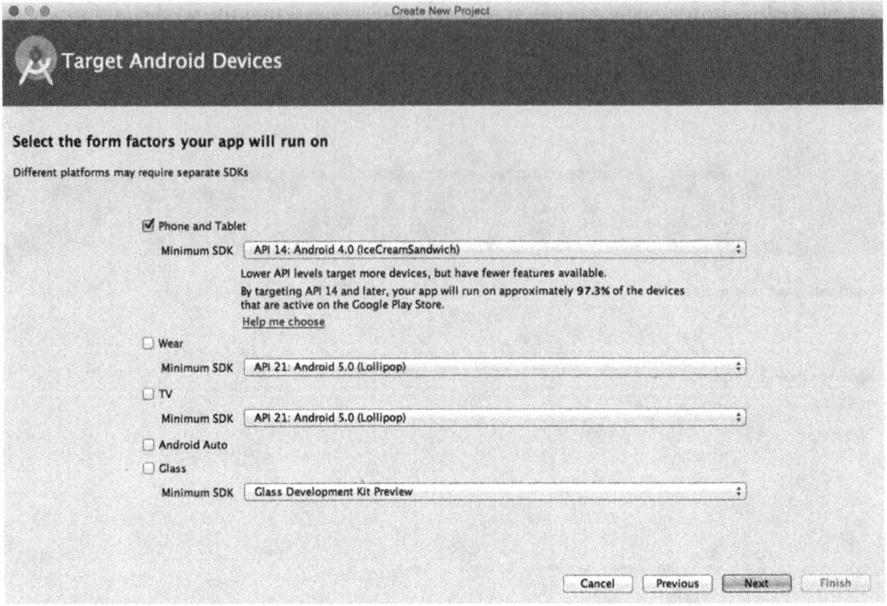

Figure 6-8. *Android device selection screen*

Your app requires a screen where users can tap to turn lights on or off. To accomplish this, you need to create an activity. So, from the Activity Template selection screen, choose Blank Activity, as shown in Figure 6-9. Click Next.

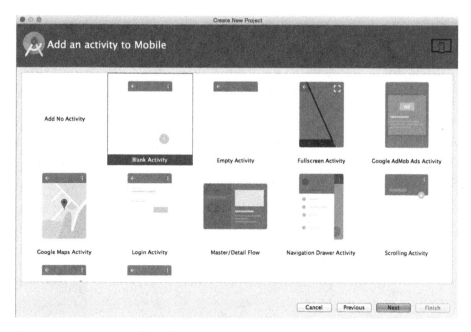

Figure 6-9. *Activity template selection screen*

Leave the default values for Activity Name, Layout Name, Title, and Menu Resource Name, as shown in Figure 6-10. The rest of the chapter references them with these same names.

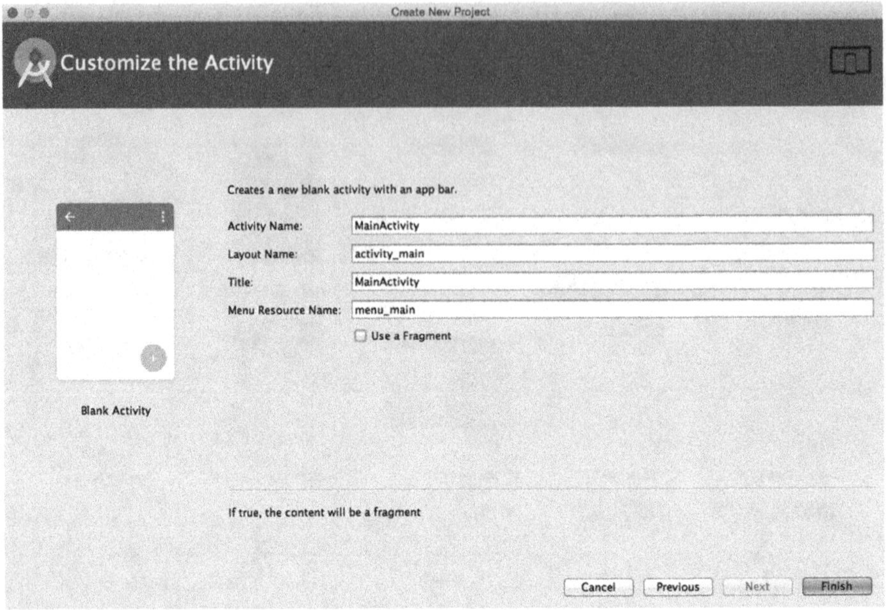

Figure 6-10. *Activity customization screen*

Click on Finish. Android Studio will create quite a few folders and files, as shown in Figure 6-11. These are the most important ones:

- `app > manifests > AndroidManifest.xml`: A mandatory file required by the system that contains application information such as required permissions, screens and services, etc. Most of the elements in this file are system-generated, but you can update it manually as well.

- `app > java > *.* - package-hierarchy`: This folder contains all Java code and unit tests.

- `app > res > layout > *.xml`: This folder contains layout XMLs for all screens, including how each screen will look, fonts, colors, position, etc. You can access any layout XML in Java using the auto-generated Java class R, such as `R.layout.activity_main`. To access an individual element in layout XML, you can use syntax `R.id.updated_field`.

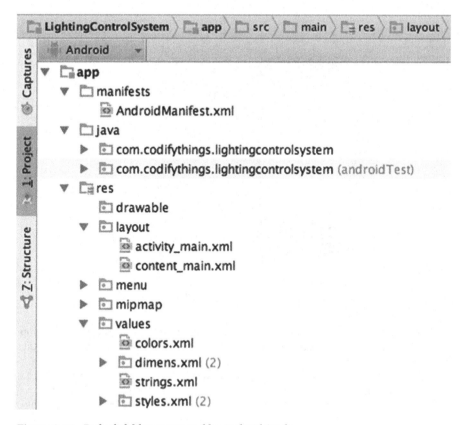

Figure 6-11. *Default folders generated by Android Studio*

Screen Layout

To start designing the layout of the screen, click on the activity_main.xml file in the App ➤ Res ➤ Layout folder, which will open the Main Activity screen. The default screen in Design view will look like Figure 6-12.

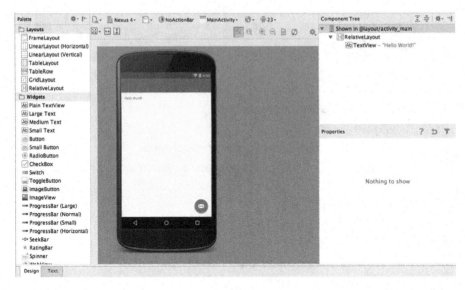

Figure 6-12. *Default development view of Android Studio*

There are two options to customize screen layout—you can either use the drag-and-drop feature in Design view or manually edit the XML file in Text view. We are going to directly edit the XML in the Text view.

Switch from Design view to Text view and you will be able to see the screen layout in XML, as shown in Listing 6-1. This layout file acts as a container for other sublayout files. As you can see in Listing 6-1, content_main is included in the `activity_main.xml` layout file.

Listing 6-1. Default Text View of activity_main.xml

```
<?xml version="1.0" encoding="utf-8"?>
<android.support.design.widget.CoordinatorLayout xmlns:android="http://
schemas.android.com/apk/res/android"
    xmlns:app="http://schemas.android.com/apk/res-auto"
    xmlns:tools="http://schemas.android.com/tools"
    android:layout_width="match_parent"
    android:layout_height="match_parent"
    android:fitsSystemWindows="true"
    tools:context="com.codifythings.lightingcontrolsystem.MainActivity">

    <android.support.design.widget.AppBarLayout
        android:layout_width="match_parent"
        android:layout_height="wrap_content"
        android:theme="@style/AppTheme.AppBarOverlay">

        <android.support.v7.widget.Toolbar
            android:id="@+id/toolbar"
            android:layout_width="match_parent"
```

```
        android:layout_height="?attr/actionBarSize"
        android:background="?attr/colorPrimary"
        app:popupTheme="@style/AppTheme.PopupOverlay" />

</android.support.design.widget.AppBarLayout>

<include layout="@layout/content_main" />

<android.support.design.widget.FloatingActionButton
        android:id="@+id/fab"
        android:layout_width="wrap_content"
        android:layout_height="wrap_content"
        android:layout_gravity="bottom|end"
        android:layout_margin="@dimen/fab_margin"
        android:src="@android:drawable/ic_dialog_email" />
```

```
</android.support.design.widget.CoordinatorLayout>
```

The activity_main.xml file adds a toolbar and a floating action button on the view. None of these widgets is required in this app, so you can remove those two. After removing the toolbar and floating action button, activitiy_main.xml should look similar to Listing 6-2.

Listing 6-2. activity_main.xml Without Toolbar and Floating Action Button

```
<?xml version="1.0" encoding="utf-8"?>
<android.support.design.widget.CoordinatorLayout xmlns:android="http://
schemas.android.com/apk/res/android"
    xmlns:app="http://schemas.android.com/apk/res-auto"
    xmlns:tools="http://schemas.android.com/tools"
    android:layout_width="match_parent"
    android:layout_height="match_parent"
    android:fitsSystemWindows="true"
    tools:context="com.codifythings.lightingcontrolsystem.MainActivity">

    <include layout="@layout/content_main" />

</android.support.design.widget.CoordinatorLayout>
```

It is recommended to add custom content in the content_main.xml file. Listing 6-3 shows the default code of content_main.xml.

Listing 6-3. Default Text View of content_main.xml

```
<?xml version="1.0" encoding="utf-8"?>
<RelativeLayout xmlns:android="http://schemas.android.com/apk/res/android"
    xmlns:app="http://schemas.android.com/apk/res-auto"
    xmlns:tools="http://schemas.android.com/tools"
    android:layout_width="match_parent"
    android:layout_height="match_parent"
```

```
        android:paddingBottom="@dimen/activity_vertical_margin"
        android:paddingLeft="@dimen/activity_horizontal_margin"
        android:paddingRight="@dimen/activity_horizontal_margin"
        android:paddingTop="@dimen/activity_vertical_margin"
        app:layout_behavior="@string/appbar_scrolling_view_behavior"
        tools:context="com.codifythings.lightingcontrolsystem.MainActivity"
        tools:showIn="@layout/activity_main">

    <TextView
        android:layout_width="wrap_content"
        android:layout_height="wrap_content"
        android:text="Hello World!" />
</RelativeLayout>
```

You can start by first removing the existing TextView element for Hello World shown in Listing 6-4.

Listing 6-4. Remove Default Element from content_main.xml

```
<TextView
        android:layout_width="wrap_content"
        android:layout_height="wrap_content"
        android:text="Hello World!" />
```

Next, add the ImageView element provided in Listing 6-5 to content_main.xml; this will display an image of a light bulb.

Listing 6-5. Add ImageView Element to content_main.xml

```
<ImageView
    android:id="@+id/light_icon"
    android:src="@drawable/light_icon"
    android:layout_width="wrap_content"
    android:layout_height="wrap_content"
    android:layout_centerHorizontal="true"
    android:layout_centerVertical="true"
    />
```

The element references an image called light_icon, so you need to provide an image named light_icon.png in the App ➤ Res ➤ Drawable folder, as shown in Figure 6-13. You can upload your image or download the same that has been used in the example from https://openclipart.org/detail/220988/light-bulb-on-off.

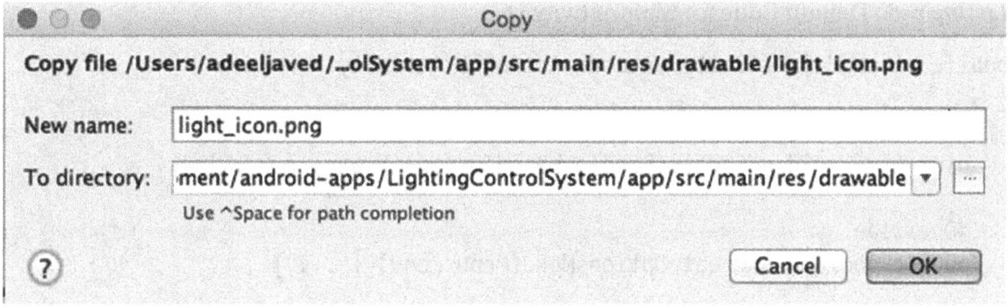

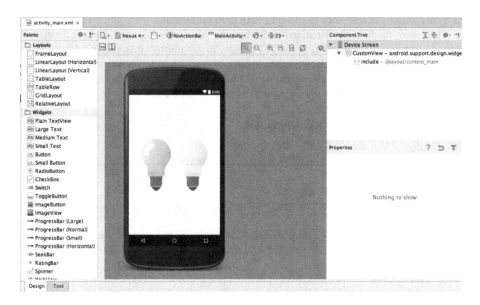

Figure 6-13. Dialog box for adding an image to an app

Your app's screen layout is ready, and it should look similar to Figure 6-14.

Figure 6-14. Final screen layout of app

Screen Logic

Next you are going to make the screen interactive so that app users can tap on the light bulb icon to turn the lights on or off. This app does not display if the lights are currently on or off; instead, it simply switches the state from on to off and from off to on.

Open the MainActivity.java file from the App ➤ Java ➤ com.codifythings. lightingcontrolsystem package. By default, there will be three methods auto-generated by Android Studio as shown in Listing 6-6.

125

Listing 6-6. Default Code for MainActivity.java

```java
public class MainActivity extends ActionBarActivity
{
    @Override
    protected void onCreate(Bundle savedInstanceState) { ... }

    @Override
    public boolean onCreateOptionsMenu(Menu menu) { ... }

    @Override
    public boolean onOptionsItemSelected(MenuItem item) { ... }
}
```

Since you removed toolbar and floating action button from activity_main.xml, you need to remove the reference in the onCreate method as well.

You want the light bulb icon to be interactive so that when an app user taps on the icon, a message is published to the MQTT broker. To accomplish this, you need to update the onCreate() method, as shown in Listing 6-7. You are going to register an onClick() listener which will be called whenever someone taps on the light bulb icon. For now the implementation of onClick() is empty and will be updated later.

Listing 6-7. Screen Tap/Click Listener Code

```java
@Override
protected void onCreate(Bundle savedInstanceState)
{
    super.onCreate(savedInstanceState);
    setContentView(R.layout.activity_main);

    ImageView lightIcon = (ImageView) findViewById(R.id.light_icon);
    lightIcon.setOnClickListener(new View.OnClickListener()
    {
        @Override
        public void onClick(View v)
        {
            //TODO - add action
        }
    });
}
```

MQTT Client

The final piece of this app is the MQTT client that will connect to an MQTT server and publish to the codifythings/lightcontrol topic.

In order to communicate with an MQTT broker, your app requires an MQTT library that can be download from https://eclipse.org/paho/clients/java/.

Once you have downloaded the library, switch the view of Android Studio from Android to Project, as shown in Figure 6-15.

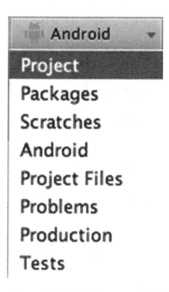

Figure 6-15. Switch perspective from Android to Project

Expand LightingControlSystem ➤ App and paste the MQTT library in the `libs` folder. Figure 6-16 shows the `libs` folder where all libraries need to be pasted.

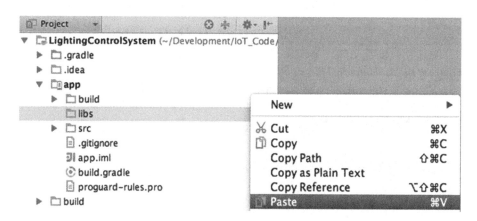

Figure 6-16. Import library to resolve dependencies

Figure 6-17 shows the dialog box that will be presented when you paste the MQTT library.

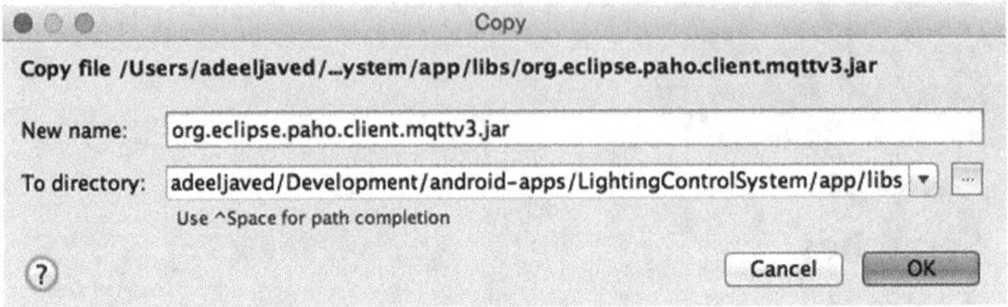

Figure 6-17. *Import MQTT library*

As shown in Figure 6-18, right-click on the newly added library and click on the Add As Library option.

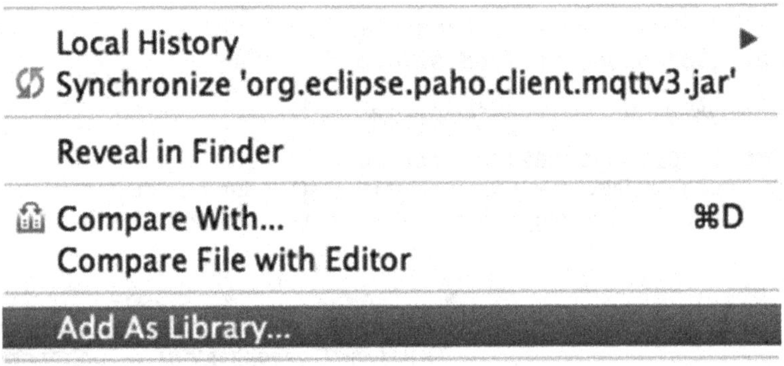

Figure 6-18. *Add imported files as libraries*

As shown in Figure 6-19, select App from the Add to Module option. Click OK and switch back to Android view.

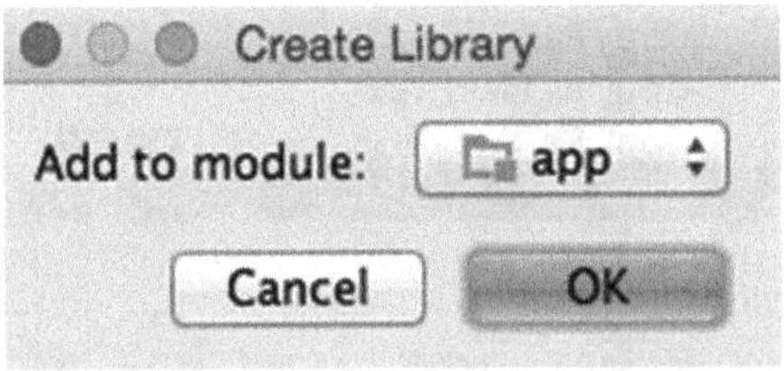

Figure 6-19. *Add libraries to the app module*

Next you are going to write code to communicate with the MQTT broker. As shown in Figure 6-20, right-click on the top-level package (in the example, it is com.codifythings. lightingcontrolsystem) and choose New ➤ Java Class.

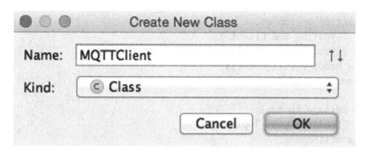

Figure 6-20. *Add a new class*

Enter MQTTClient in the Name field and click OK, as shown in Figure 6-21.

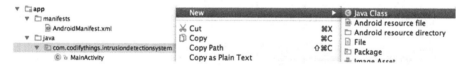

Figure 6-21. *Enter new class name*

Android Studio will generate an empty class with the default code shown in Listing 6-8.

Listing 6-8. Default Code for MQTTClient.java

```
public class MQTTClient
{
        ...
}
```

Next you are going to add code to the MQTTClient that will connect and publish to an MQTT broker whenever the user taps on the app screen. Listing 6-9 provides the complete implementation of the MQTTClient class.

Listing 6-9. Complete Code of MQTTClient.java

```
package com.codifythings.lightingcontrolsystem;
import android.util.Log;

import org.eclipse.paho.client.mqttv3.MqttClient;
import org.eclipse.paho.client.mqttv3.MqttConnectOptions;
import org.eclipse.paho.client.mqttv3.MqttException;
import org.eclipse.paho.client.mqttv3.MqttMessage;
import org.eclipse.paho.client.mqttv3.persist.MemoryPersistence;
```

```
public class MQTTClient {
    private static final String TAG = "MQTTClient";
    private String mqttBroker = "tcp://iot.eclipse.org:1883";
    private String mqttTopic = "codifythings/lightcontrol";
    private String deviceId = "androidClient";
    private String messageContent = "SWITCH";

    public void publishToMQTT() throws MqttException {
        // Request clean session in the connection options.
        Log.i(TAG, "Setting Connection Options");
        MqttConnectOptions options = new MqttConnectOptions();
        options.setCleanSession(true);

        // Attempt a connection to MQTT broker using the values
        // of connection variables.
        Log.i(TAG, "Creating New Client");
        MqttClient client = new MqttClient(mqttBroker, deviceId,
                new MemoryPersistence());
        client.connect(options);

        // Publish message to topic
        Log.i(TAG, "Publishing to Topic");
        MqttMessage mqttMessage =
                new MqttMessage(messageContent.getBytes());
        mqttMessage.setQos(2);
        client.publish(mqttTopic, mqttMessage);
        Log.i(TAG, "Publishing Complete");

        Log.i(TAG, "Disconnecting from MQTT");
        client.disconnect();
    }
}
```

In Listing 6-9, the variable TAG will be used while logging so that you can identify your apps messages in the log.

The mqttBroker, mqttTopic, and deviceId variables define the MQTT broker your app will connect to, the topic that your app will publish to, and the device ID that will show up on the server when your app successfully connects. If you do not have an MQTT broker installed on your machine, you can use the openly available MQTT broker from the Eclipse Foundation.

In this project, you are only switching the state of a single light, such as from on to off and vice versa. You are not controlling multiple lights or multiple appliances; therefore, you do not need to create specific commands for all actions. You are going to publish the following message whenever the user taps on the app screen.

The code for connecting and publishing to an MQTT broker goes in the publishToMQTT() method. Initialize a new MqttClient and connect to the iot.eclipse.org:1883 server with a clean session. Create an MqttMessage object and publish it to the

MQTT broker when the user taps on the app screen. Finally, disconnect the app from the MQTT broker, as you do not need an active connection throughout.

Now that the MQTT connectivity and publish code is ready, you are going to go back to the MainActivity class and update the onCreate() method. Earlier you had added a listener to the light icon that would be called whenever a user taps on the app screen. You are going to provide the missing implementation of the listener. You are just going to initialize a new MQTTClient object and call its publishToMQTT() method inside the listener. Listing 6-10 provides the complete code of the MainActivity class within the onCreate() method highlighted.

Listing 6-10. Complete Code of MainActivity.java

```java
package com.codifythings.lightingcontrolsystem;

import android.os.Bundle;
import android.support.v7.app.AppCompatActivity;
import android.util.Log;
import android.view.Menu;
import android.view.MenuItem;
import android.view.View;
import android.widget.ImageView;

public class MainActivity extends AppCompatActivity {

    private static final String TAG = "MainActivity";

    @Override
    protected void onCreate(Bundle savedInstanceState) {
        super.onCreate(savedInstanceState);
        setContentView(R.layout.activity_main);

        ImageView lightIcon = (ImageView) findViewById(R.id.light_icon);
        lightIcon.setOnClickListener(new View.OnClickListener() {
            @Override
            public void onClick(View v) {
                try {
                    new MQTTClient().publishToMQTT();
                } catch (Exception ex) {
                    Log.e(TAG, ex.getMessage());
                }
            }
        });
    }

    @Override
    public boolean onCreateOptionsMenu(Menu menu) {
        // Inflate the menu; this adds items to the action bar if it
```

```
    //is present.
    getMenuInflater().inflate(R.menu.menu_main, menu);
    return true;
}

@Override
public boolean onOptionsItemSelected(MenuItem item) {
    // Handle action bar item clicks here. The action bar will
    // automatically handle clicks on the Home/Up button, so long
    // as you specify a parent activity in AndroidManifest.xml.
    int id = item.getItemId();

    //noinspection SimplifiableIfStatement
    if (id == R.id.action_settings) {
        return true;
    }

    return super.onOptionsItemSelected(item);
}
}
```

Finally, you need to update AndroidManifest.xml under the App ➤ Manifests folder. Your app needs to access the Internet for connecting to the MQTT broker, so you need to add Internet permissions in AndroidManifest.xml as well. Listing 6-11 provides the code that needs to be updated in AndroidManifest.xml.

Listing 6-11. Add App Permissions in AndroidManifest.xml

```
<uses-permission android:name="android.permission.INTERNET" />
```

Code (Arduino)

Next, you are going to write code for connecting Arduino to the Internet using WiFi, subscribing to an MQTT broker, and controlling the attached LED.

Start your Arduino IDE and either type the code provided here or download it from the site and open it. All the code goes into a single source file (*.ino), but in order to make it easy to understand and reuse, it has been divided into five sections.

- External libraries

- Internet connectivity (WiFi)

- MQTT (subscribe)

- Control LED

- Standard functions

External Libraries

The first section of code includes all the external libraries required to run the code. This sketch has two main dependencies—for Internet connectivity, you need to include the <WiFi.h> (assuming you are using a WiFi shield) and for the MQTT broker communication, you need to include <PubSubClient.h>.

Listing 6-12 provides the first section of the code with all the required libraries.

Listing 6-12. Code for Including External Dependencies

```
#include <SPI.h>
#include <WiFi.h>
#include <PubSubClient.h>
```

Internet Connectivity (Wireless)

The second section of the code defines variables, constants, and functions that are going to be used for connecting to the Internet. Use the code from Listings 2-7, 2-8, and 2-9 (in Chapter 2) here.

Data Subscribe

The third section of the code defines variables, constants, and functions that are going to be used for connecting to an MQTT broker and callback when a new message arrives (for details, see Chapter 3).

This is the same code that you saw in Chapter 3. You do not need to make any changes for the code to work, but it is recommended that you customize some of the code so that your messages do not get mixed up with someone else who is using the same values. All values that can be changed have been highlighted in bold in Listing 6-13. If you are using your own MQTT server, make sure to change the server and port values. The two recommended changes include the value of the topic variable and the name of client that you need to pass while connecting to the MQTT broker.

Whenever a new message is received, the callback() function is called. It extracts payload and calls the turnLightsOnOff() function.

Listing 6-13. Code for Subscribing to an MQTT Broker

```
// IP address of the MQTT broker
char server[] = {"iot.eclipse.org"};
int port = 1883;
char topic[] = {"codifythings/lightcontrol"};

PubSubClient pubSubClient(server, port, callback, client);
```

```
void callback(char* topic, byte* payload, unsigned int length)
{
  // Print payload
  String payloadContent = String((char *)payload);
  Serial.println("[INFO] Payload: " + payloadContent);

  // Turn lights on/off
  turnLightsOnOff();
}
```

Control Lights

The fourth section of the code defines variables, constants, and functions that are going to be used for controlling the LED.

The code provided in Listing 6-14 checks if the LED is already on or off and simply switches the state of the LED. If the value of the digital port 3 is HIGH, that means LED is on. In that case, it's changed to LOW, which turns the LED off.

Listing 6-14. Code for Controlling LED Light

```
int ledPin = 3;

void turnLightsOnOff()
{
  // Check if lights are currently on or off
  if(digitalRead(ledPin) == LOW)
  {
    //Turn lights on
    Serial.println("[INFO] Turning lights on");
    digitalWrite(ledPin, HIGH);
  }
  else
  {
    // Turn lights off
    Serial.println("[INFO] Turning lights off");
    digitalWrite(ledPin, LOW);
  }
}
```

Standard Functions

Finally, the code in the fifth and final section is shown in Listing 6-15. It implements Arduino's standard setup() and loop() functions.

In the setup() function, the code initializes the serial port, connects to the Internet, and subscribes to the MQTT topic.

The MQTT broker has already been initialized and subscribed, so in loop() function, you only need to wait for new messages from the MQTT broker.

Listing 6-15. Code for Standard Arduino Functions

```
void setup()
{
  // Initialize serial port
  Serial.begin(9600);

  // Connect Arduino to internet
  connectToInternet();

  // Set LED pin mode
  pinMode(ledPin, OUTPUT);

  //Connect MQTT Broker
  Serial.println("[INFO] Connecting to MQTT Broker");
  if (pubSubClient.connect("arduinoClient"))
  {
    Serial.println("[INFO] Connection to MQTT Broker Successful");
    pubSubClient.subscribe(topic);
  }
  else
  {
    Serial.println("[INFO] Connection to MQTT Broker Failed");
  }
}

void loop()
{
  // Wait for messages from MQTT broker
  pubSubClient.loop();
}
```

Your Arduino code is now complete.

The Final Product

To test the application, verify and upload the Arduino code as discussed in Chapter 1. Once the code has been uploaded, open the Serial Monitor window. You will start seeing log messages similar to ones shown in Figure 6-22.

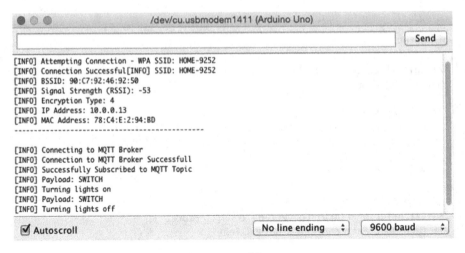

Figure 6-22. *Log messages from Lighting Control System*

In your Android Studio, deploy and run the app on your Android device by choosing Run ➤ Run 'App' from the menu bar, as shown in Figure 6-23.

Figure 6-23. *Deploy and run the app from Android Studio*

If you have an Android device connected to your computer, Android Studio will prompt you to either use your existing running device or launch a new emulator to run the app. As shown in Figure 6-24, select the emulator or device that you want to test your app on and click OK.

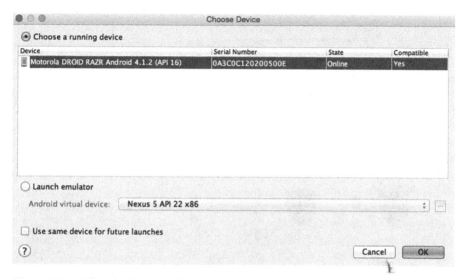

Figure 6-24. *Select the device to deploy and run the app*

Open the device where your app was deployed. If your app is not already running, locate your app and run it. Figure 6-25 shows the default view of your app.

Figure 6-25. *The default view of the Android app*

Tap on the screen and check the LED attached to your Arduino. Its state should change every time you tap.

Summary

In this chapter you learned about the remote control pattern of IoT applications. This pattern lets users control their devices remotely using handheld or web-based interfaces. You also built an Android app that acts as a remote control for your Arduino device.

As mentioned in Chapter 5, an Android app is just one example. Remote controls can be made from many different types such as iOS, wearables, and web-based apps.

CHAPTER 7

IoT Patterns: On-Demand Clients

Compared to realtime IoT patterns that provide end users with data instantaneously, on-demand patterns provide end users with data only when it's requested. IoT applications built using this pattern get information by directly accessing the device or by getting it from a pre-stored location. On-demand patterns are useful when your application is not actively looking for data and only accesses it when needed.

In this chapter, you are going to build an example of this pattern, called a smarter parking system. Figure 7-1 shows a high-level diagram of all components involved in building this system. The first component is an Arduino device that monitors the status of parking spots with a proximity sensor and publishes it to a server using an HTTP request. The second component is a server with services to store parking spot data and an interface service that provides the number of open parking spots. The final component is an iOS app that accesses open parking spot data and displays it to users when requested.

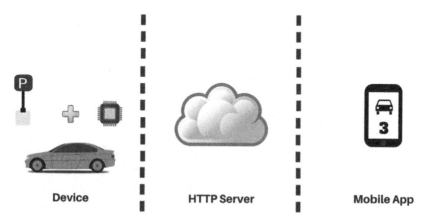

Device   **HTTP Server**   **Mobile App**

Figure 7-1. *Components of the smarter parking system*

Since this is just an example to help you better understand the pattern, it's purposely simple. You are going to check the status of only a single parking spot. The project can be easily scaled for multiple parking spots.

Learning Objectives

At the end of this chapter, you will be able to:

- Read data from a proximity sensor

- Send sensor data to a server using HTTP

- Display sensor data in an iOS app using HTTP

Hardware Required

Figure 7-2 provides a list of all hardware components required for building this smarter parking system.

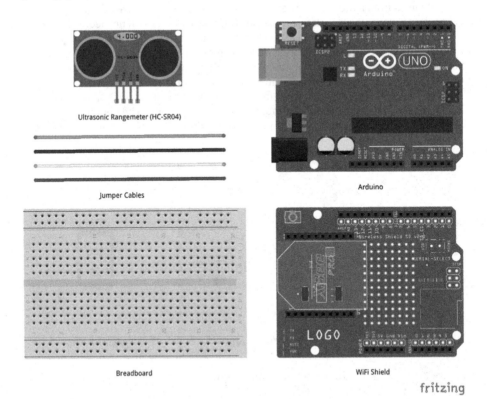

Figure 7-2. Hardware required for the smarter parking system

Software Required

In order to develop the smarter parking system, you need the following software:

- Arduino IDE 1.6.4 or later
- PHP server (installed or hosted)
- MySQL server (installed or hosted)
- Text editor
- Xcode

Circuit

In this section, you are going to build the circuit required for the smarter parking system. This circuit uses an ultrasonic proximity sensor to detect objects. The sensor sends an ultrasonic burst, which reflects from objects in front of it. The circuit reads the echo that is used to calculate the distance to nearest object.

1. Make sure Arduino is not connected to a power source, such as to a computer via a USB or a battery.

2. Attach a WiFi shield to the top of the Arduino. All the pins should align.

3. Use jumper cables to connect the power (5V) and ground (GND) ports on Arduino to the power (+) and ground (-) ports on the breadboard.

4. Now that your breadboard has a power source, use jumper cables to connect the power (+) and ground (-) ports of your breadboard to the power and ground ports of the proximity sensor.

5. To trigger an ultrasonic burst, connect a jumper cable from the TRIG pin of the sensor to the digital port 2 of Arduino. Your code will set the value of this port to LOW, HIGH, and LOW in order to trigger the burst.

6. To read the echo, connect a jumper cable from the ECHO pin of the sensor to the digital port 3 of Arduino. Your code will read values from this port to calculate distance of the object.

Your circuit is now complete and should look similar to Figures 7-3 and 7-4.

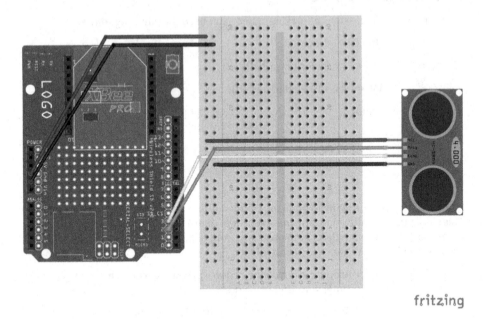

Figure 7-3. *Circuit diagram of the smarter parking system*

Figure 7-4. *Actual circuit of the smarter parking system*

Database Table (MySQL)

Before you can send HTTP requests from Arduino, you need to build a service that will receive the data.

The data received from Arduino needs to be stored so that your iOS app can access and display this information to users. Data storage requirements for this project are relatively simple. You just need to create a two-column table that can store the count of open parking spots and a timestamp to track when it was last updated.

This book uses MySQL as the database. Create a new table called PARKING_SPOTS_DATA using the SQL script provided in Listing 7-1. Run this script in an existing database or create a new one. The first column will contain a count of parking spots and the second column will be an auto-generated timestamp. In addition to create table sql, Listing 7-1 also contains an insert statement. This statement initializes the count of parking spots, which will then be updated as data is received from the sensors.

Listing 7-1. Create and Initialize Table SQL

```
CREATE TABLE `PARKING_SPOTS_DATA` (
  `PARKING_SPOTS_COUNT` int(11) NOT NULL,
  `TIMESTAMP` timestamp NOT NULL DEFAULT CURRENT_TIMESTAMP
)

INSERT INTO `PARKING_SPOTS_DATA`(`PARKING_SPOTS_COUNT`) VALUES (1)
```

Figure 7-5 shows structure of the PARKING_SPOTS_DATA table.

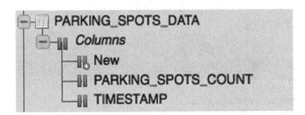

Figure 7-5. *PARKING_SPOTS_DATA table structure*

Code (PHP)

Now that the database table is ready, you need to build two services. The first service will receive the Arduino sensor data in an HTTP request and accordingly update the open parking spots count to the database. The second service will act as an interface for the iOS app—it will return data in a format that the iOS app can parse and display.

This project uses PHP for building the data storage and the interface services. PHP is a simple and open source server-side processing language that can process HTTP requests and send HTTP responses.

Create a new folder called smartparking in the public/root folder of your PHP server. All of the PHP source code for this project will go in the smartparking folder.

Start a text editor of your choice.

■ **Note** All the PHP code was developed using Brackets, which is an open source text editor. Visit http://brackets.io/ for more information.

Database Connection

Both PHP scripts for data storage and interface need to connect to the database. As shown in Figure 7-6, create a new file called util-dbconn.php in the smartparking folder. This file will be used by both scripts instead of repeating the code.

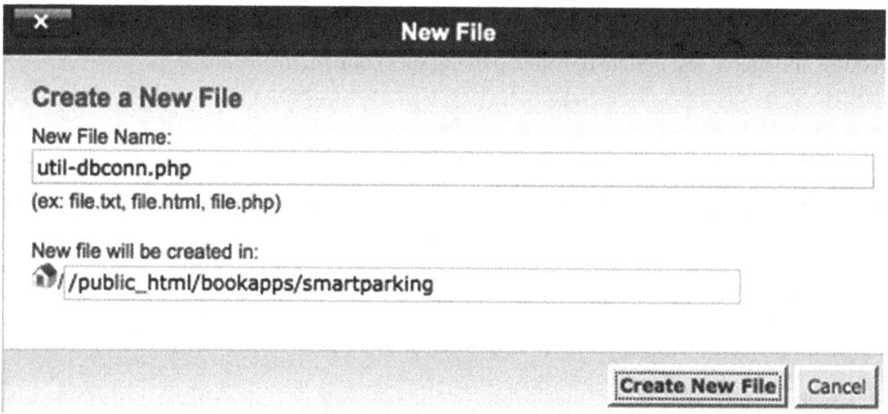

Figure 7-6. Common database connectivity file called util-dbconn.php

Open the file in a text editor and copy or type the code from Listing 7-2. As you can see, there is not much code in this file. The four variables $servername, $username, $password, and $dbname contain the connection information. Create a new connection by passing these four variables and storing the connection reference in the $mysqli variable.

The IF condition in the code simply checks for errors during the connection attempt and prints them if there were any.

Listing 7-2. Common Database Connectivity Code util-dbconn.php

```php
<?php
    $servername = "SERVER_NAME";
    $dbname = "DB_NAME";
    $username = "DB_USERNAME";
    $password = "DB_PASSWORD";
```

```
//Open a new connection to MySQL server
$mysqli = new mysqli($servername, $username, $password, $dbname);

//Output connection errors
if ($mysqli->connect_error)
{
    die("[ERROR] Connection Failed: " . $mysqli->connect_error);
}
?>
```

Receive and Store Sensor Data

As shown in Figure 7-7, you can create a new file called update.php within the smartparking folder. This script will perform two tasks—it will first fetch information from the HTTP request and then it will update the open parking spot count in the database.

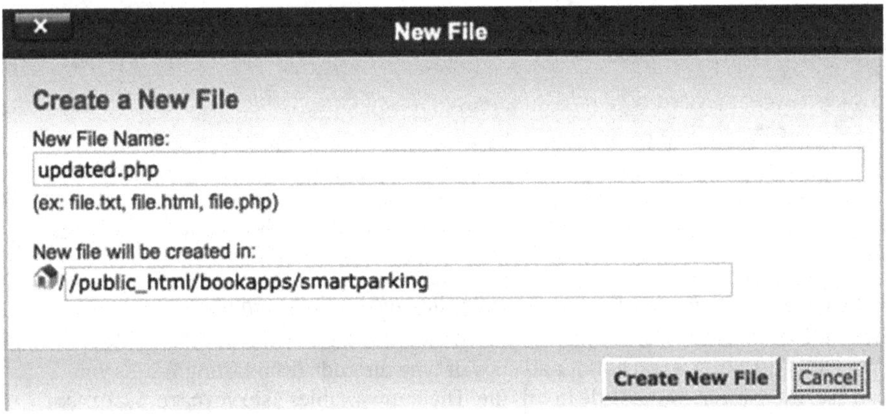

Figure 7-7. File to receive and update stored data called update.php

Open the newly created file in a text editor and copy or type the code provided in Listing 7-3. As mentioned in the previous step, in order to store data, a database connection needs to be established, and you created util-dbconn.php to perform that task, so in this file you need to include util-dbconn.php. The util-dbconn.php provides access to the $mysqli variable, which contains the connection reference and will be used to run the SQL queries.

The example in this book is hosted at http://bookapps.codifythings.com/smartparking, and Arduino will be sending open parking spot data to update.php using an HTTP GET method. As discussed in Chapter 2, HTTP GET uses a query string to send request data. So, the complete URL with the query string that Arduino will be using becomes http://bookapps.codifythings.com/smartparking/update. php?parkingUpdate=OPEN. Your PHP code will need to extract parkingUpdate from the query string using a $_GET['parkingUpdate'] statement.

Since you are only checking status of a single parking spot, the default value of $currentParkingCount in the code is set as 1, which is the same value with which the database was initialized. If you were monitoring multiple parking spots, you would simply add to or subtract from the count based on the data from the proximity sensor. For this project, the code simply sets the value as 1 whenever Arduino sends OPEN as a value of the parkingUpdate parameter and sets the value to 0 if Arduino sends OCCUPIED as the parameter value.

To update this count in the database table, prepare an UPDATE SQL statement in the $sql variable. You just need to pass the $currentParkingCount value and the TIMESTAMP value will be auto-generated.

Finally, execute the UPDATE SQL statement using $mysqli->query($sql) and check the $result variable for success or failure.

Listing 7-3. Code to Receive and Update Stored Data in update.php

```php
<?php
    include('util-dbconn.php');

    $parkingUpdate = $_GET['parkingUpdate'];

    echo "[DEBUG] Parking Update: " . $parkingUpdate . "\n";

    $currentParkingCount = 1;

    if($parkingUpdate == "OPEN")
    {
        $currentParkingCount = 1;
    }
    else
    {
        $currentParkingCount = 0;
    }

    $sql = "UPDATE `PARKING_SPOTS_DATA` SET PARKING_SPOTS_COUNT =
$currentParkingCount";

    if (!$result = $mysqli->query($sql))
    {
        echo "[Error] " . mysqli_error() . "\n";
        exit();
    }

    $mysqli->close();

    echo "[DEBUG] Updated Parking Spots Counter Successfully\n";

?>
```

Get the Parking Spot Count

Your app is not going to directly query the database for the parking spot count; instead you are going to create a PHP service that returns the information over HTTP. As shown in Figure 7-8, you should create a new file called getcount.php in the smartparking folder. Once the iOS app calls the http://bookapps.codifythings.com/smartparking/getcount.php URL, the PHP service will return the open parking spots count from the database in JSON format as part of the HTTP response.

x   **New File**

Create a New File

New File Name:

getcount.php

(ex: file.txt, file.html, file.php)

New file will be created in:

/ /public_html/bookapps/smartparking

Create New File   Cancel

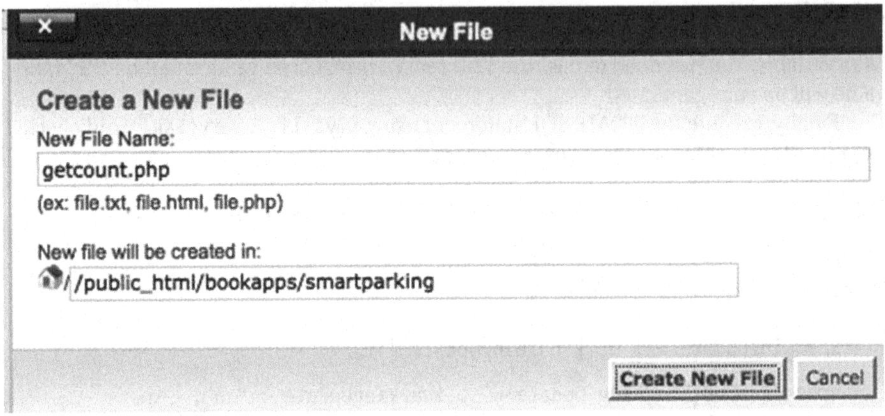

Figure 7-8. File for interface to database is getcount.php

Listing 7-4 provides the complete code for getcount.php, so copy or write the code in getcount.php. The code requires access to the database so include util-dbconn.php, create a new SELECT sql statement, and execute it using $mysqli->query($sql). Check if any results were returned and pass all the results in JSON format as part of the HTTP response.

Listing 7-4. Code for Interface to Database in getcount.php

```php
<?php
    include('util-dbconn.php');

    $sql = "SELECT PARKING_SPOTS_COUNT FROM `PARKING_SPOTS_DATA`";
    $result = $mysqli->query($sql);
    $resultCount = $result->num_rows;

    if ($resultCount > 0)
    {
        $row = $result->fetch_assoc();
        print(json_encode($row));
    }
```

```
    else
    {
        echo "0 results";
    }
    $mysqli->close();
?>
```

Code (Arduino)

The second component of this project is the Arduino code. This code connects Arduino to the Internet using WiFi, checks if parking spot is open or not, and publishes this information to a server.

Start your Arduino IDE and either type the code provided or download it from book's site and open it. All the code goes into a single source file (*.ino), but in order to make it easy to understand and reuse, it has been divided into five sections.

- External libraries
- Internet connectivity (WiFi)
- Read sensor data
- HTTP (publish)
- Standard functions

External Libraries

The first section of code, as provided in Listing 7-5, includes all external libraries required to run the code. Since you are connecting to the Internet wirelessly, the main dependency of the code is on <WiFi.h>.

Listing 7-5. Code for Including External Dependencies

```
#include <SPI.h>
#include <WiFi.h>
```

Internet Connectivity (Wireless)

The second section of the code defines variables, constants, and functions that are going to be used for connecting to the Internet. Use the code from Listings 2-7, 2-8, and 2-9 (in Chapter 2) here.

Read Sensor Data

The third section of the code, as provided in Listing 7-6, defines the variables, constants, and functions that are going to be used for reading sensor data.

The calibrateSensor() function waits for the proximity sensor to calibrate properly. Once calibration is complete, the proximity sensor is active and can start detection. If you do not give it enough time to calibrate, the proximity sensor might return incorrect readings.

The readSensorData() function generates a burst to detect if the parking spot is empty. It triggers a burst on Digital Pin 2 by sending alternate signals—LOW, HIGH, and LOW again. Then it reads the echo from Digital Pin 3, which provides a distance of the closest object. Finally, it checks if the echo value is less than the threshold. If it is, that means an object is occupying the parking spot. Since this is just a prototype, the echo value of 500 has been used, so when you use this sensor in real life you will need to adjust the value by doing a few tests. If the parking spot is occupied, it calls publishSensorData(...) with a OCCUPIED parameter; otherwise, it sends OPEN in the parameter.

Listing 7-6. Code for Detecting if Parking Spot Is Empty

```
int calibrationTime = 30;
#define TRIGPIN 2        // Pin to send trigger pulse
#define ECHOPIN 3        // Pin to receive echo pulse

void calibrateSensor()
{
  //Give sensor some time to calibrate
  Serial.println("[INFO] Calibrating Sensor ");

  for(int i = 0; i < calibrationTime; i++)
  {
    Serial.print(".");
    delay(1000);
  }

  Serial.println("");
  Serial.println("[INFO] Calibration Complete");
  Serial.println("[INFO] Sensor Active");

  delay(50);
}

void readSensorData()
{
  // Generating a burst to check for objects
  digitalWrite(TRIGPIN, LOW);
  delayMicroseconds(10);
  digitalWrite(TRIGPIN, HIGH);
  delayMicroseconds(10);
  digitalWrite(TRIGPIN, LOW);
```

```
// Distance Calculation
float distance = pulseIn(ECHOPIN, HIGH);

Serial.println("[INFO] Object Distance: " + String(distance));

if(distance < 500)
{
  Serial.println("[INFO] Parking Spot Occupied");

  // Publish sensor data to server
  publishSensorData("OCCUPIED");
}
else
{
  Serial.println("[INFO] Parking Spot Open");

  // Publish sensor data to server
  publishSensorData("OPEN");
}
}
```

Data Publish

The fourth section of the code, as provided in Listing 7-7, defines the variables, constants, and functions that are going to be used for creating and sending an HTTP request to the server. This code is a slightly modified version of the HTTP GET developed in Chapter 3.

The main modification in this code is its ability to open and close a connection to the server repeatedly. Apart from that make sure to change the server and port values to your PHP server's values. Make sure to change the server, port, and requestData variables and the URL values.

Listing 7-7. Code for Sending an HTTP Request

```
//IP address of the server
char server[] = {"bookapps.codifythings.com"};
int port = 80;

unsigned long lastConnectionTime = 0;

const unsigned long postingInterval = 10L * 1000L;

void publishSensorData(String updateParkingSpot)
{
  // Read all incoming data (if any)
  while (client.available())
  {
```

```
    char c = client.read();
    Serial.write(c);
  }

  if (millis() - lastConnectionTime > postingInterval)
  {
    client.stop();

    Serial.println("[INFO] Connecting to Server");

    String requestData = "parkingUpdate=" + updateParkingSpot;

    // Prepare data or parameters that need to be posted to server
    if (client.connect(server, port))
    {
      Serial.println("[INFO] Server Connected - HTTP GET Started");

      // Make HTTP request:
      client.println("GET /smartparking/update.php?" + requestData + "
HTTP/1.1");
      client.println("Host: " + String(server));
      client.println("Connection: close");
      client.println();

      lastConnectionTime = millis();

      Serial.println("[INFO] HTTP GET Completed");
    }
    else
    {
      // Connection to server:port failed
      Serial.println("[ERROR] Connection Failed");
    }
  }

  Serial.println("-----------------------------------------------");
}
```

Standard Functions

The fifth and final code section is shown in Listing 7-8. It implements Arduino's standard setup() and loop() functions.

The setup() function initializes the serial port, sets the pin modes for the trigger and echo pins, connects to the Internet, and calibrates the proximity sensor.

The loop() function needs to call readSensorData() at regular intervals as it internally calls the publishSensorData() function.

Listing 7-8. Code for Standard Arduino Functions

```
void setup()
{
  // Initialize serial port
  Serial.begin(9600);

  // Set pin mode
  pinMode(ECHOPIN, INPUT);
  pinMode(TRIGPIN, OUTPUT);

  // Connect Arduino to internet

  connectToInternet();

  // Calibrate sensor
  calibrateSensor();
}

void loop()
{
  // Read sensor data
  readSensorData();

  delay(5000);

}
```

Your Arduino code is now complete.

Code (iOS)

The final component of your IoT application is an iOS app that will show the number of open parking spots to the user. The app will fetch the count of open parking spots from the PHP service whenever the user taps on the Refresh button.

Project Setup

In this section, you are going to set up your Xcode project for the iOS app. You can download Xcode from https://developer.apple.com/xcode/download/. Xcode can also be downloaded directly from the Mac App Store. Developing and testing iOS apps in Xcode is free. You can use built-in simulators to test your apps. In order to test your apps on an iOS device or publish them to the App Store, you need a paid developer account (https://developer.apple.com/programs/). This chapter uses built-in emulator for testing, so you do not need a paid developed account to complete this chapter.

Start Xcode from Applications and, as shown in Figure 7-9, click on Create a New Xcode Project.

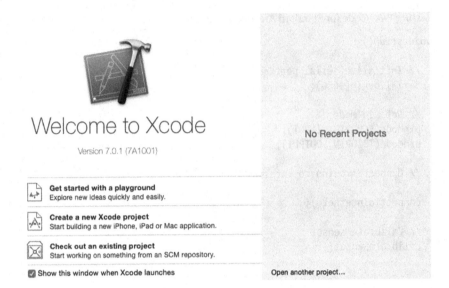

Figure 7-9. *Create new Xcode project*

Select Single View Application for the project, as shown in Figure 7-10. Screen requirements for this app are very simple and the Single View Application template accomplishes them. If you are interested in building more complicated applications, you can use one of the other templates that Xcode provides. Click on Next.

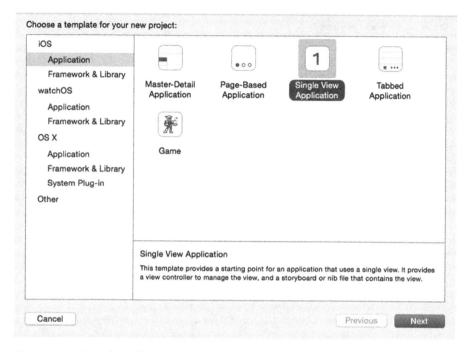

Figure 7-10. *Template selection screen*

Fill out the details of your project as shown in Figure 7-11. You need to provide the Product Name, Organization Name, and Organization Identifier. The Organization Identifier can be your company or personal domain name, which is used for creating the Bundle Identifier. This project will be developed using Swift, so select that option from the Language dropdown. If you want your application to run on all types of iOS devices, then select Universal. Uncheck all other options as they are not required for this project. Click Next.

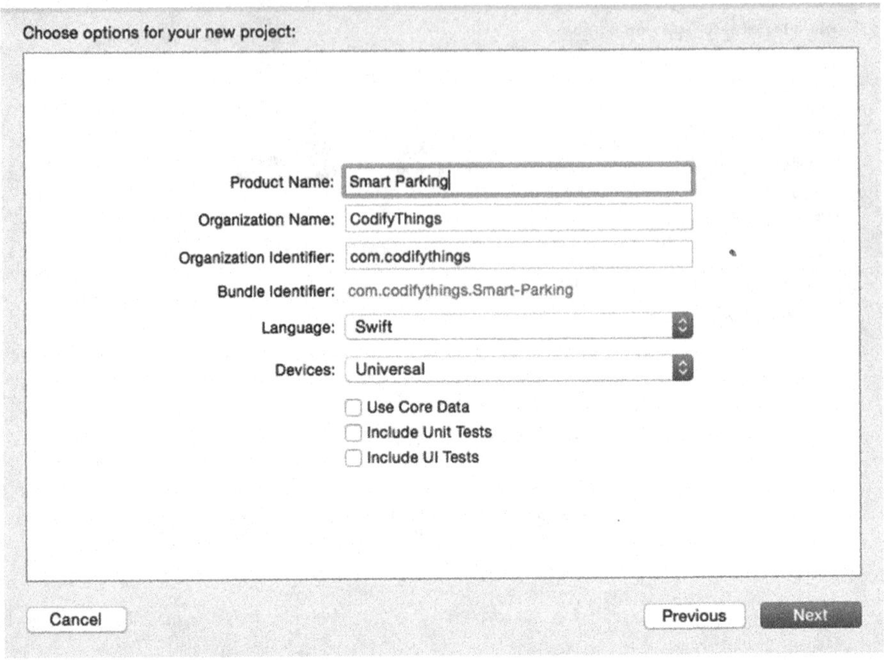

Figure 7-11. *New project configuration*

Select the location on your machine where you want to save the project and click Create. Xcode will create quite a few folders and files, as shown in Figure 7-12. The following are the most important ones:

- Smart Parking > Main.storyboard: This file provides a main entry point for your app and is used for designing the visual interface.

- Smart Parking > ViewController.swift: This file contains all the Swift code for making your app dynamic and interactive.

- Smart Parking > Assets.xcassets: This file contains all assets to be used by the app (images).

- Smart Parking > Info.plist: This file contains important information about the runtime of the app.

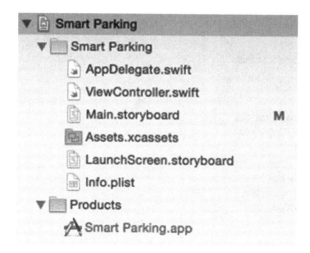

Figure 7-12. *Default files generated by Xcode*

Screen Layout

To start designing the layout of the screen, click on Main.storyboard under the main Smart Parking folder. This will open the default storyboard, as shown in Figure 7-13. Storyboard is where you drag and drop different widgets to create a user interface of your application.

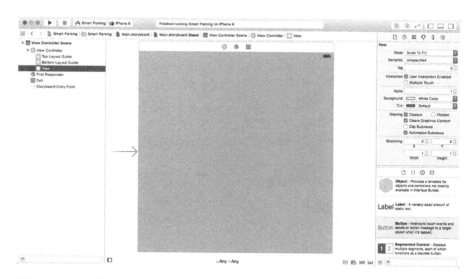

Figure 7-13. *Default development view of Xcode*

All widgets are available in the Object Library on the bottom-right side of the storyboard. Figure 7-14 shows the Object Library from where you can drag and drop widgets on storyboard.

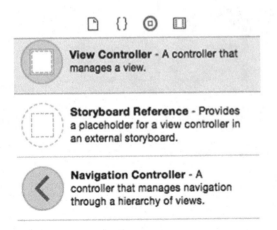

Figure 7-14. Object library with user interface widgets

This application needs three widgets on the screen—the first one is an optional ImageView to display image of a car, the second is a Label to display open parking spots, and the third is a button that users can click to recheck open parking spots.

Drag these widgets from the Object Library on to the storyboard; do not worry about alignment or size of widgets right now. Your screen should look similar to Figure 7-15.

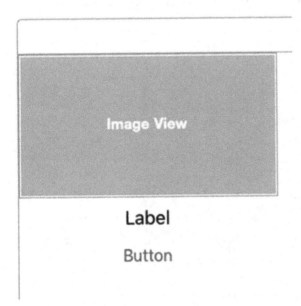

Figure 7-15. Screen with required widgets

Since the first widget is an `ImageView`, you need to set an image in properties. You need to import an image in `Assets.xcassets`. As shown in Figure 7-16, select `Assets.xcassets` and right-click to see the menu, then select Import. You can either provide your own image or use the same that has been used in the example from `https://openclipart.org/detail/122965/car-pictogram`. Select an image and click on Open.

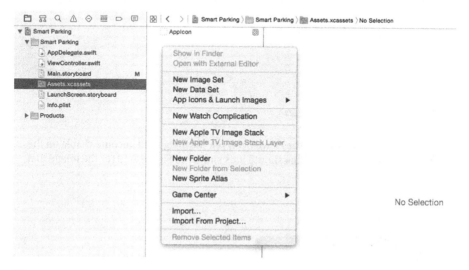

Figure 7-16. *Import an image asset*

Once imported, the image becomes available in the application, as shown in Figure 7-17.

Figure 7-17. *Available/imported assets*

Now that the image is available in the assets, you need to set this image in the `ImageView` widget that you added on the storyboard. Switch back to `Main.storyboard` and select `ImageView` from the storyboard. As shown in Figure 7-18, from the Attribute Inspector on the right, choose ParkedCar (or the name of your image) in the Image and Highlighted dropdowns. You can always set two different images when the image is highlighted versus normal scenarios.

159

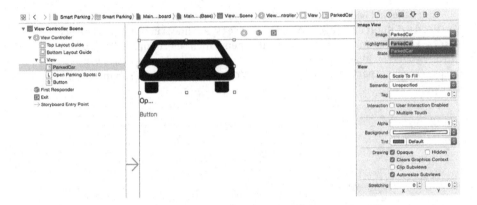

Figure 7-18. *ImageView properties*

Once the ImageView properties have been set, the image will become visible on the storyboard as well. Your ImageView should look similar to Figure 7-19 (or the image that you selected).

Figure 7-19. *ImageView with newly imported image*

Just like with ImageView, you need to update the properties of the Label and Button as well.

Select Label and, from the Attribute Inspector, change the Text property to Open Parking Spots: 0, as shown in Figure 7-20.

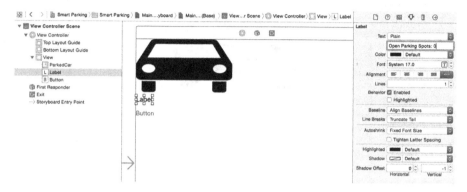

Figure 7-20. *Label properties*

Next, select Button and, from the Attribute Inspector, change the Title property to Click to Refresh, as shown in Figure 7-21.

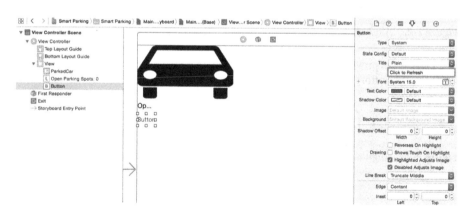

Figure 7-21. *Button properties*

You are almost done with the screen layout. The final steps involve aligning the widgets. As shown in Figure 7-22, select all three widgets.

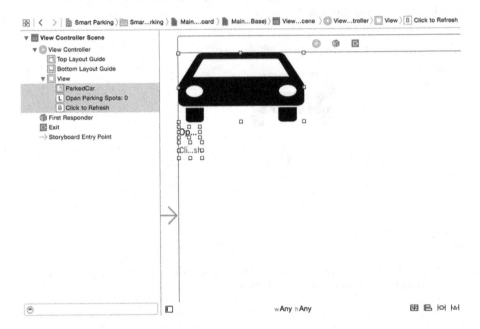

Figure 7-22. *Align widgets*

Figure 7-23 provides a magnified version of alignment and constrains the menu visible on the bottom-right side of storyboard.

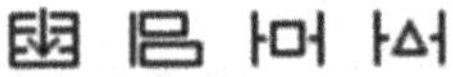

Figure 7-23. *Alignment and constraints menu*

While all three widgets are selected, click on the Stack (▤) button. This will stack all selected widgets together in a vertical fashion, as shown in Figure 7-24.

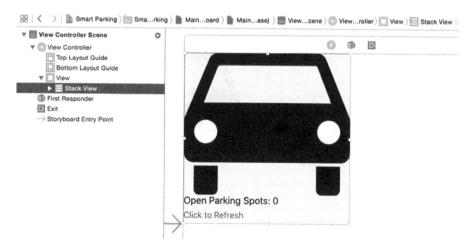

Figure 7-24. *Vertically stacked widgets*

To complete screen alignment, you need to add some constraints to the widgets so that, even when they run on different devices, their behavior is consistent. As shown in Figure 7-24, make sure you have the Stack View selected in the View Controller. Drag the Stack View into center of the screen so that the horizontal and vertical alignment guides are visible, as shown in Figure 7-25.

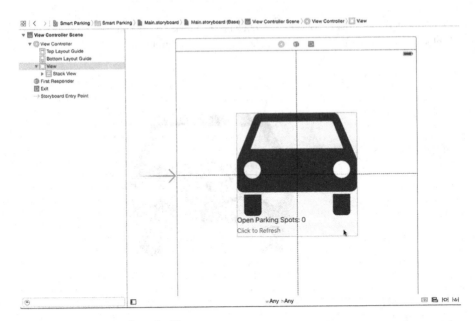

Figure 7-25. *Center-aligned widgets*

While Stack View is selected from the alignment and constraints menu shown in Figure 7-24, click on the Resolve Auto Layout Issues (├△┤) button. Select Add Missing Constraints for Selected Views, as shown in Figure 7-26.

Figure 7-26. *Add missing constraints*

Your screen layout is ready and should look similar to Figure 7-27.

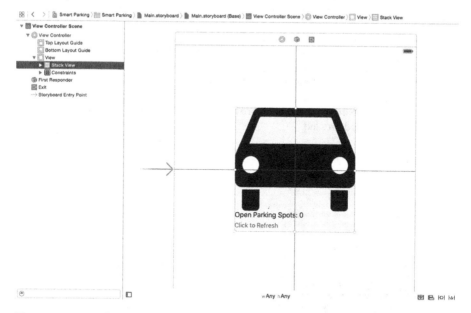

Figure 7-27. *Final screen layout of app*

Screen Logic

Next you are going to add some logic that will make the screen interactive. Whenever the user taps on the Click to Refresh button, the app will check the server for open parking spot information.

Open the ViewController.swift file side by side with the storyboard. As shown in Listing 7-9, by default there will be two functions, called viewDidLoad() and didReceiveMemoryWarning(), that were auto-generated by the system. You are not going to make any changes to these functions.

Listing 7-9. Default Code for ViewController.swift

```
import UIKit

class ViewController: UIViewController {

    override func viewDidLoad() {
        super.viewDidLoad()
        // Do any additional setup after loading the view, typically
        // from a nib.
    }
```

165

```
override func didReceiveMemoryWarning() {
    super.didReceiveMemoryWarning()
    // Dispose of any resources that can be recreated.
}
```

}

In order to update the values of the open parking spots on the screen, you need a reference of the `Open Parking Spots: 0` label in your `ViewController.swift` file. Xcode provides a very easy way to do this, as shown in Figure 7-28. You simply drag and drop the label from the storyboard on the `ViewController.swift` file. Make sure you keep the Ctrl button on the keyboard pressed.

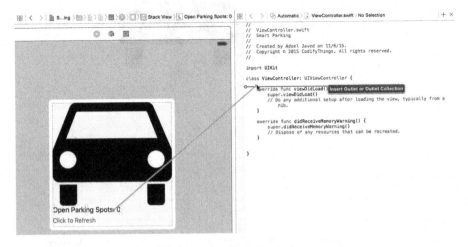

Figure 7-28. *Drag and drop label from storyboard*

When you drop the label on the code, Xcode will display a popup to enter the name of this property. As shown in Figure 7-29, enter a name and make sure you leave Connection set to Outlet. Click Connect to add a new property to `ViewController.swift`.

Connection	Outlet
Object	⊙ View Controller
Name	parkingSpots
Type	UILabel
Storage	Weak

| Cancel | | Connect |

Figure 7-29. *Outlet properties*

Similarly drag and drop the Click to Refresh button from the storyboard on the ViewController.swift file, as shown in Figure 7-30.

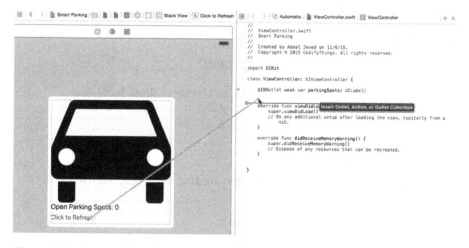

Figure 7-30. *Drag and drop button from storyboard*

As shown in Figure 7-31, from the properties popup, select Action from Connection as you need to add code to respond whenever the user taps on the button. In the Name field, enter refreshParkingSpotsCount and click Connect.

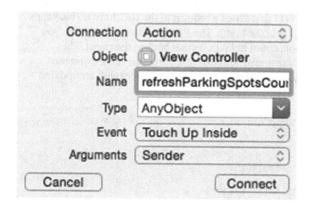

Figure 7-31. *Action properties*

At this point, your `ViewController.swift` should look similar to Listing 7-10.

Listing 7-10. Action Code in ViewController.swift

```
import U]IKit

class ViewController: UIViewController {

    @IBOutlet weak var parkingSpots: UILabel!

    @IBAction func refreshParkingSpotsCount(sender: AnyObject) {

    }

    override func viewDidLoad() {
        super.viewDidLoad()
        // Do any additional setup after loading the view, typically
        // from a nib.
    }

    override func didReceiveMemoryWarning() {
        super.didReceiveMemoryWarning()
        // Dispose of any resources that can be recreated.
    }
}
```

Now you are going to add code that needs to execute in response to a `Button` clicked action. Add all the code in the `refreshParkingSpotsCount(sender: AnyObject)` function.

The code provided in Listing 7-11 first sends a request to the URL `http://bookapps.codifythings.com/smartparking/getcount.php`. The PHP response service that you wrote earlier sends the parking spots count in JSON format back to the client. The next piece of code parses this JSON response and extracts the count value using the `PARKING_SPOTS_COUNT` key. Finally, it updates the `parkingSpots` label with an updated count of open parking spots.

Listing 7-11. Complete Code for ViewController

```
import UIKit

class ViewController: UIViewController {

    @IBOutlet weak var parkingSpots: UILabel!

    @IBAction func refreshParkingSpotsCount(sender: AnyObject) {

        let url = NSURL(string: "http://bookapps.codifythings.com/
smartparking/getcount.php")
        let request = NSURLRequest(URL: url!)
        NSURLConnection.sendAsynchronousRequest(request, queue:
NSOperationQueue.mainQueue()) {(response, data, error) in
```

```
        let jsonResponse: NSDictionary!=(try! NSJSONSerialization.
JSONObjectWithData(data!, options: NSJSONReadingOptions.MutableContainers))
as! NSDictionary

        self.parkingSpots.text = "Open Parking Spots: " +
String(jsonResponse["PARKING_SPOTS_COUNT"]!)
      }
   }

   override func viewDidLoad() {
      super.viewDidLoad()
      // Do any additional setup after loading the view, typically from a nib.
   }

   override func didReceiveMemoryWarning() {
      super.didReceiveMemoryWarning()
      // Dispose of any resources that can be recreated.
   }

}
```

Before your iOS app can make any Internet calls, you need to add a property in Info.plist. As shown in Figure 7-32, click on the + on the top-level parent Information Property List.

Figure 7-32. *Info.plist properties list*

A new property will be added to the list. As shown in Figure 7-33, select App Transport Security Settings.

Key		Type	Value
▼ Information Property List	⊕	Dictionary	(17 items)
App Transport Security Settings ⬍ ⊕ ⊖		String ⬍	
▶ App Transport Security Settings	⬍	Dictionary	(0 items)
Application can be killed imme...	⬍	String	en
Application Category	⬍	String	$(EXECUTABLE_NAME)
Application does not run in ba...	⬍	String	$(PRODUCT_BUNDLE_IDENTIFIER)
Application fonts resource path	⬍	String	6.0
Application has localized displ...	⬍	String	$(PRODUCT_NAME)
Application is agent (UIElement)	⬍	String	APPL
Application is background only	⬍	String	1.0
Application is visible in Classic	⬍	String	????
Application prefers Carbon env...	⬍	String	1
Application requires iPhone envir...	⬍	Boolean	YES
Launch screen interface file base...	⬍	String	LaunchScreen
Main storyboard file base name	⬍	String	Main
▶ Required device capabilities	⬍	Array	(1 item)
▶ Supported interface orientations	⬍	Array	(3 items)
▶ Supported interface orientations (...	⬍	Array	(4 items)

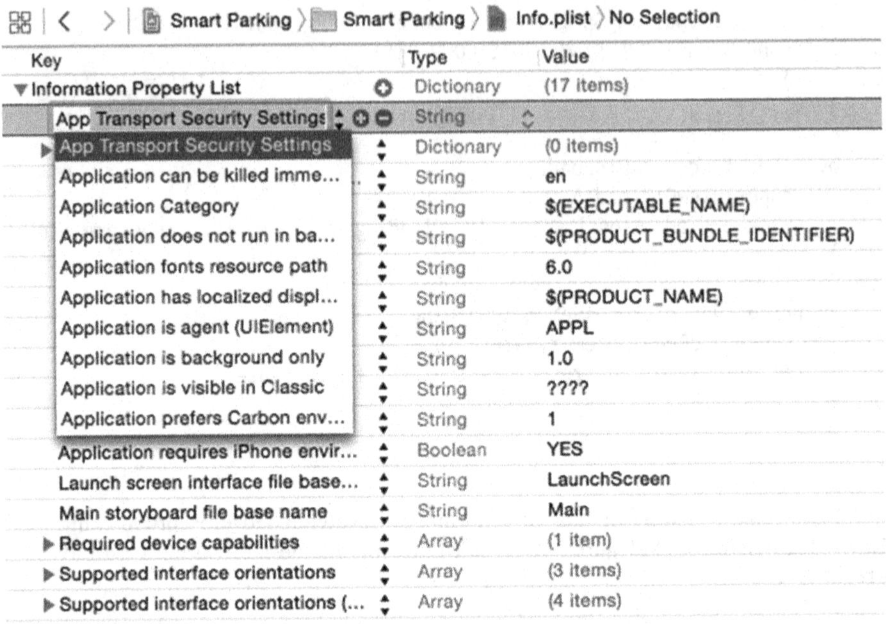

Figure 7-33. Select the App Transport Security Settings property

Click on + in the newly added property of App Transport Security Settings, as shown in Figure 7-34. This will add a child property. Select the Allow Arbitrary Loads property from the list and change its value from NO to YES.

Key	Type	Value
▼ Information Property List	Dictionary	(17 items)
▼ App Transport Security Settings ↕	Dictionary	(1 item)
Allow Arbitrary Loads ↕ ⊕ ⊖	Boolean	⌄ YES
▶ Application Category ↕	Dictionary	(0 items)
Localization native development r... ↕	String	en
Executable file ↕	String	$(EXECUTABLE_NAME)
Bundle identifier ↕	String	$(PRODUCT_BUNDLE_IDENTIFIER)
InfoDictionary version ↕	String	6.0
Bundle name ↕	String	$(PRODUCT_NAME)
Bundle OS Type code ↕	String	APPL
Bundle versions string, short ↕	String	1.0
Bundle creator OS Type code ↕	String	????
Bundle version ↕	String	1
Application requires iPhone envir... ↕	Boolean	YES
Launch screen interface file base... ↕	String	LaunchScreen
Main storyboard file base name ↕	String	Main
▶ Required device capabilities ↕	Array	(1 item)
▶ Supported interface orientations ↕	Array	(3 items)
▶ Supported interface orientations (... ↕	Array	(4 items)

Top bar: 🔲 < > | 📄 Smart Parking ⟩ 📁 Smart Parking ⟩ 📄 Info.plist ⟩ No Selection

Figure 7-34. *Select the Allow Arbitrary Loads property*

This completes the implementation of your iOS app.

The Final Product

To test the application, make sure your MySQL and PHP servers are up and running with the code deployed.

Also verify and upload the Arduino code as discussed in Chapter 1. Make sure initially there is no object in front of your proximity sensor. Once the code has been uploaded, open the Serial Monitor window. You will start seeing log messages similar to the ones shown in Figure 7-35.

Figure 7-35. *Log messages from the smarter parking system*

Next, open your iOS app in Xcode. Click on the Play button from menu visible on top-left side of storyboard shown in Figure 7-36 to launch your app in a simulator.

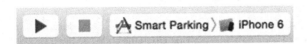

Figure 7-36. *Screen simulation menu*

Once the app launches, click on the Click to Refresh button to fetch the latest count of the open parking spots. Figure 7-37 shows how the screen will look in the simulator. The screen will show 1 because you have not placed any object in front of the proximity sensor.

Figure 7-37. *App screen in simulator with one open spot*

As shown in Figure 7-38, place an object in front of your proximity sensor.

Figure 7-38. Object in front of proximity sensor

As soon as your Arduino sends the next HTTP request to the server, the count will change. Click the Refresh button on your iOS app. As shown in Figure 7-39, it will show no open spots.

Open Parking Spots: 0

Click to Refresh

Figure 7-39. *App screen in simulator with no open spots*

Summary

In this chapter, you learned about the on-demand pattern of IoT applications. This pattern is a good fit if your users are not required to be fed data and instead are provided the latest data only when they request it. The smarter parking system that you built in this chapter is a good example of this pattern, because users are only concerned with open parking spot information when they are looking for a parking spot; otherwise, they are not concerned.

CHAPTER 8

■ ■ ■

IoT Patterns: Web Apps

As most of our day-to-day tasks and interactions move to mobile devices, web applications will still have a place. In the IoT space, they will mainly be used for monitoring and controlling large-scale implementations.

In this chapter, you are going to build a temperature monitoring system. Figure 8-1 shows a high-level diagram of all components involved in this system. The first component is an Arduino device that gathers temperature data and publishes it to a server using an HTTP request. The second component is a server that receives temperature data and stores it in a database. The final component accesses temperature data from the server and presents it to users in a web-based analytics dashboard. This web-based analytics dashboard is going to reside in the server as well.

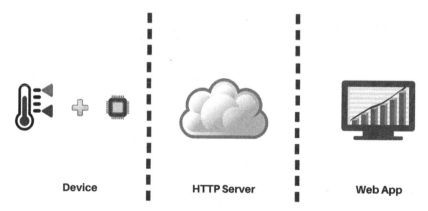

Device   **HTTP Server**   **Web App**

Figure 8-1. *Components of the temperature monitoring system*

Learning Objectives

At the end of this chapter, you will be able to:

- Read data from a temperature sensor

- Publish sensor data to a server

- Display sensor data in a web-based dashboard

© Adeel Javed 2016
A. Javed, *Building Arduino Projects for the Internet of Things*,
DOI 10.1007/978-1-4842-1940-9_8

Hardware Required

Figure 8-2 provides a list of all hardware components required for building this temperature monitoring system.

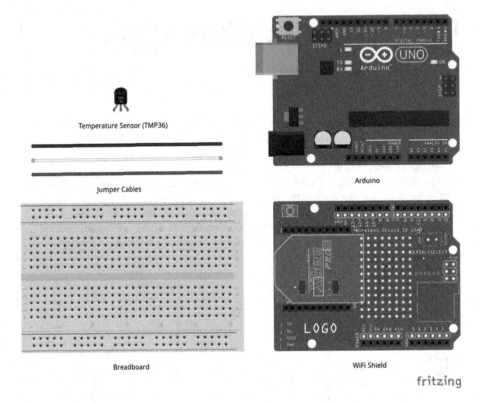

Figure 8-2. Hardware required for the temperature monitoring system

Software Required

In order to develop the temperature monitoring system, you need the following software:

- Arduino IDE 1.6.4 or later
- PHP server (installed or hosted)
- MySQL server (installed or hosted)
- Text editor

Circuit

In this section, you are going to build the circuit required for the temperature monitoring system. This circuit uses a low-cost and easy-to-use TMP36 temperature sensor. The sensor returns its values in voltage, which is converted into Celsius and Fahrenheit.

1. Make sure Arduino is not connected to a power source, such as to a computer via USB or a battery.

2. Attach a WiFi shield to the top of the Arduino. All the pins should align.

3. Use jumper cables to connect the power (5V) and ground (GND) ports on Arduino to the power (+) and ground (-) ports on the breadboard.

4. Now that your breadboard has a power source, use jumper cables to connect the power (+) and ground (-) ports of your breadboard to the power and ground ports of the temperature sensor. The left pin of the sensor is the power (+) and the right pin is the ground (-).

5. To read values from the temperature sensor, you will need to connect a jumper cable from the analog voltage port (middle pin) of the temperature sensor to the A0 (Analog) port of Arduino. Your code will read the voltage from this port to calculate the temperature in Celsius and Fahrenheit.

Your circuit is now complete and should look similar to Figures 8-3 and 8-4.

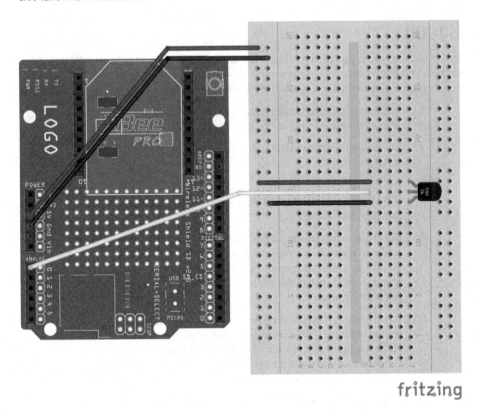

Figure 8-3. *Circuit diagram of the temperature monitoring system*

Figure 8-4. *Actual circuit of the temperature monitoring system*

Database Table (MySQL)

As discussed in the previous chapter, before you can send HTTP requests from Arduino, you need to build a service that will receive data.

This chapter also uses MySQL as a database. The application needs a very simple three-column table. So create a new table called TEMPERATURE_MONITORING_DATA using the SQL script provided in Listing 8-1. Run this script in an existing database or create a new one.

The first column will be an auto-generated ID, the second column will be an auto-generated timestamp, and the third column will be used to store the temperature readings.

Listing 8-1. Create Table SQL

```
CREATE TABLE `TEMPERATURE_MONITORING_DATA`
(
  `ID` int(11) NOT NULL AUTO_INCREMENT,
  `TIMESTAMP` timestamp NOT NULL DEFAULT CURRENT_TIMESTAMP ON UPDATE
  CURRENT_TIMESTAMP,
  `TEMPERATURE` double NOT NULL,
  PRIMARY KEY (`ID`)
)
```

Figure 8-5 shows the structure of the TEMPERATURE_MONITORING_DATA table.

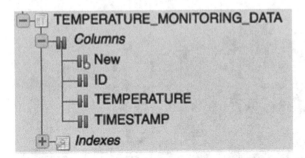

Figure 8-5. *TEMPERATURE_MONITORING_DATA table structure*

Code (PHP)

Now that the database table is ready, you need to build two services. The first service will receive the Arduino sensor data and store it in the newly created database table. The second service will show historical sensor data in a dashboard.

This project also uses PHP for building data storage and interface services.

Create a new folder called tempmonitor in the public/root folder of your PHP server. All of the PHP source code for this project will go in this tempmonitor folder.

Start a text editor of your choice.

■ **Note**   All the PHP code was developed using Brackets, which is an open source text editor. See http://brackets.io/ for more information.

Database Connection

The PHP scripts for storing and displaying data will need to connect to the database. As shown in Figure 8-6, create a new file called util-dbconn.php in the tempmonitor folder. This file will be used by both scripts instead of repeating the code.

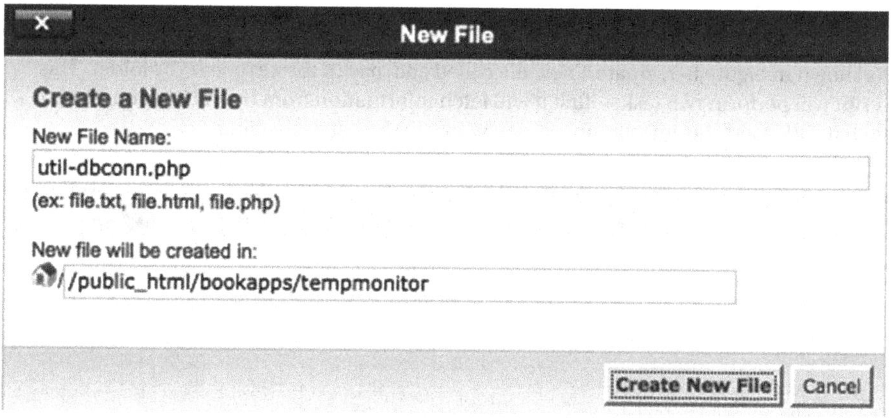

Figure 8-6. Common database connectivity file called util-dbconn.php

Open the file in a text editor and copy or type code from Listing 8-2. As you can see, there is not much code in this file. The four variables $servername, $username, $password, and $dbname contain the connection information. Create a new connection by passing these four variables and store the connection reference in the $mysqli variable.

The IF condition in the code simply checks for errors during the connection attempt and prints them if there were any.

Listing 8-2. Common Database Connectivity Code util-dbconn.php

```php
<?php
    $servername = "SERVER_NAME";
    $dbname = "DB_NAME";
    $username = "DB_USERNAME";
    $password = "DB_PASSWORD";

    //Open a new connection to MySQL server
    $mysqli = new mysqli($servername, $username, $password, $dbname);

    //Output connection errors
    if ($mysqli->connect_error)
    {
        die("[ERROR] Connection Failed: " . $mysqli->connect_error);
    }
?>
```

Receive and Store Sensor Data

As shown in Figure 8-7, create a new file called add.php in the tempmonitor folder. This script will perform two tasks—first it will fetch information from the HTTP request and then it will insert this information as a new row in the database table.

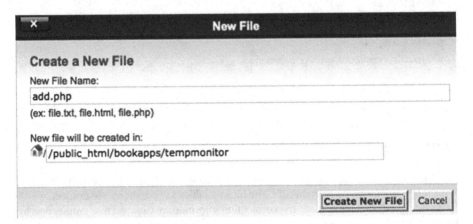

Figure 8-7. File to receive and store data in add.php

Open the newly created file in a text editor and copy or type the code provided in Listing 8-3. As mentioned in the previous step, in order to store data, a database connection needs to be established. You created util-dbconn.php to perform that task, so in this file you need to include util-dbconn.php. The util-dbconn.php file provides access to the $mysqli variable, which contains connection references and will be used to run the SQL queries.

The example in this book is hosted at http://bookapps.codifythings.com/tempmonitor, and Arduino will be sending temperature data to add.php using an HTTP GET method. As discussed in Chapter 2, HTTP GET uses a query string to send request data. So, the complete URL with the query string that Arduino will be using becomes http://bookapps.codifythings.com/tempmonitor/add.php?temperature=79.5. Your PHP code will need to extract temperature values from the query string using the $_GET['temperature'] statement.

Now you need to store this temperature value in the database table as a new row. Prepare an INSERT SQL statement in $sql variable. You just need to pass the temperature value, as ID and TIMESTAMP are both auto-generated, so the database will take care of that for you.

Finally, execute the INSERT SQL statement using $mysqli->query($sql) and check the $result variable for success or failure.

Listing 8-3. Code to Receive and Store Data in add.php

```php
<?php
    include('util-dbconn.php');

    $temperature = $_GET['temperature'];
    echo "[DEBUG] Temperature Sensor Data: " . $temperature . "\n";
    $sql = "INSERT INTO `TEMPERATURE_MONITORING_DATA`(`TEMPERATURE`) VALUES
    ($temperature)";

    if (!$result = $mysqli->query($sql))
    {
        echo "[Error] " . mysqli_error() . "\n";
        exit();
    }

    $mysqli->close();

    echo "[DEBUG] New Temperature Sensor Data Added Successfully\n";

?>
```

Dashboard

All the data that is being captured by the sensor and stored in database is not visible to anyone. So next, you are going to build an analytics dashboard that will load the last 30 entries from the database and display them in a bar chart format. As shown in Figure 8-8, create a new file called index.php in the tempmonitor folder.

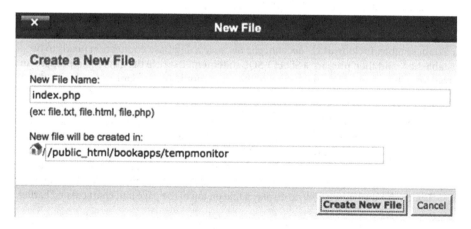

Figure 8-8. *The file for analytics dashboard is index.php*

185

Listing 8-4 provides the structure of the index.php file. The structure is standard HTML, so in the <head> tag you are going to load data from database table, load dependencies and initialize the chart. The <body> tag will simply display the chart.

Listing 8-4. Code Structure for Analytics Dashboard in index.php

```
<html>
        <head>
                <title>...</title>

                <?php
                ?>

                <script src="..." />

                <script>
                        // chart customization code
                </script>
        </head>

        <body>
                // chart display
        </body>
</html>
```

Listing 8-5 provides the complete code for index.php, so copy or write the code in index.php. For developing the bar chart, you will be using Dojo, which is a very popular JavaScript toolkit. You do not need to download or install any code. The toolkit is accessible over the Internet so your script tag just needs to point to //ajax.googleapis.com/ajax/libs/dojo/1.10.4/dojo/dojo.js as its source.

To populate the chart, you first need to load data from the database in an array variable called chartData. In the <script> tag, add the PHP code for loading data from a database table. Include util-dbconn.php because a database connection needs to be established, and then prepare a SELECT SQL statement. Execute the query and prepare an array from the results. The final format of the array should be similar to var chartData = [Val1, Val2, Val3].

To use Dojo toolkit resources, you need to load all the dependencies using require(). For chart development, the two most important dependencies are the chart resource dojox/charting/Chart and a theme dojox/charting/themes/PlotKit/orange. The remaining dependencies are included for customizing the chart.

Inside function(Chart, theme){...}, create a new chart, set its theme, customize its plot area and x/y axis, add a chartData series to the chart. Finally, render the chart.

The <body> tag has the code to display a title on top of the page and chart created earlier.

Listing 8-5. Complete Code for the Analytics Dashboard in index.php

```html
<html lang="en">

<head>

        <title>Temperature Monitoring System - Dashboard</title>

        <script src="//ajax.googleapis.com/ajax/libs/dojo/1.10.4/dojo/dojo.js"
                data-dojo-config="async: true"></script>

        <script>
                <?php
                include('util-dbconn.php');

                $sql = "SELECT * FROM (SELECT * FROM
                        `TEMPERATURE_MONITORING_DATA`
                        ORDER BY ID DESC LIMIT 30) sub ORDER BY id ASC";
                $result = $mysqli->query($sql);
                $resultCount = $result->num_rows;

                if ($resultCount > 0)
                {
                        $currentRow = 0;
                        echo "var chartData = [";
                        // output data of each row
                        while($row = $result->fetch_assoc())
                        {
                            $currentRow = $currentRow + 1;

                            echo $row["TEMPERATURE"];

                            if($currentRow < $resultCount)
                            {
                                echo ",";
                            }
                        }
                        echo "];";
                        }
                else
                {
                        echo "0 results";
                }

                $mysqli->close();

                ?>
```

```
                require([
                "dojox/charting/Chart",
                "dojox/charting/themes/PlotKit/orange",
                "dojox/charting/plot2d/Columns",
                "dojox/charting/plot2d/Markers",
                "dojox/charting/axis2d/Default",
                "dojo/domReady!"
                ], function(Chart, theme) {
                        var chart = new Chart("chartNode");

                        chart.setTheme(theme);

                        chart.addPlot("default", {type: "Columns",
                                        gap: 5 , labels: true,
                                        labelStyle: "outside"});

                        chart.addAxis("x", {title: "Readings (#)",
                                         titleOrientation: "away"});
                        chart.addAxis("y", {title: "Temperature (F)",
                                        titleOrientation: "axis" , min: 0,
                                        max: 270, vertical: true, fixLower:
                                        "major",
                                        fixUpper: "major" });

                        chart.addSeries("TemperatureData",chartData);

                        chart.render();
                });
        </script>
</head>

<body style="background-color: #F5EEE6">
        <div style="align: center;">
        <font size="5px">
                Temperature Monitoring System - Dashboard
                </font></div>
        <div id="chartNode" style="width: 100%; height: 50%; margin-top: 50px;">
        </div>

        <script type="text/javascript">
                init();
        </script>
</body>
</html>
```

Code (Arduino)

The final component of this project is the Arduino code for connecting to the Internet using WiFi, reading data from the temperature sensor, and publishing it to a server.

Start your Arduino IDE and either type the code provided here or download it from book's site and open it. All the code goes into a single source file (*.ino), but in order to make it easy to understand and reuse, it has been divided into five sections.

- External libraries
- Internet connectivity (WiFi)
- Read sensor data
- HTTP (publish)
- Standard functions

External Libraries

The first section of code, as provided in Listing 8-6, includes all the external libraries required to run the code. Since you are connecting to the Internet wirelessly, the main dependency of code is on <WiFi.h>.

Listing 8-6. Code for Including External Dependencies

```
#include <SPI.h>
#include <WiFi.h>
```

Internet Connectivity (Wireless)

The second section of the code defines variables, constants, and functions that are going to be used for connecting to the Internet. Use the code from Listings 2-7, 2-8, and 2-9 (in Chapter 2) here.

Read Sensor Data

The third section of code, as provided in Listing 8-7, defines the variables, constants, and functions that are going to be used for reading sensor data.

The readSensorData() function reads data from Analog Pin A0 and the result is between 0 and 1023. The greater the value returned, the higher the temperature. The sensor value does not directly provide the temperature in Celsius or Fahrenheit, so a formula, as highlighted in Listing 8-7, is used to convert the sensor value into the required formats.

Listing 8-7. Code for Reading Temperatures

```
int TEMP_SENSOR_PIN = A0;

float temperatureC = 0.0;
float temperatureF = 0.0;

void readSensorData()
{
    //Read Temperature Sensor Value
    int temperatureSensorValue = analogRead(TEMP_SENSOR_PIN);

    float voltage = temperatureSensorValue * 5.0 / 1024;

    //Converting reading to Celsius
    temperatureC = (voltage - 0.5) * 100;

    //Converting reading to Fahrenheit
    temperatureF = (temperatureC * 9.0 / 5.0) + 32.0;

    //Log Sensor Data on Serial Monitor
    Serial.print("[INFO] Temperature Sensor Reading (F): ");
    Serial.println(temperatureF);
}
```

Data Publish

The fourth section of code as provided in Listing 8-8 defines the variables, constants, and functions that are going to be used for creating and sending an HTTP request to the server. This code is a slightly modified version of the HTTP GET that you developed in Chapter 3.

The main modification in this code is its ability to open and close a connection to the server repeatedly. Apart from that, make sure to change the server and port values to your PHP server's values, requestData variables and the URL values.

Listing 8-8. Code for Sending an HTTP Request

```
//IP address of the server
char server[] = {"bookapps.codifythings.com"};
int port = 80;

unsigned long lastConnectionTime = 0;
const unsigned long postingInterval = 10L * 1000L;
```

```
void transmitSensorData()
{
  // Read all incoming data (if any)
  while (client.available())
  {
    char c = client.read();
    Serial.write(c);
  }

  if (millis() - lastConnectionTime > postingInterval)
  {
    client.stop();

    Serial.println("[INFO] Connecting to Server");

    String requestData = "temperature=" + String(temperatureF);

    // Prepare data or parameters that need to be posted to server
    if (client.connect(server, port))
    {
      Serial.println("[INFO] Server Connected - HTTP GET Started");

      // Make a HTTP request:
      client.println("GET /tempmonitor/add.php?" + requestData +
                                                    " HTTP/1.1");
      client.println("Host: " + String(server));
      client.println("Connection: close");
      client.println();

      lastConnectionTime = millis();

      Serial.println("[INFO] HTTP GET Completed");
    }
    else
    {
      // Connection to server:port failed
      Serial.println("[ERROR] Connection Failed");
    }
  }

  Serial.println("-----------------------------------------------");

}
```

Standard Functions

The code in the last section is provided in Listing 8-9. It implements Arduino's standard setup() and loop() functions.

The setup() function initializes the serial port and connects to the Internet.

The loop() function calls readSensorData() for reading temperature data and then publishes the data to the server using HTTP by calling transmitSensorData() at regular intervals.

Listing 8-9. Code for Standard Arduino Functions

```
void setup()
{
  // Initialize serial port
  Serial.begin(9600);

  //Connect Arduino to internet
  connectToInternet();
}

void loop()
{
  // Read sensor data
  readSensorData();

  // Transmit sensor data
  transmitSensorData();

  // Delay
  delay(6000);
}
```

Your Arduino code is now complete.

The Final Product

To test the application, make sure your MySQL and PHP servers are up and running with the code deployed.

Also verify and upload the Arduino code as discussed in Chapter 1. Once the code has been uploaded, open the Serial Monitor window. You will start seeing log messages similar to ones shown in Figure 8-9.

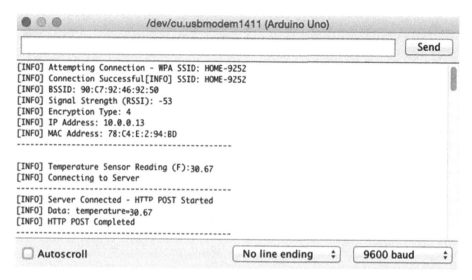

Figure 8-9. *Log messages from the temperature monitoring system*

Let your Arduino run for a couple of minutes so that enough data is sent to the server. Check your dashboard by accessing the project URL, in this case it was `http://bookapps.codifythings.com/tempmonitor`. Your dashboard should look similar to Figure 8-10.

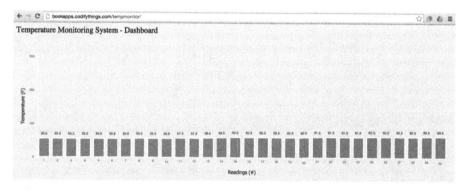

Figure 8-10. *Dashboard of the temperature monitoring system*

Summary

In this chapter, you learned about building custom web apps. Web apps are being extensively used for monitoring IoT applications and large-scale implementations, as well as for creating dashboards.

CHAPTER 9

■ ■ ■

IoT Patterns: Location Aware

Location-aware devices are going to be one of the largest contributors of savings from an IoT implementation. The IoT pattern is seen in various types of scenarios, including optimal route planning, endangered wildlife tracking, and pinpointing crash locations.

In this chapter, you are going to build a livestock tracking system. Figure 9-1 shows a high-level diagram of all the components involved in this system. The first component is an Arduino device that captures the current coordinates and publishes them to a server using an HTTP request. The second component is a server that receives GPS coordinates and stores them in a database. The final component is a web page that shows stored GPS coordinates on a map. This web page resides on the server as well.

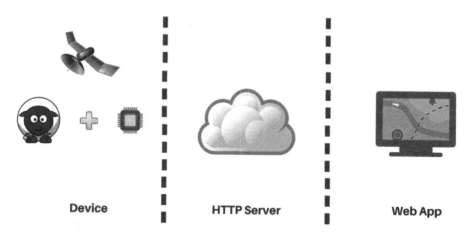

Device   **HTTP Server**   **Web App**

Figure 9-1. *The components of livestock tracking system*

For the purposes of this project, you are going to be tracking only one animal.

© Adeel Javed 2016
A. Javed, *Building Arduino Projects for the Internet of Things*,
DOI 10.1007/978-1-4842-1940-9_9

Learning Objectives

At the end of this chapter, you will be able to:

- Read GPS coordinates

- Publish GPS coordinates to a server

- Display GPS coordinates in a map

Hardware Required

Figure 9-2 provides a list of all the hardware components required for building the livestock tracking system.

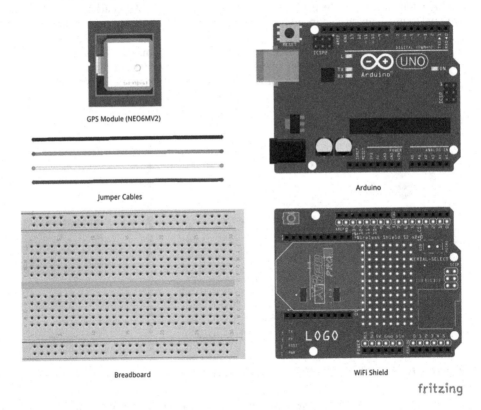

Figure 9-2. Hardware required for the livestock tracking system

Software Required

In order to develop this livestock tracking system, you need the following software:

- Arduino IDE 1.6.4 or later
- PHP server (installed or hosted)
- MySQL server (installed or hosted)
- Text editor

Circuit

In this section, you are going to build the circuit required for the livestock tracking system. This circuit uses the NEO6MV2 GPS module for getting current latitude and longitude data. The GPS module has a positional accuracy of 5 meters.

1. Make sure Arduino is not connected to a power source, such as to a computer via USB or a battery.

2. Attach a WiFi shield to the top of the Arduino. All the pins should align.

3. Use jumper cables to connect the power (3.3V) and ground (GND) ports on Arduino to the power (+) and ground (-) ports on the breadboard.

4. Now that your breadboard has a power source, use jumper cables to connect the power (+) and ground (-) ports of your breadboard to the power and ground ports of the GPS.

5. To read the GPS data, you will need to connect a jumper cable from the RX (Receive) port of the GPS to Digital Port 3 of Arduino. Your code will use data from this port to find the latitude and longitude information.

6. Similar to Step 5, you also need to connect a jumper cable from the TX (Transmit) port of the GPS to Digital Port 2 of Arduino. Your code will use data from this port to find the latitude and longitude information.

■ **Note** Other GPS modules might have different power requirements and circuits. Check the datasheet of your GPS module to confirm its requirements.

Your circuit is now complete and should look similar to Figures 9-3 and 9-4.

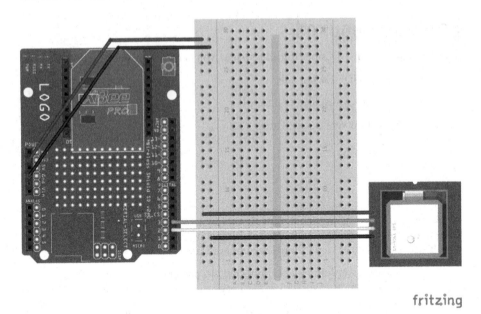

Figure 9-3. *Circuit diagram of the livestock tracking system*

Figure 9-4. *Actual circuit of the livestock tracking system*

Database Table (MySQL)

As discussed in the previous two chapters, before you can send HTTP requests from Arduino, you need to build a service that will receive the data.

The livestock tracking system will be displaying the latest GPS coordinates on a map, so you need to create a database table that will store those GPS coordinates.

This chapter also uses MySQL as the database. Even though you are only going to track a single device, the table structure will be the same as if you were tracking multiple devices. So create a new table called GPS_TRACKER_DATA using the SQL script provided in Listing 9-1. Run this script in an existing database or create a new one.

The first column will store the ID of the animal/device sending the coordinates; the second column will store the latitude; the third column will store longitude; and the fourth column will contain an auto-generated timestamp.

Listing 9-1. Create Table SQL

```
CREATE TABLE `GPS_TRACKER_DATA`
(
  `CLIENT_ID` varchar(40) NOT NULL,
  `LATITUDE` varchar(40) NOT NULL,
  `LONGITUDE` varchar(40) NOT NULL,
  `LAST_UPDATED` timestamp NOT NULL DEFAULT CURRENT_TIMESTAMP
  ON UPDATE CURRENT_TIMESTAMP,
  PRIMARY KEY (`CLIENT_ID`)
)
```

Figure 9-5 shows the structure of the GPS_TRACKER_DATA table.

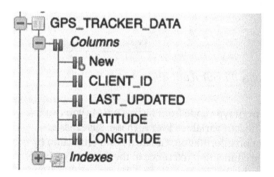

Figure 9-5. *GPS_TRACKER_DATA table structure*

Code (PHP)

Now that the database table is ready, you need to build two services. The first service that will receive the GPS coordinates and store them in the newly created database table. The second service will show the stored GPS coordinates on a map.

This project also uses PHP for building the storage and user interface services.

Create a new folder called gpstracker in the public/root folder of your PHP server. All of the PHP source code for this project will go in this gpstracker folder.

Start the text editor of your choice.

■ **Note** All the PHP code was developed using Brackets, which is an open source text editor. See http://brackets.io/ for more information.

Database Connection

Both PHP scripts for storing and displaying data will need to connect to the database. As shown in Figure 9-6, create a new file called util-dbconn.php in the gpstracker folder. This file will be used by both scripts instead of repeating the code.

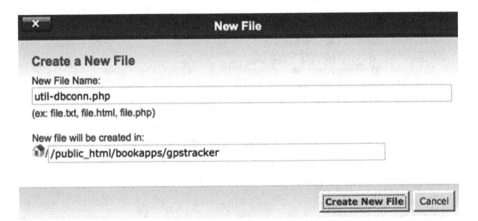

Figure 9-6. Common database connectivity file called util-dbconn.php

Open the file in a text editor and copy or type code from Listing 9-2. As you can see, there is not much code in this file. The four variables $servername, $username, $password, and $dbname contain connection information. Create a new connection by passing these four variables and store the connection reference in the $mysqli variable.

The IF condition in the code simply checks for errors during the connection attempt and prints them if there are any.

Listing 9-2. Common Database Connectivity Code util-dbconn.php

```php
<?php
    $servername = "SERVER_NAME";
    $dbname = "DB_NAME";
    $username = "DB_USERNAME";
```

```
$password = "DB_PASSWORD";

//Open a new connection to MySQL server
$mysqli = new mysqli($servername, $username, $password, $dbname);

//Output connection errors
if ($mysqli->connect_error)
{
    die("[ERROR] Connection Failed: " . $mysqli->connect_error);
}
?>
```

Receive and Store Sensor Data

As shown in Figure 9-7, create a new file called update.php in the gpstracker folder. This script will perform two tasks—first it will fetch information from an HTTP request and then it will update this information in the database table.

Open the newly created file in a text editor and copy or type the code provided

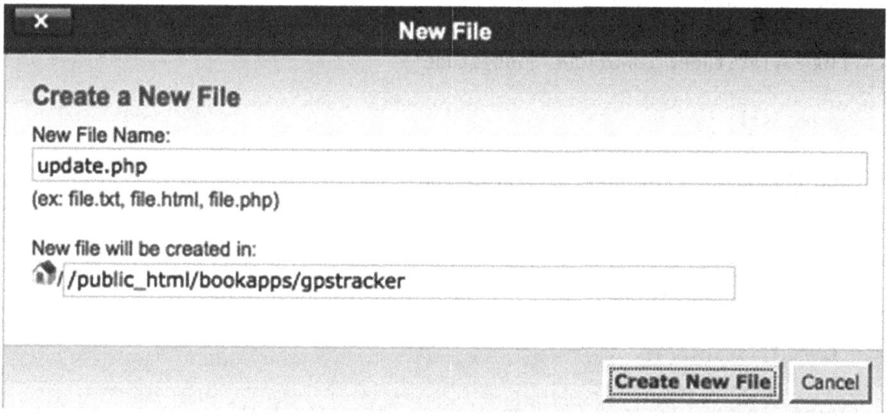

Figure 9-7. *File to receive and add/update data in update.php*

in Listing 9-3. As mentioned in the previous step, in order to store data, a database connection needs to be established. You created util-dbconn.php to perform that task, so in this file you need to include util-dbconn.php. The util-dbconn.php file provides access to the $mysqli variable, which contains connection references and will be used to run the SQL queries.

The example in this book is hosted at http://bookapps.codifythings.com/gpstracker/, and Arduino will be sending GPS coordinates to update.php using an HTTP GET method. As discussed in Chapter 2, HTTP GET uses a query string to send request data. So, the complete URL with the query string that Arduino will be using becomes http://bookapps.codifythings.com/gpstracker/update.php?clientID=Sheep1&lat

itude=41.83&longitude=-87.68. Your PHP code will need to extract client ID and GPS coordinates from the query string using $_GET['parameterName'] statement.

Now you need to store these GPS coordinates in the database table, either in an existing row or by inserting them in a new row. Prepare an INSERT OR UPDATE SQL statement in the $sql variable. You will need to pass the CLIENT_ID, LATITUDE, and LONGITUDE values in the SQL query while TIMESTAMP will be auto-generated by the database.

Finally, execute the INSERT OR UPDATE SQL statement using $mysqli->query($sql) and check the $result variable for success or failure.

Listing 9-3. Code to Receive and Add/Update Data in update.php

```php
<?php
    include('util-dbconn.php');

    $clientID = $_GET['clientID'];
    $latitude = $_GET['latitude'];
    $longitude = $_GET['longitude'];

    $sql = "INSERT INTO `GPS_TRACKER_DATA` (CLIENT_ID, LATITUDE, LONGITUDE)
VALUES('$clientID', $latitude, $longitude) ";
    $sql = $sql . "ON DUPLICATE KEY UPDATE CLIENT_ID='$clientID',
LATITUDE=$latitude, LONGITUDE=$longitude";

    echo $sql;

    if (!$result = $mysqli->query($sql))
    {
        echo "[Error] " . mysqli_error() . "\n";
        exit();
    }

    $mysqli->close();

    echo "[DEBUG] Updated GPS Coordinates Successfully\n";

?>
```

Map

All the GPS coordinates being stored in the database are not visible to anyone yet. Next, you are going to build a web page that will display all coordinates on a map. As shown in Figure 9-8, create a new file called `index.php` in the `gpstracker` folder.

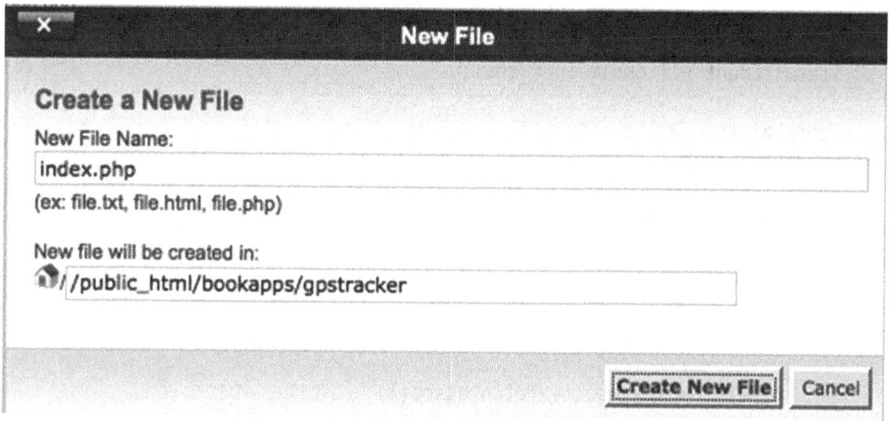

Figure 9-8. *The file for displaying a map is index.php*

Listing 9-4 provides the complete code for `index.php`, so copy or write the code in `index.php`. This code uses the Google Maps API for creating a map and displaying all the coordinates. You do not need to download or install any code; the API is accessible over the Internet so your `script` tag just needs to point to `http://maps.googleapis.com/maps/api/js?sensor=false` as its source.

To populate the map, you first need to load data from the database in the `location` array variable. Add your PHP code for loading data from a database table inside the `init()` JavaScript function. Include `util-dbconn.php` because the database connection needs to be established first, and then prepare a `SELECT` SQL statement. Execute the query and prepare a `locations` array from the results.

After the PHP code and inside the `init()` function, initialize a new map. Set its zoom level, default coordinates, and map type. Next read the array in a loop and mark all the coordinates on the map.

The `<body>` tag has the code to display a title on top of the page and map created earlier.

Listing 9-4. Code Structure for Map in index.php

```
<html lang="en">

<head>
<title>Livestock Tracking System</title>

<script type="text/javascript" src="http://maps.googleapis.com/maps/api/
js?sensor=false"></script>
```

```php
<script>
function init()
{
    <?php
    include('util-dbconn.php');

    $sql = "SELECT * FROM `GPS_TRACKER_DATA`";
    $result = $mysqli->query($sql);
    $resultCount = $result->num_rows;

    $zoomLatitude = "";
    $zoomLongitude = "";

    echo "var locations = [";

    if ($resultCount > 0)
    {
        $currentRow = 0;

        while($row = $result->fetch_assoc())
        {
            $currentRow = $currentRow + 1;
            $clientID=$row["CLIENT_ID"];
            $latitude=$row["LATITUDE"];
            $longitude=$row["LONGITUDE"];

            if($currentRow == 1)
            {
                $zoomLatitude = $latitude;
                $zoomLongitude = $longitude;
            }

            echo "['".$clientID."',".$latitude.",".$longitude."]";

            if($currentRow < $resultCount)
            {
                echo ",";
            }
        }
    }

    echo "];";

    echo "var latitude = '$zoomLatitude';";
    echo "var longitude = '$zoomLongitude';";
```

```
    $mysqli->close();

    ?>

    map = new google.maps.Map(document.getElementById('map'),
                              {
                              zoom: 10,
                              center: new google.maps.LatLng(latitude,
                                                             longitude),
                              mapTypeId: google.maps.MapTypeId.ROADMAP
            ▴                });

    var infowindow = new google.maps.InfoWindow();

    var marker, i;

    for (i = 0; i < locations.length; i++)
    {
        marker = new google.maps.Marker({
                         position: new
                                    google.maps.LatLng(locations[i][1],
                                    locations[i][2]),map: map});

        google.maps.event.addListener(marker, 'click',
                (function(marker, i)
                {
                        return function()
                                {
                                  infowindow.setContent(locations[i][0]);
                                  infowindow.open(map, marker);
                                }
                })(marker, i));
    }
}
</script>
</head>

<body style="background-color: #9bcc59">
<div style="align: center;"><font size="5px" color="white">Livestock
Tracking System</font></div>
<div id="map" style="width: 100%; height: 50%; margin-top: 50px;"></div>

<script type="text/javascript">
init();
</script>
</body>
</html>
```

Code (Arduino)

The final component of this project is the Arduino code for connecting to the Internet using WiFi, getting the current GPS coordinates, and publishing them to a server.

Start your Arduino IDE and either type the code provided here or download it from the site and open it. All the code goes into a single source file (*.ino), but in order to make it easy to understand and reuse, it has been divided into five sections.

- External libraries
- Internet connectivity (WiFi)
- Read GPS coordinates
- HTTP (publish)
- Standard functions

External Libraries

The first section of code, as provided in Listing 9-5, includes all the external libraries required to run the code. This sketch has multiple dependencies—for Internet connectivity, you need to include the <WiFi.h>, for communication with the GPS module, you need to include <SoftwareSerial.h>, and for reading the GPS coordinates, you need to include <TinyGPS.h>. You can download <TinyGPS.h> from https://github.com/mikalhart/TinyGPS/releases/tag/v13.

Listing 9-5. Code for Including External Dependencies

```
#include <SPI.h>
#include <WiFi.h>
#include <TinyGPS.h>
#include <SoftwareSerial.h>
```

Internet Connectivity (Wireless)

The second section of the code defines the variables, constants, and functions that are going to be used for connecting to the Internet. Use the code from Listings 2-7, 2-8 , and 2-9 (Chapter 2) here.

Get GPS Coordinates

The third section of the code, as provided in Listing 9-6, defines the variables, constants, and functions that are going to be used for reading the GPS coordinates.

Once the GPS module is connected to Arduino and it is powered on, it will look for a satellite and start sending data on serial ports D2 and D3 to Arduino. This data won't make much sense, so in order to find the latitude and longitude information, you will use

TinyGPS library. This library parses data coming from the GPS module and provides an easy way to retrieve the required information. So initialize a variable of the TinyGPS library.

The getGPSCoordinates() function reads the GPS data from serial ports D2 and D3. The GPS module might take a few seconds to find a satellite, so the latitude and longitude values returned might not be valid. If latitude and longitude are equal to TinyGPS::GPS_INVALID_F_ANGLE, that means the coordinates are invalid, so until the code receives valid coordinates, it keeps printing Searching for Satellite on the serial monitor. Once the valid coordinates are received, the transmitSensorData(latitude, longitude) function is called.

Listing 9-6. Code for Reading GPS Coordinates

```
TinyGPS gps;
SoftwareSerial ss(2, 3); // GPS TX = Arduino D2, GPS RX = Arduino D3

static void smartdelay(unsigned long ms)
{
  unsigned long start = millis();
  do
  {
    while (ss.available())
      gps.encode(ss.read());
  } while (millis() - start < ms);
}

void getGPSCoordinates()
{
  float latitude;
  float longitude;
  unsigned long age = 0;

  gps.f_get_position(&latitude, &longitude, &age);

  smartdelay(10000);

  // Transmit sensor data
  if(latitude != TinyGPS::GPS_INVALID_F_ANGLE &&
                        longitude != TinyGPS::GPS_INVALID_F_ANGLE)
  {
    transmitSensorData(latitude, longitude);
  }
  else
  {
    Serial.println("[INFO] Searching for Satellite");
  }
}
```

Data Publish

The fourth section of code, as provided in Listing 9-7, defines the variables, constants, and functions that are going to be used for creating and sending an HTTP request to the server. This code is a slightly modified version of the HTTP GET that you developed in Chapter 3.

The main modification in this code is its ability to open and close a connection to the server repeatedly. Apart from that, make sure to change the server and port values to your PHP server's values, requestData variables and the URL values.

Listing 9-7. HTTP Publish

```
//IP address of the server
char server[] = {"bookapps.codifythings.com"};
int port = 80;

unsigned long lastConnectionTime = 0;
const unsigned long postingInterval = 10L * 1000L;

void transmitSensorData(float latitude, float longitude)
{
  // Read all incoming data (if any)
  while (client.available())
  {
    char c = client.read();
  }

  if (millis() - lastConnectionTime > postingInterval)
  {
    client.stop();

    Serial.println("[INFO] Connecting to Server");

    String requestData = "clientID=Sheep1&latitude=" + String(latitude)
                              + "&longitude=" + String(longitude);
    Serial.println("[INFO] Query String: " + requestData);

    // Prepare data or parameters that need to be posted to server
    if (client.connect(server, port))
    {
      Serial.println("[INFO] Server Connected - HTTP GET Started");

      // Make a HTTP request:
      client.println("GET /gpstracker/update.php?" + requestData +
                                              " HTTP/1.1");
      client.println("Host: " + String(server));
```

```
      client.println("Connection: close");
      client.println();

      lastConnectionTime = millis();

      Serial.println("[INFO] HTTP GET Completed");
    }
    else
    {
      // Connection to server:port failed
      Serial.println("[ERROR] Connection Failed");
    }
  }

  Serial.println("-----------------------------------------------");

}
```

Standard Functions

The final code section is provided in Listing 9-8. It implements Arduino's standard setup() and loop() functions.

The setup() function initializes the serial port. Note that the baud rate is 115200, which is different from what you have been using so far. The reason for difference will be clear when you look at the next line of code: ss.begin(9600). This statement initializes communication with the GPS module on serial ports D2 and D3 (ss is the instance of SoftwareSerial library that you initialized in Listing 9-6). The GPS module used in this project communicates at 9600 baud rate by default, therefore 115200 was used for serial monitor logs. The GPS module that you are using might have a different default baud rate, so make sure to check the manufacturer's datasheet to find the correct one. Next, connect to the Internet using WiFi.

The loop() function just needs to call the getGPSCoordinates() function. It reads the GPS coordinates and, at regular intervals, calls the transmitSensorData() function to publish the GPS coordinates to the server.

Listing 9-8. Code for Standard Arduino Functions

```
void setup()
{
  // Initialize serial port
  Serial.begin(115200);

  // Initialize serial port for GPS data
  ss.begin(9600);

  //Connect Arduino to internet
  connectToInternet();
}
```

```
void loop()
{
  // Get GPS Coordinates
  getGPSCoordinates();
}
```

Your Arduino code is now complete.

The Final Product

To test the application, make sure your MySQL and PHP servers are up and running with the code deployed.

Also verify and upload the Arduino code as discussed in Chapter 1. Once the code has been uploaded, open the Serial Monitor window. You will start seeing log messages similar to ones shown in Figure 9-9.

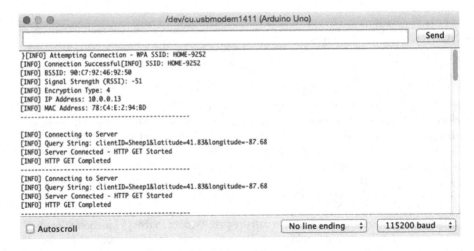

Figure 9-9. Log messages from the livestock tracking system

Once the GPS has initialized, which might take a few seconds, it will publish the current coordinates to the server. Check your web app by accessing the project URL; in this case it was http://bookapps.codifythings.com/gpstracker. Your web app should look similar to Figure 9-10.

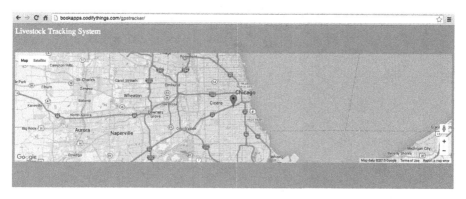

Figure 9-10. *The final version of the livestock tracking system*

Summary

In this chapter you learned about location-aware things. They have many great uses, and, when combined with other sensors, they can improve so many aspects of our lives, such as emergency response, maintenance and optimized routing, and more.

You developed an IoT application that published livestock tracking data to a server where this information was displayed on a map. You can improve quite a few other applications that you developed in previous chapters by making them location-aware, including:

- The intrusion detection system from Chapter 5. When an intrusion is detected, you can send alerts to the security company with the exact coordinates so that they can send someone to investigate.

- The smart parking system from Chapter 7. You can provide exact coordinates of a parking spot so that drivers looking for parking spots can enter the coordinates in their GPS for directions.

Not all scenarios will need a purpose-built GPS module. Smartphones are location-aware as well and can be used for building IoT applications. For scenarios such as livestock tracking, you need to attach purpose-built GPS modules, but for other scenarios, such as a car mileage tracker, you have the option to use smartphones as well.

211

CHAPTER 10

IoT Patterns: Machine to Human

Due to regulatory requirements or lack of technology, there will be scenarios where human intervention is required to respond to sensor-generated alerts.

In this chapter, you are going to build a simple waste management system to elaborate this use case. Figure 10-1 shows a high-level diagram of all components involved in this system. The first component is an Arduino device that monitors garbage levels with a proximity sensor and publishes a message to an MQTT broker. The second component is a Node-RED flow that subscribes to an MQTT broker. The final component is a workflow that is initiated whenever the garbage levels are high and a pickup needs to be scheduled.

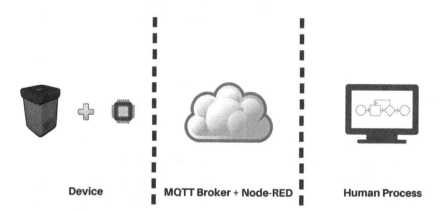

| Device | MQTT Broker + Node-RED | Human Process |

Figure 10-1. Components of the waste management system

© Adeel Javed 2016
A. Javed, *Building Arduino Projects for the Internet of Things*,
DOI 10.1007/978-1-4842-1940-9_10

Learning Objectives

At the end of this chapter, you will be able to:

- Read data from a proximity sensor

- Publish message to an MQTT broker

- Build a workflow in Effektif (renamed to Signavio Workflow)

- Create a Node-RED flow and initiate it from Arduino

Hardware Required

Figure 10-2 provides a list of all hardware components required for building the waste management system.

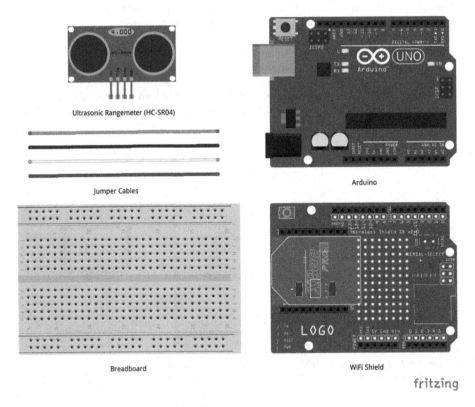

Figure 10-2. *Hardware required for the waste management system*

Software Required

In order to develop this waste management system, you need the following software:

- Arduino IDE 1.6.4 or later
- Effektif (hosted)
- Node-RED 0.13.2 or later

Circuit

In this section, you are going to build the circuit required for the waste management system. This circuit uses an ultrasonic proximity sensor to detect objects, as illustrated in Chapter 7. The sensor is attached to the top of a garbage can and sends an ultrasonic burst that reflects off of the garbage in the can. The circuit reads the echo, which is used to calculate the level of garbage.

1. Make sure Arduino is not connected to a power source, such as to a computer via a USB or a battery.

2. Attach a WiFi shield to the top of the Arduino. All the pins should align.

3. Use jumper cables to connect the power (5V) and ground (GND) ports on Arduino to the power (+) and ground (-) ports on the breadboard.

4. Now that your breadboard has a power source, use jumper cables to connect the power (+) and ground (-) ports of your breadboard to the power and ground ports of the proximity sensor.

5. To trigger an ultrasonic burst, connect a jumper cable from the TRIG pin of the sensor to Digital Port 2 of Arduino. Your code will set the value of this port to LOW, HIGH, and then LOW in order to trigger the burst.

6. To read the echo, connect a jumper cable from the ECHO pin of the sensor to Digital Port 3 of Arduino. Your code will read the values from this port to calculate the level of garbage in the can.

Your circuit is now complete and should look similar to Figures 10-3 and 10-4.

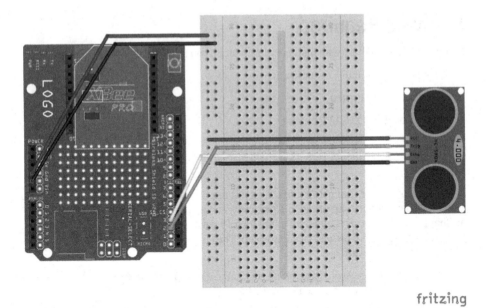

Figure 10-3. *Circuit diagram of the waste management system*

Figure 10-4. *Actual circuit of the waste management system*

Code (Arduino)

Next you are going to write the code for the first component of this application. This code will connect Arduino to the Internet using WiFi, read the proximity sensor data to get garbage levels, and publish that information to an MQTT broker.

Start your Arduino IDE and type the code provided here or download it from the site and open it. All the code goes into a single source file (*.ino), but in order to make it easy to understand and reuse, it has been divided into five sections.

- External libraries
- Internet connectivity (WiFi)
- Read sensor data
- MQTT (publish)
- Standard functions

External Libraries

The first section of code, as provided in Listing 10-1, includes all the external libraries required to run the code. This sketch has two main dependencies—for Internet connectivity, you need to include <WiFi.h> (assuming you are using a WiFi shield) and for MQTT broker communication, you need to include <PubSubClient.h>.

Listing 10-1. Code for Including External Dependencies

```
#include <SPI.h>
#include <WiFi.h>
#include <PubSubClient.h>
```

Internet Connectivity (Wireless)

The second section of the code defines the variables, constants, and functions that are going to be used for connecting to the Internet. Use the code from Listings 2-7, 2-8, and 2-9 (Chapter 2) here.

Read Sensor Data

The third section of code, as provided in Listing 10-2, defines the variables, constants, and functions that are going to be used for reading the sensor data.

The calibrateSensor() function waits for the proximity sensor to calibrate properly. Once the calibration is complete, the proximity sensor is active and can start detecting. If you do not give it enough time to calibrate, the proximity sensor might return incorrect readings.

The readSensorData() function generates a burst to detect garbage level in the can. It triggers a burst on Digital Pin 2 by sending alternate signals—LOW, HIGH, and LOW again. Then it reads the echo from Digital Pin 3, which provides the distance between the sensor and the garbage. Finally, it checks if the distance is less than a threshold, and if it is, that means the garbage can is close to being full and a pickup needs to be scheduled. Since this is just a prototype, the echo value of 700 has been used. When you use this sensor in real life, you need to adjust the value by doing a few tests. If the garbage level is above the threshold, then call publishSensorData(...) with HIGH.

Listing 10-2. Code for Detecting the Garbage Level

```
int calibrationTime = 30;
#define TRIGPIN 2          // Pin to send trigger pulse
#define ECHOPIN 3          // Pin to receive echo pulse

void calibrateSensor()
{
  //Give sensor some time to calibrate
  Serial.println("[INFO] Calibrating Sensor ");

  for(int i = 0; i < calibrationTime; i++)
  {
    Serial.print(".");
    delay(1000);
  }

  Serial.println("");
  Serial.println("[INFO] Calibration Complete");
  Serial.println("[INFO] Sensor Active");

  delay(50);

}

void readSensorData()
{
  // Generating a burst to check for objects
  digitalWrite(TRIGPIN, LOW);
  delayMicroseconds(10);
  digitalWrite(TRIGPIN, HIGH);
  delayMicroseconds(10);
  digitalWrite(TRIGPIN, LOW);

  // Distance Calculation
  float distance = pulseIn(ECHOPIN, HIGH);

  Serial.println("[INFO] Garbage Level: " + String(distance));
```

```
  if(distance < 700)
  {
    Serial.println("[INFO] Garbage Level High");

    // Publish sensor data to server
    publishSensorData("HIGH");
  }
}
```

Data Publish

The fourth section of code, provided in Listing 10-3, defines the variables, constants, and functions that are going to be used for publishing data to an MQTT broker.

This code is a slightly modified version of MQTT publish that you developed in Chapter 3. You do not need to make any changes for the code to work, but it is recommended that you customize some of the messages so that they do not get mixed up with someone else using the same values. All values that can be changed have been highlighted in bold in Listing 10-3. If you are using your own MQTT server, make sure to change the server and port values. The two recommended changes include the value of the topic variable and the name of client that you need to pass while connecting to the MQTT broker.

Listing 10-3. Code for Publishing Messages to an MQTT Broker

```
// IP address of the MQTT broker
char server[] = {"iot.eclipse.org"};
int port = 1883;
char topic[] = {"codifythings/garbagelevel"};

void callback(char* topic, byte* payload, unsigned int length)
{
  //Handle message arrived
}

PubSubClient pubSubClient(server, port, 0, client);

void publishSensorData(String garbageLevel)
{
  // Connect MQTT Broker
  Serial.println("[INFO] Connecting to MQTT Broker");

  if (pubSubClient.connect("arduinoIoTClient"))
  {
    Serial.println("[INFO] Connection to MQTT Broker Successful");
  }
  else
  {
    Serial.println("[INFO] Connection to MQTT Broker Failed");
  }
```

```
// Publish to MQTT Topic
if (pubSubClient.connected())
{
  Serial.println("[INFO] Publishing to MQTT Broker");
  pubSubClient.publish(topic, "Garbage level is HIGH, schedule pickup");
  Serial.println("[INFO] Publish to MQTT Broker Complete");
}
else
{
  Serial.println("[ERROR] Publish to MQTT Broker Failed");
}

pubSubClient.disconnect();

}
```

Standard Functions

The final code section is shown in Listing 10-4. It implements Arduino's standard setup() and loop() functions.

The setup() function initializes the serial port, sets the pin modes for the trigger and echo pins, connects to the Internet, and calibrates the proximity sensor.

The loop() function simply needs to call readSensorData() at regular intervals.

Listing 10-4. Code for Standard Arduino Functions

```
void setup()
{
  // Initialize serial port
  Serial.begin(9600);

  // Set pin mode
  pinMode(ECHOPIN, INPUT);
  pinMode(TRIGPIN, OUTPUT);

  // Connect Arduino to internet
  connectToInternet();

  // Calibrate sensor
  calibrateSensor();
}
```

```
void loop()
{
  // Read sensor data
  readSensorData();

  // Delay
  delay(5000);
}
```

Your Arduino code is now complete.

Effektif Workflow

Effektif is a cloud-based platform that lets you automate routine workflows and processes into applications within minutes. For the purposes of this project, you can sign up for their free 30-day trial membership. You are going to define a very simple single step workflow that allows a person to enter a garbage pickup schedule.

Effektif is just one example of a workflow and process management solution; you can use one of the many other solutions available as well.

Process Creation

Log in using your credentials at https://app.effektif.com/. Once you are logged in, choose Processes from the menu shown in Figure 10-5.

Figure 10-5. *Effektif menu*

This will take you to list of all existing processes and give you the option to create a new one. Figure 10-6 shows the screen where you will see all existing processes.

Figure 10-6. *List of existing processes*

221

From the Processes tab shown in Figure 10-6, click on the Create New Process button. As shown in Figure 10-7, enter `Schedule Garbage Pickup` as the process name. Press Enter to create process and move to next screen.

Figure 10-7. *New process name*

Process Configurations

Next you need to configure the newly created process. Figure 10-8 shows the process configuration screen, which is where you can define all aspects of your process, including:

- Trigger: Select how the process can be started

- Actions: Specify what human and system actions will happen in the process and their orders

- Details: Choose who will be involved in the process

- Versions: View a list of all versions of processes published till date

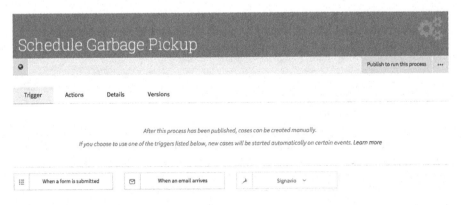

Figure 10-8. *Process configuration screen*

First you are going to select a *trigger* for your process. For this project, you are going to select e-mail as a trigger. As shown in Figure 10-9 under the Triggers tab, click on When an Email Arrives as the trigger option. Once you select an e-mail trigger, Effektif provides an auto-generated e-mail address. Any person or a system can send an e-mail to this auto-generated address and a new instance of process will be started in Effektif.

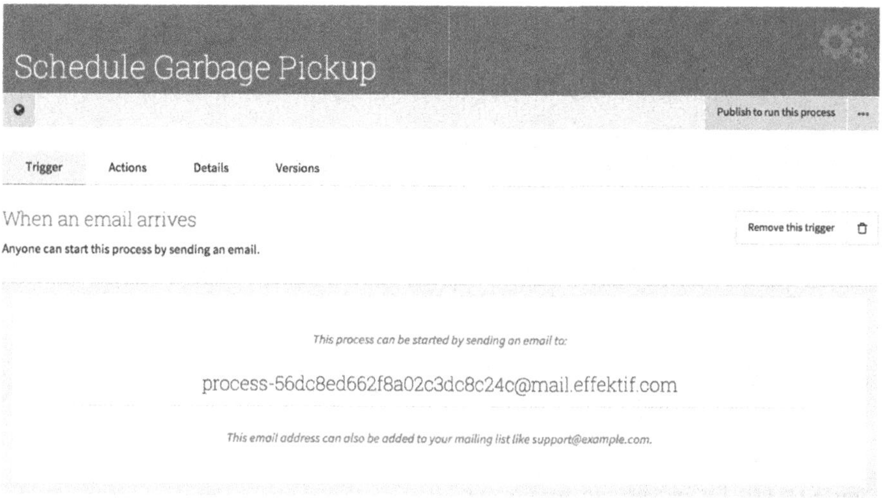

Schedule Garbage Pickup

Publish to run this process •••

Trigger   Actions   Details   Versions

When an email arrives   Remove this trigger 🗑

Anyone can start this process by sending an email.

This process can be started by sending an email to:

process-56dc8ed662f8a02c3dc8c24c@mail.effektif.com

This email address can also be added to your mailing list like support@example.com.

Figure 10-9. *Process trigger options*

Next you will create and configure the one-step scheduling process. As shown in Figure 10-10, the Actions tab lets you choose type of tasks you want the process to do.

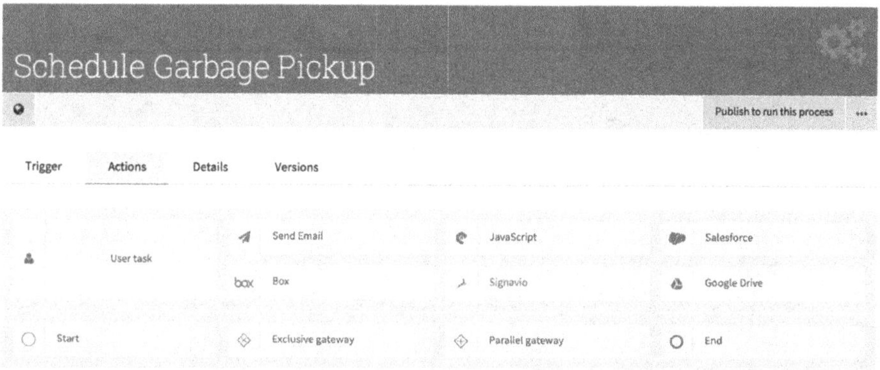

Schedule Garbage Pickup

Publish to run this process •••

Trigger   Actions   Details   Versions

▲ User task   ◁ Send Email   ↻ JavaScript   Salesforce

                     box Box   ↗ Signavio   ▲ Google Drive

○ Start   ◇ Exclusive gateway   ◈ Parallel gateway   ○ End

Figure 10-10. *Process actions*

From the Actions tab shown in Figure 10-10, click on User Task to create an action that a person needs to perform.

As shown in Figure 10-11, enter the title of this task as `Schedule Garbage Pickup`. You will also need to specify Assignment information, such as whether a single user or a group of users can perform this task. These candidates can be defined in the My Organization screen under Profile. For simplicity, select the name that you used when creating your Effektif account.

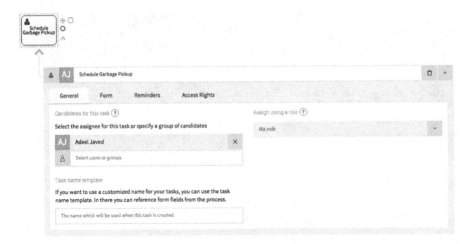

Figure 10-11. *Action type and assignment*

Next you are going to configure how the screen is going to look. This is a simple point-and-click activity. Click on the Form tab.

There are two ways to add fields to a screen—you can either create new fields using one of the provided controls or you can use an existing field (system generated or previously defined). Figure 10-12 shows list of controls currently available in Effektif.

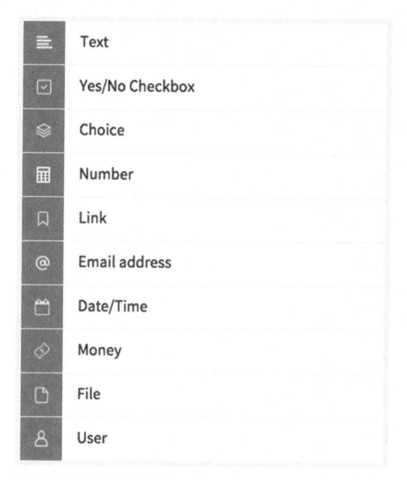

Figure 10-12. List of available controls

Figure 10-13 shows a list of existing fields that can be reused. Since you selected e-mail as trigger option, the trigger e-mail fields become available in the list.

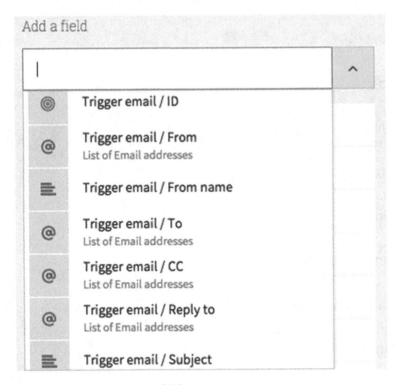

Figure 10-13. *List of existing fields*

For this process, you will be using new and existing fields. Since the process is being triggered by an e-mail, you need to display some information from the e-mail. Select Trigger Email/Subject and Trigger Email/Body from Add a Field list. These will be added to your form. Change their names to Title and Description, respectively.

You also need to add a new Date/Time field for someone to enter the garbage pickup date/time. As shown in Figure 10-14, select Date/Time from Add a Field list, set its name to Pickup Data/Time, and make it a mandatory field.

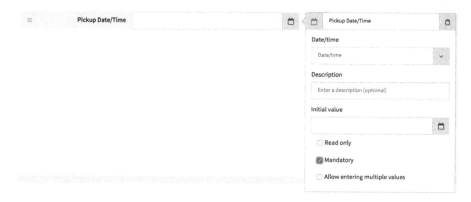

Figure 10-14. *Add a new field on the form*

You can rearrange the order of all the fields on the form and change their properties to make them more understandable. The final screen layout of your action should look similar to Figure 10-15.

Figure 10-15. *Final form layout*

Next click on the Reminders tab and, as shown in Figure 10-16, you have the option to define different types of reminders for the task. For now you can leave them as-is for all types of reminders.

- **Due date:** When is the task due?

- **Reminder:** When should a reminder be sent to the user that the task is getting delayed?

- **Continue reminding every:** Until when should the system keep sending reminders?

- **Escalation:** If the user still does not take action, to whom should the task be reassigned or delegated?

227

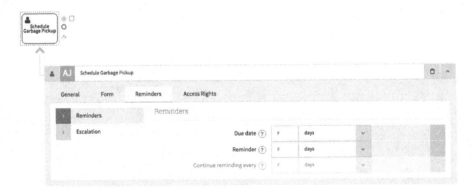

Figure 10-16. *Task reminders*

The Schedule Garbage Pickup action is fully configured, so now you need to define the flow. From the Actions tab, select the Start action to add it in the flow right before the Schedule Garbage Pickup action, as shown in Figure 10-17.

Figure 10-17. *Start action added to flow*

Connect the Start action to the Schedule Garbage Pickup action, as shown in Figure 10-18.

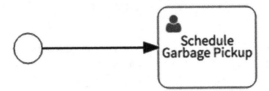

Figure 10-18. *Connect the Start and Schedule Garbage Pickup actions*

Next, select the Schedule Garbage Pickup action and, from the available options, click on End action, as shown in Figure 10-19.

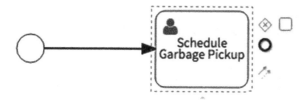

Figure 10-19. *Connect Start and Schedule Pickup activities*

A new End action will be added to the flow, right after Schedule Pickup action, as shown in Figure 10-20. This will make sure that the process ends once a user enters the pickup date/time on the form.

Figure 10-20. *Connect Schedule Pickup and End activities*

The final step is to make the process available. To do this, switch to the Versions tab, as shown in Figure 10-21.

Figure 10-21. *Publish process changes*

Next, click on the Publish Changes button and a new version of the process will immediately show up in Versions list, as shown in Figure 10-22.

Figure 10-22. *Process versions*

This completes configuration of your process.

Node-RED Flow

The final component of your IoT application is a Node-RED flow that will subscribe to an MQTT topic that Arduino is publishing messages to and then kick off the process in Effektif.

Start the Node-RED server and designer, as explained in Chapter 4. As shown in Figure 10-23, click on the + to create a new flow.

Figure 10-23. *Create a new Node-RED flow*

Double-click the flow tab name to open the properties dialog box. As shown in Figure 10-24, rename the flow Waste Management System and click OK to save your changes.

Figure 10-24. *Rename flow sheet*

Drag and drop the mqtt input node from palette in the flow tab; your flow should look similar to Figure 10-25.

Figure 10-25. *MQTT subscribe node*

Double-click the mqtt node to open the properties dialog box, as shown in Figure 10-26. You need to configure a new MQTT broker, select Add New mqtt-Broker... from the Broker field and click on the Pencil icon.

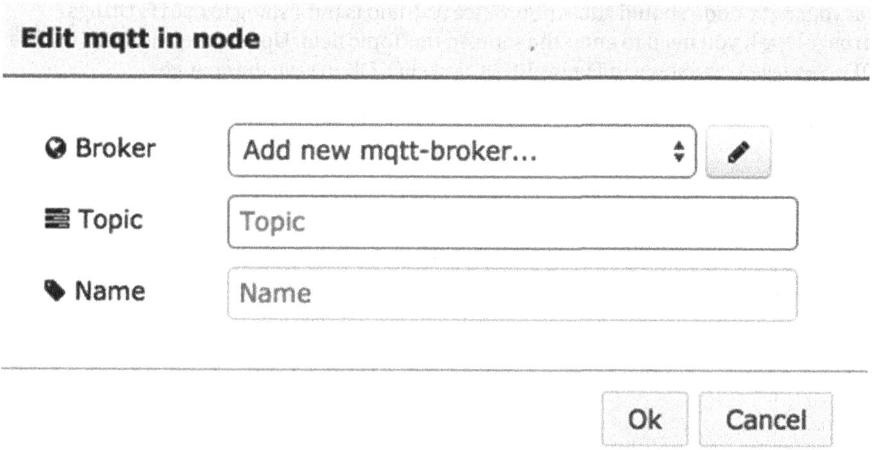

Edit mqtt in node

⊘ Broker	Add new mqtt-broker...
≣ Topic	Topic
🏷 Name	Name

Ok   Cancel

Figure 10-26. *MQTT node properties*

The MQTT configuration dialog box will open, as shown in Figure 10-27. You need to configure the same MQTT broker where Arduino is publishing messages, which in this case is the publicly available broker from Eclipse Foundation. Enter iot.eclipse.org in the Broker field, 1883 in the Port field, and nodeRedClient in the Client ID field. Click Add to add the newly configured MQTT broker.

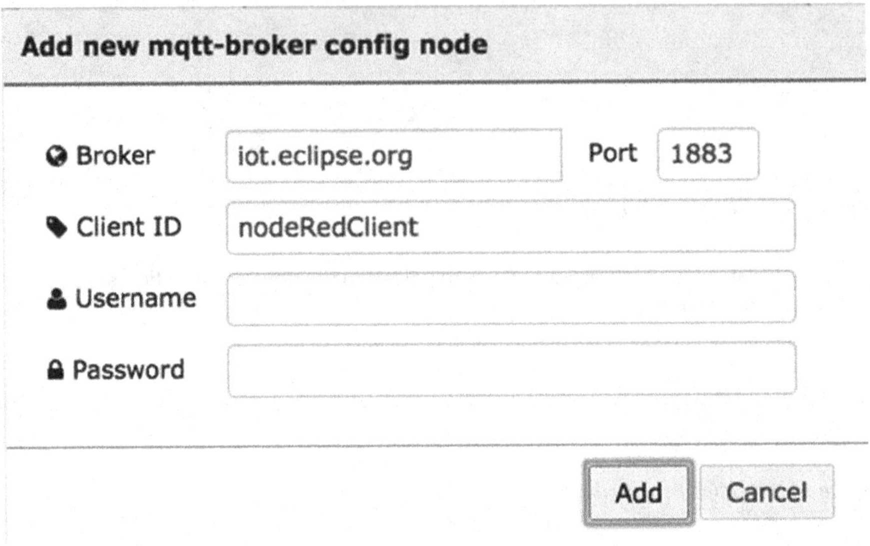

Add new mqtt-broker config node

❏ Broker	iot.eclipse.org	Port 1883
❏ Client ID	nodeRedClient	
❏ Username		
❏ Password		

Add   Cancel

Figure 10-27. *MQTT broker configuration*

Now that you have configured the MQTT broker, you will need to enter a topic that your mqtt node should subscribe. Since Arduino is publishing to codifythings/ garbagelevel, you need to enter the same in the Topic field. Update the name to Receive MQTT Messages, as shown in Figure 10-28, and click OK to save the changes.

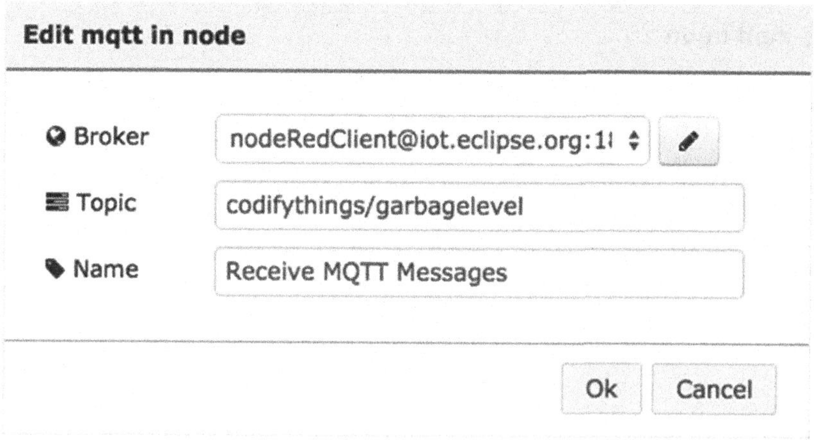
Edit mqtt in node
Broker
nodeRedClient@iot.eclipse.org:1
Topic
codifythings/garbagelevel
Name
Receive MQTT Messages
Ok
Cancel

Figure 10-28. *MQTT broker topic*

Drag and drop an `email` node from the social palette and place it in the flow tab after the `Receive MQTT Messages` node. Your flow should look similar to Figure 10-29 at this point.

Receive MQTT Messages
email

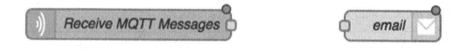

Figure 10-29. *Email node*

An `email` node lets you send an e-mail message to the provided address. Double-click the `email` node to open the properties dialog box shown in Figure 10-30.

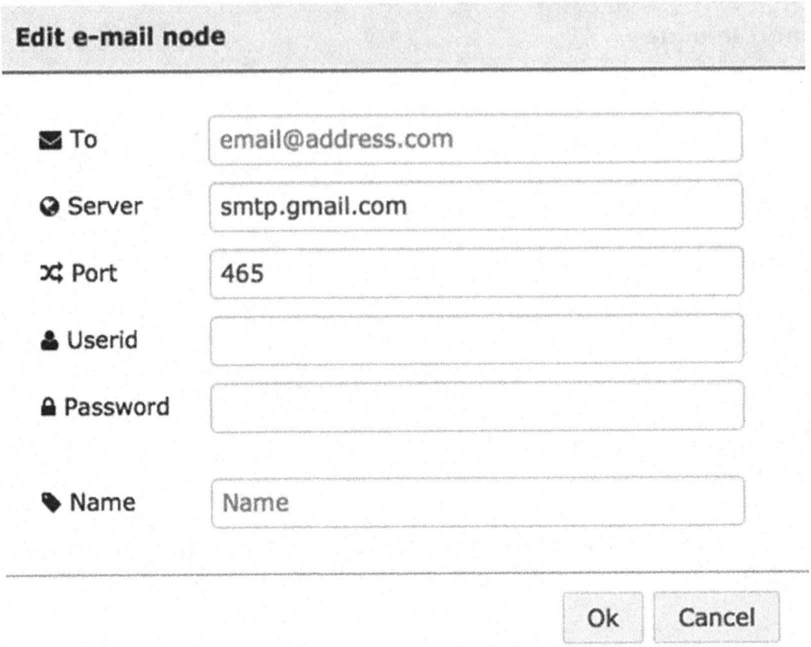

Edit e-mail node

✉ To   email@address.com

🌐 Server   smtp.gmail.com

⤫ Port   465

👤 Userid

🔒 Password

🏷 Name   Name

Ok   Cancel

Figure 10-30. E-mail node properties

Update the email node properties as shown in Figure 10-31. In the To field, enter the e-mail address that was auto-generated by Effketif BPM. In the Server, Port, Userid, and Password fields, provide information about the the SMTP server that Node-RED can use to send this e-mail. By default, the email node has Gmail properties. Update the Name to Send Email/Start New Process option. Click OK to save your changes.

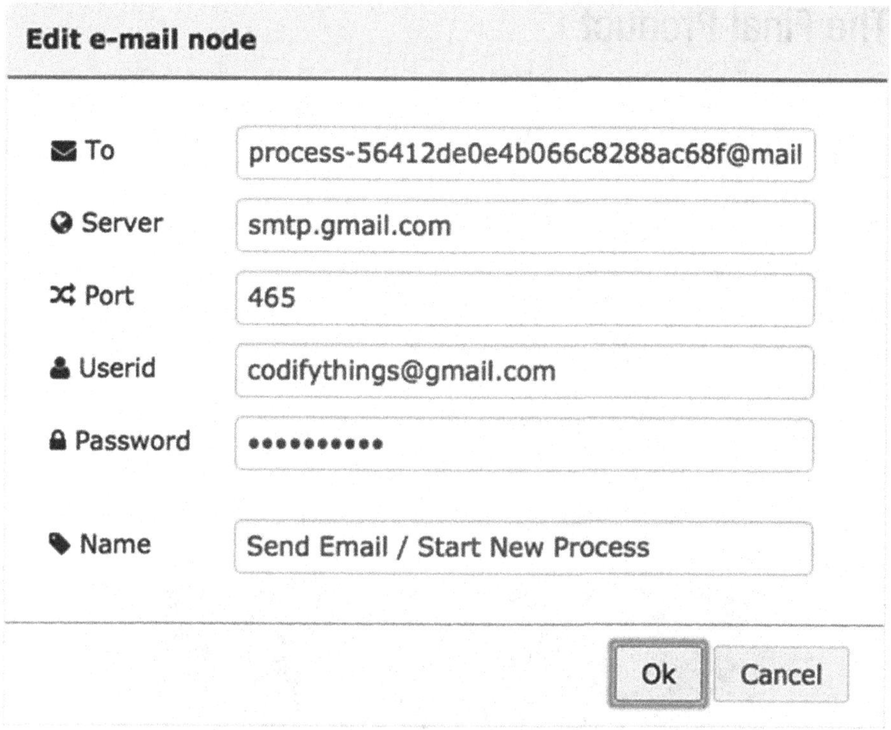
Edit e-mail node
To
process-56412de0e4b066c8288ac68f@mail
Server
smtp.gmail.com
Port
465
Userid
codifythings@gmail.com
Password
••••••••••
Name
Send Email / Start New Process
Ok
Cancel

Figure 10-31. *Updated email node properties*

You have added all the required nodes, so you can now connect the `Receive MQTT Messages` node to the `Send Email/Start New Process` node. This completes your Node-RED flow and it should look similar to Figure 10-32. Click on the Deploy button to make this flow available.

Receive MQTT Messages
Send Email / Start New Process

Figure 10-32. *Final Node-RED flow*

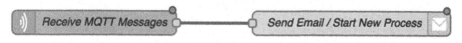

The Final Product

To test the application, verify and upload the Arduino code as discussed in Chapter 1. Place your proximity sensor on top of a trash can or an empty cardboard box, as shown in Figures 10-33 and 10-34. Make sure there is no garbage in the can initially.

Figure 10-33. *Circuit of the waste management system*

Figure 10-34. *Close-up of the waste management system circuit*

Once the code has been uploaded, open the Serial Monitor window. You will start seeing log messages similar to ones shown in Figure 10-35.

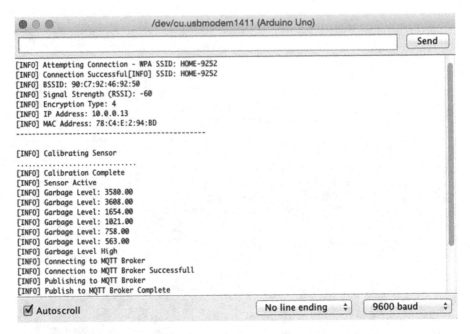

Figure 10-35. *Log messages from the waste management system*

Your Node-RED server should be up and running and the waste management system flow should be deployed. The final component is the Effektif process, and you should have already published that in previous steps.

Start adding stuff to your garbage can/box, and as soon as it reaches a certain level (set at 700 in Arduino code), a message will be published to the MQTT broker. Your Node-RED flow is listening to the MQTT broker for new messages and, as soon as it receives a new one, an e-mail will be sent out that starts the Effektif process. Log in to Effektif using your credentials and, as shown in Figure 10-36, you should see a new task for the Schedule Garbage Pickup process available under the Tasks tab.

Figure 10-36. *New task available in Effektif*

Click on the task link to see the details. As you can see in Figure 10-37, Title contains the MQTT topic name and Description contains the message that was sent by Arduino. Enter a pickup date/time and click Done. This will complete the process and the task will be removed from your Tasks list.

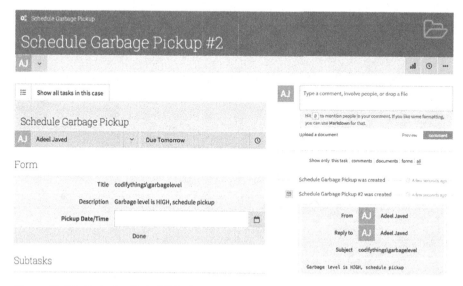

Figure 10-37. Task details in Effektif

This completes the end-to-end testing of this project.

Summary

In this chapter, you learned about the IoT pattern that will be used when a human response is required to device generated alerts.

The project you developed was one example where Arduino sends alerts and a process is started in response to them.

Initiating a process is just one way to respond. Processes provide you with a more streamlined and structured response, but depending on the requirement, you can always use e-mail, SMS, etc.

Due to regulatory requirements or lack of response technology, human intervention will continue to be a requirement for some IoT applications. As IoT progresses, the amount of human intervention will be reduced as well.

CHAPTER 11

IoT Patterns: Machine to Machine

As IoT technology evolves and machines become smarter and more capable, the need for human intervention will reduce. Machines will be able to autonomously respond to alerts generated by other machines.

In this chapter, you are going to build an energy conservation system that will show how two machines can communicate. Figure 11-1 shows a high-level diagram of all components involved in this system. The first component is an Arduino device that monitors light brightness levels and sends an alert whenever the levels are low. The second component is an MQTT broker that helps avoid point-to-point communication. Multiple devices can communicate with each other without knowing each other's identities.

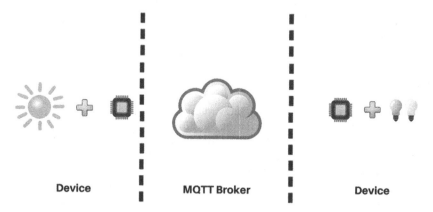

Device   **MQTT Broker**   **Device**

Figure 11-1. Components of an energy conservation system

© Adeel Javed 2016
A. Javed, *Building Arduino Projects for the Internet of Things*,
DOI 10.1007/978-1-4842-1940-9_11

The final component is another Arduino device that controls lights. If the light sensor publishes a message to the MQTT broker that light brightness level is LOW, the device will automatically turn the lights on. In real life, this system could be utilized to turn street lights on or off only when they are required instead of doing it at scheduled times, regardless of how bright it is.

Learning Objectives

At the end of this chapter, you will be able to:

- Read data from a light sensor
- Publish messages to an MQTT broker
- Control LEDs
- Subscribe Arduino to an MQTT broker

Light Sensor Device

The first component of your IoT application is an Arduino device that will monitor the light brightness levels and publish a message when they are low.

■ **Note** You already built this circuit in Chapter 4, so for the hardware and software requirements and circuit instructions, refer back to Chapter 4. Changes are in Arduino code only, which in this case publishes a message to an MQTT broker instead of starting a Node-RED flow.

Code (Arduino)

Next you are going to write code for connecting Arduino to the Internet using WiFi, reading light sensor data, and publishing it to an MQTT broker.

Start your Arduino IDE and type the code provided here or download it from the site and open it. All the code goes into a single source file (*.ino), but in order to make it easy to understand and reuse, it has been divided into five sections:

- External libraries
- Internet connectivity (WiFi)
- Read sensor data
- MQTT (publish)
- Standard functions

External Libraries

The first section of the code, as provided in Listing 11-1, includes all the external libraries required to run the code. This sketch has two main dependencies—for Internet connectivity you need to include <WiFi.h> (assuming you are using a WiFi shield), and for MQTT broker communication, you need to include <PubSubClient.h>.

Listing 11-1. Code for Including External Dependencies

```
#include <SPI.h>
#include <WiFi.h>
#include <PubSubClient.h>
```

Internet Connectivity (Wireless)

The second section of the code defines the variables, constants, and functions that are going to be used for connecting to the Internet. Use the code from Listings 2-7, 2-8, and 2-9 (in Chapter 2) here.

Read Sensor Data

The third section of code, as provided in Listing 11-2, defines the variables, constants, and functions that are going to be used for reading the sensor data.

The readSensorData() function reads the data from Analog Pin A0; the result is between 0 and 1023. The greater the value returned, the brighter the light source. The light sensor value is assigned to the lightValue variable. Based on the lightValue variable, the corresponding LOW or HIGH value is passed as a parameter to the publishSensorData() function.

Listing 11-2. Code for Reading the Light Sensor Data

```
int lightValue;

void readSensorData()
{
  //Read Light Sensor Value
  lightValue = analogRead(A0);

  Serial.print("[INFO] Light Sensor Reading: ");
  Serial.println(lightValue);

  if(lightValue < 500)
  {
    publishSensorData("LOW");
  }
```

```
else
{
  publishSensorData("HIGH");
}
Serial.println("---------------------------------------------------");
}
```

Data Publish

The fourth section of the code defines the variables, constants, and functions that are going to be used for publishing data to an MQTT broker (for details, see Chapter 3).

This code is similar to what you saw in Chapter 3. There are a few changes that you need to make. All the changes are highlighted in bold in Listing 11-3. Make sure to change the server, port, and topic variables and the name of client that you need to pass while connecting to the MQTT broker. The other main change includes an IF/ELSE condition that publishes different messages based on the lightLevel parameter passed by the readSensorData() function.

Listing 11-3. Code for Publishing an MQTT Message

```
// IP address of the MQTT broker
char server[] = {"iot.eclipse.org"};
int port = 1883;
char topic[] = {"codifythings/lightlevel"};

void callback(char* topic, byte* payload, unsigned int length)
{
  //Handle message arrived
}

PubSubClient pubSubClient(server, port, 0, client);

void publishSensorData(String lightLevel)
{
  // Connect MQTT Broker
  Serial.println("[INFO] Connecting to MQTT Broker");

  if (pubSubClient.connect("arduinoIoTClient"))
  {
    Serial.println("[INFO] Connection to MQTT Broker Successful");
  }
  else
  {
    Serial.println("[INFO] Connection to MQTT Broker Failed");
  }
```

```
// Publish to MQTT Topic
if (pubSubClient.connected())
{
  Serial.println("[INFO] Publishing to MQTT Broker");
  if(lightLevel == "LOW")
  {
    Serial.println("[INFO] Light Level is LOW");
    pubSubClient.publish(topic, "LOW");
  }
  else
  {
    Serial.println("[INFO] Light Level is HIGH");
    pubSubClient.publish(topic, "HIGH");
  }

  Serial.println("[INFO] Publish to MQTT Broker Complete");
}
else
{
  Serial.println("[ERROR] Publish to MQTT Broker Failed");
}

pubSubClient.disconnect();

}
```

Standard Functions

The final section is provided in Listing 11-4. It implements Arduino's standard setup() and loop() functions.

The setup() function initializes the serial port and connects to the Internet. The loop() function calls readSensorData() only, as it internally calls the publishSensorData() function when light levels are low.

Listing 11-4. Code for Standard Arduino Functions

```
void setup()
{
  // Initialize serial port
  Serial.begin(9600);

  // Connect Arduino to internet
  connectToInternet();
}
```

```
void loop()
{
  // Read sensor data
  readSensorData();

  // Delay
  delay(5000);
}
```

Your Arduino code for the light sensor device is now complete.

Lighting Control Device

The other component of your IoT application is an Arduino device that will the control lights—it will turn them on or off depending on the messages received from the MQTT broker. The circuit and code for this device is basically the same as the circuit and device that you developed in Chapter 6.

■ **Note**   You already built this circuit in Chapter 6, so for hardware and software requirements and circuit instructions, refer to Chapter 6. Changes are in Arduino code only, which in this case uses a different logic to publish a message to MQTT broker.

Code (Arduino)

Next you are going to write code for connecting Arduino to the Internet using WiFi, subscribing to an MQTT broker, and controlling the attached LED.

Start your Arduino IDE and type the code provided here or download it from the site and open it. All the code goes into a single source file (*.ino), but in order to make it easy to understand and reuse, it has been divided into five sections:

- External libraries
- Internet connectivity (WiFi)
- MQTT (subscribe)
- Control LED
- Standard functions

External Libraries

The first section of code, as provided in Listing 11-5, includes all the external libraries required to run the code. This sketch has two main dependencies—for Internet connectivity you need to include <WiFi.h> (assuming you are using a WiFi shield) and for the MQTT broker communication, you need to include <PubSubClient.h>.

Listing 11-5. Code for Including External Dependencies

```
#include <SPI.h>
#include <WiFi.h>
#include <PubSubClient.h>
```

Internet Connectivity (Wireless)

The second section of the code defines the variables, constants, and functions that are going to be used for connecting to the Internet. Use the code from Listings 2-7, 2-8, and 2-9 (in Chapter 2) here.

Data Subscribe

The third section of code defines the variables, constants, and functions that are going to be used for connecting to an MQTT broker and callback when a new message arrives (for details, see Chapter 3).

This code is similar to what you saw in Chapter 3. There are only few changes that you need to make for the code to work. All changes have been highlighted in bold in Listing 11-6. Make sure to change the server, port, and topic variable values to your MQTT server's values.

Whenever a new message is received, the callback(...) function is called. It extracts the payload and calls the turnLightsOnOff() function. One addition to this code is the IF/ELSE condition, which checks for the value of the payloadContent and if it is LOW, sends ON as the parameter to the turnLightsOnOff(...) function. Otherwise, OFF is sent as the parameter.

Listing 11-6. Code for Subscribing to an MQTT Broker

```
// IP address of the MQTT broker
char server[] = {"iot.eclipse.org"};
int port = 1883;
char topic[] = {"codifythings/lightlevel"};

PubSubClient pubSubClient(server, port, callback, client);

void callback(char* topic, byte* payload, unsigned int length)
{
  // Print payload
  String payloadContent = String((char *)payload);
  Serial.println("[INFO] Payload: " + payloadContent);

  if(payloadContent.substring(0,3) == "LOW")
  {
    // Turn lights on/off
    turnLightsOnOff("ON");
  }
```

```
  else
  {
    // Turn lights on/off
    turnLightsOnOff("OFF");
  }
}
```

Control Lights

The fourth section of code, as provided in Listing 11-7, defines the variables, constants, and functions that are going to be used for controlling the LED.

This code switches the state of the LED based on the value of the action parameter.

Listing 11-7. Code for Controlling the LED

```
int ledPin = 3;

void turnLightsOnOff(String action)
{
  // Check if lights are currently on or off
  if(action == "ON")
  {
    //Turn lights on
    Serial.println("[INFO] Turning lights on");
    digitalWrite(ledPin, HIGH);
  }
  else
  {
    // Turn lights off
    Serial.println("[INFO] Turning lights off");
    digitalWrite(ledPin, LOW);
  }
}
```

Standard Functions

The final code section is provided in Listing 11-8. It implements Arduino's standard setup() and loop() functions.

The setup() function initializes the serial port, connects to the internet, and subscribes to the MQTT topic.

The MQTT broker has already been initialized and subscribed, so in loop() function, you only need to wait for new messages from the MQTT broker.

Listing 11-8. Code for Standard Arduino Functions

```
void setup()
{
  // Initialize serial port
  Serial.begin(9600);

  // Connect Arduino to internet
  connectToInternet();

  // Set LED pin mode
  pinMode(ledPin, OUTPUT);

  //Connect MQTT Broker
  Serial.println("[INFO] Connecting to MQTT Broker");
  if (pubSubClient.connect("arduinoClient"))
  {
    Serial.println("[INFO] Connection to MQTT Broker Successful");
    pubSubClient.subscribe(topic);
  }
  else
  {
    Serial.println("[INFO] Connection to MQTT Broker Failed");
  }
}

void loop()
{
  // Wait for messages from MQTT broker
  pubSubClient.loop();
}
```

Your Arduino code for the lighting control device is now complete.

The Final Product

To test the application, make sure both your devices—the light sensor device and the lighting control device—are powered on and the code has already been deployed (see Chapter 1 for the deployment process).

Open the Serial Monitor window for both of your devices. Figure 11-2 shows the Serial Monitor window with log messages generated from the light sensor device. As soon as you move this device from bright light to a dark area, it will publish a message to the MQTT broker.

```
●  ●  ●              /dev/cu.usbmodem1411 (Arduino Uno)

[                                                      ]   Send

---------------------------------------------------
[INFO] Light Sensor Reading: 1023
[INFO] Connecting to MQTT Broker
[INFO] Connection to MQTT Broker Successfull
[INFO] Publishing to MQTT Broker
[INFO] Light Level is HIGH
[INFO] Publish to MQTT Broker Complete
---------------------------------------------------
[INFO] Light Sensor Reading: 280
[INFO] Connecting to MQTT Broker
[INFO] Connection to MQTT Broker Successfull
[INFO] Publishing to MQTT Broker
[INFO] Light Level is LOW
[INFO] Publish to MQTT Broker Complete
---------------------------------------------------
[INFO] Light Sensor Reading: 311
[INFO] Connecting to MQTT Broker
[INFO] Connection to MQTT Broker Successfull
[INFO] Publishing to MQTT Broker
[INFO] Light Level is LOW
[INFO] Publish to MQTT Broker Complete
---------------------------------------------------

☐ Autoscroll        No line ending  ▲▼    9600 baud  ▲▼
```

Figure 11-2. *Log messages from the light sensor device*

Figure 11-3 shows the Serial Monitor window with log messages generated from the lighting control device. As soon as the light sensor device publishes a message, the lighting control device will turn the LED ON. If you move the light sensor device back into a brighter area, the lighting control device will turn the LED OFF.

```
●  ●  ●              /dev/cu.usbmodem1411 (Arduino Uno)

[                                                      ]   Send

[INFO] Attempting Connection - WPA SSID: HOME-9252
[INFO] Connection Successful[INFO] SSID: HOME-9252
[INFO] BSSID: 90:C7:92:46:92:50
[INFO] Signal Strength (RSSI): -51
[INFO] Encryption Type: 4
[INFO] IP Address: 10.0.0.13
[INFO] MAC Address: 78:C4:E:2:94:BD
---------------------------------------------------

[INFO] Connecting to MQTT Broker
[INFO] Connection to MQTT Broker Successfull
[INFO] Payload: LOWel
[INFO] Turning lights on
[INFO] Payload: HIGHl
[INFO] Turning lights off

☐ Autoscroll        No line ending  ▲▼    9600 baud  ▲▼
```

Figure 11-3. *Log messages from the lighting control device*

Summary

In this chapter you learned how to make multiple devices communicate with each other using an MQTT broker. Brokers such as MQTT remove the need for direct communication. A device publishes a message that can be received by all devices or systems that are interested in that message and respond accordingly. The machine-to-machine pattern definitely provides maximum benefits in the IoT space. The next frontier within this area is of course developing AI (artificial intelligence) devices that can learn and adapt to an ever-changing environment.

CHAPTER 12

IoT Platforms

IoT platforms provide developers with the ability to develop, deploy, and manage their IoT applications from one central location in a secure manner. IoT platforms expedite the development process by providing required tools in a cloud-based environment, which means developers do not spend time on setups. A good IoT platform would ideally include most of the tools that we have covered in the previous 11 chapters, such as MQTT brokers, HTTP servers, REST API support, databases to store sensor data, Node-RED for complex orchestrations, device location, secure communications, reporting, analytics, and easy-to-use tools for building web and mobile apps.

This chapter covers a popular IoT platform called Xively. You are going to build a soil moisture control system that sends out an e-mail alert whenever the moisture level of the soil falls below a certain threshold. Figure 12-1 shows a high-level diagram of all components involved in this system. The first component is an Arduino device that monitors the soil moisture level and publishes a message to Xively. The second and third components reside on the Xively platform. With some basic configuration, the platform will be able to receive, store, and display data sent by the sensor.

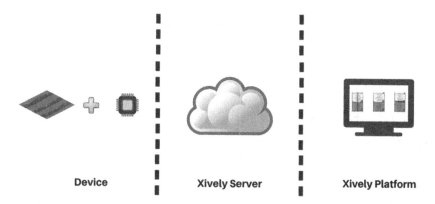

Device   **Xively Server**   **Xively Platform**

Figure 12-1. *Components of the soil moisture control system*

© Adeel Javed 2016
A. Javed, *Building Arduino Projects for the Internet of Things*,
DOI 10.1007/978-1-4842-1940-9_12

Learning Objectives

At the end of this chapter, you will be able to:

- Read soil moisture sensor data

- Set up Xively to receive moisture sensor data

- Set up a trigger in Xively to send an e-mail using a Zapier task

- Write code to read the moisture sensor data and publish it to Xively

Hardware Required

Figure 12-2 provides a list of all hardware components required for building the soil moisture control system.

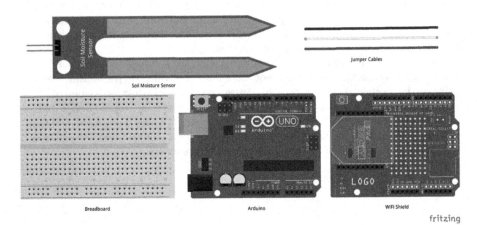

Figure 12-2. Hardware required for the soil moisture control system

Software Required

In order to develop this soil moisture control system, you need following software:

- Arduino IDE 1.6.4 or later
- Xively (hosted)
- Zapier (hosted)

Circuit

In this section, you are going to build the circuit required for the soil moisture control system. This circuit uses a soil moisture sensor to detect the amount of moisture in the soil.

1. Make sure your Arduino is not connected to a power source, such as to a computer via a USB or a battery.

2. Attach a WiFi shield to the top of the Arduino.

3. Use jumper cables to connect the power (5V) and ground (GND) ports on Arduino to the power (+) and ground (-) ports on the breadboard.

4. Now that your breadboard has a power source, use jumper cables to connect the power (+) and ground (-) ports of your breadboard to the power and ground ports of the moisture sensor.

5. To read the moisture sensor values, you need to connect a jumper cable from the analog port of the moisture sensor to the A0 (Analog) port of your Arduino. Your code will read the moisture level from this port. The sensor returns a value between 0 and 1023. Higher values correspond to lower soil moisture levels.

Your circuit is now complete and should look similar to Figures 12-3 and 12-4.

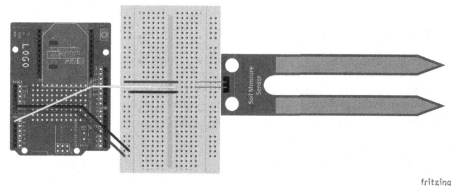

fritzing

Figure 12-3. *Circuit diagram of the soil moisture control system*

Figure 12-4. Actual circuit of the soil moisture control system

Xively Setup

As mentioned earlier, Xively is a popular IoT platform. To use Xively, you first need to set up a free account at `https://personal.xively.com/`.

Once your account is setup, log in to Xively. Upon login, you will be redirected to your account dashboard. Click on DEVELOP from the menu bar on top, as shown in Figure 12-5.

xively   DEVELOP   MANAGE   SETTINGS   DEVELOPER CENTER ▾   LOGOUT   Q ▾   👤 processramablings

Figure 12-5. Xively account dashboard

Add a new development device, as shown in Figure 12-6, by clicking on the + Add Device link.

‹› **Development Devices**

Prototype, experiment, research. more

Figure 12-6. *Add a new development device*

On the device setup screen, enter a device name and device description, as provided in Figure 12-7. Keep the privacy of your device set to Private Device. Click on Add Device to complete this step.

‹› **Add Device**

The Xively Developer Workbench will help you to get your devices, applications and services talking to each other through Xively. The first step is to create a development device. Begin by providing some basic information:

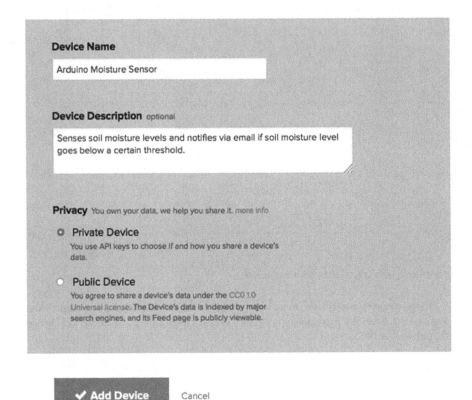

Device Name

Arduino Moisture Sensor

Device Description optional

Senses soil moisture levels and notifies via email if soil moisture level goes below a certain threshold.

Privacy You own your data, we help you share it. more info

○ Private Device
You use API keys to choose if and how you share a device's data.

○ Public Device
You agree to share a device's data under the CC0 1.0 Universal license. The Device's data is indexed by major search engines, and its Feed page is publicly viewable.

✔ **Add Device**   Cancel

Figure 12-7. *Device setup*

Xively will automatically generate a unique API key and a Feed ID, and both of these are required in the Arduino code. You can find the Feed ID on top-right side of the dashboard (see Figure 12-8).

Figure 12-8. *Feed ID*

As mentioned earlier, Xively automatically generates an API key, but you have the option to add your own key as well. In this project you are going to use the auto-generated API key. You can locate the API key in the API Keys section of the dashboard (see Figure 12-9).

API Keys

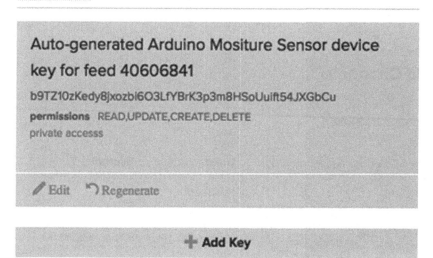

Figure 12-9. *API keys (auto-generated and custom-generated)*

Next you are going to create a channel. A *channel* will map directly to a sensor, that is, data from a sensor will be received and stored by a channel. As shown in Figure 12-10, click on the Add Channel button from the Channels section.

259

Channels Last updated a few seconds ago   *N* Graphs

+ Add Channel

Figure 12-10. Add channel

Enter the values of your channel, as shown in Figure 12-11. Channel ID is the only required field, and as you will see in later sections, it is also used in the Arduino code for sending sensor data. If you have multiple channels, then Tags will help you search. The Units and Symbol fields will be used while displaying data. Current Value is also used while displaying data as your graph starts from this point. Click on Save Channel to complete the channel's setup.

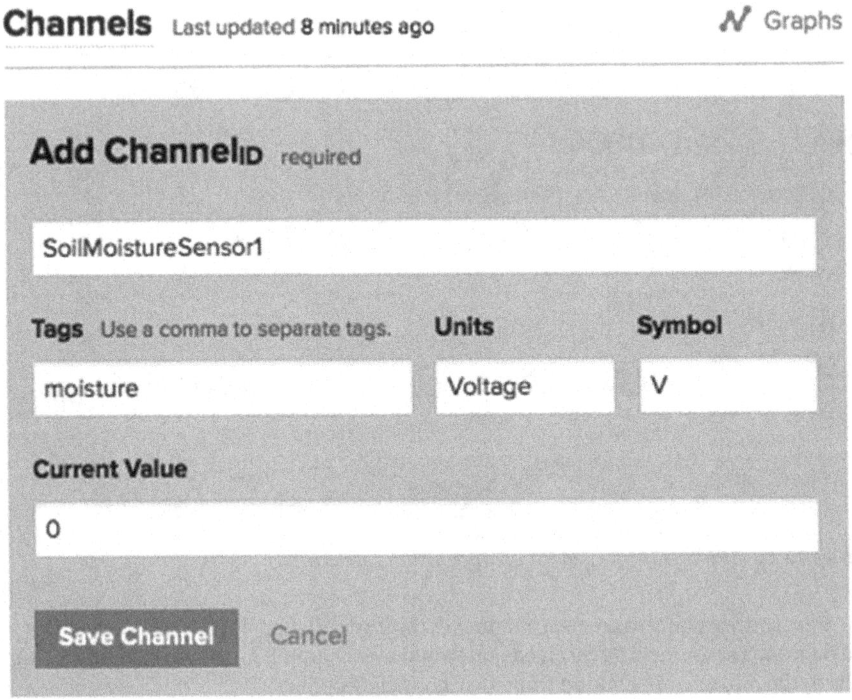

Channels Last updated 8 minutes ago   *N* Graphs

Add Channel ID required

SoilMoistureSensor1

Tags Use a comma to separate tags.   **Units**   **Symbol**

| moisture | Voltage | V |

Current Value

0

Save Channel   Cancel

Figure 12-11. New channel setup

Once you save your channel settings, Xively is ready to receive the sensor data. Figure 12-12 shows the section where each sensor's data will be displayed.

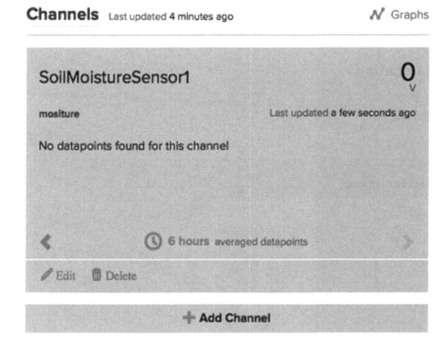

Channels Last updated 4 minutes ago $\mathcal{N}$ Graphs

Figure 12-12. SoilMoistureSensor1 channel

If the location of the device is important, you can set that from the Location section as well, as shown in Figure 12-13. In this project, you are not going to be changing it from code, so this will be just static that will show up on the dashboard.

Location

 Add location

Figure 12-13. Add location

Click on Add Location and, as shown in Figure 12-14, enter the location name and address where your sensor is physically located. Location data is always useful for maintenance purposes. Click Save.

Location

Figure 12-14. Set device location

Figure 12-15 shows how the location information will be displayed on the dashboard.

Location

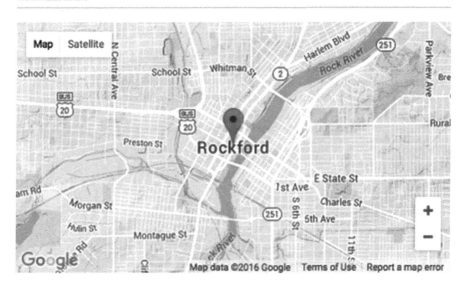

Location Name Corn Field 1

Latitude   42.2711311
Longitude   -89.0939952
Elevation

Figure 12-15. *Device location*

For now, there are no more setups needed in Xively.

Zapier Setup

Xively supports triggering external tasks; for example, if the value of a channel crosses a certain threshold, you can execute your own task. Xively uses HTTP POST to trigger an external task. All the data will be submitted to the recipient using the HTTP POST method (see Chapter 3 for more details about HTTP POST).

Xively data is available over HTTP and can be used for developing custom dashboards and generating alerts. A few of the IoT applications that you developed in Chapters 7, 8, and 9 had HTTP components. You will lose advantage of using an IoT platform if you end up writing custom code. For generating triggers in Xively, you can avoid all the coding by simply using a Zapier task. Zapier is a web-based tool that lets you automate if/then tasks. You create a task (a.k.a., a Zap) that requires a trigger and a corresponding action.

■ **Note**   You can also trigger a Zapier task from Arduino using the HTTP POST method discussed in Chapter 3.

To set up a Zap, you first need to set up a free Zapier account. Once you have completed account setup process, log in to Zapier at https://zapier.com/. Upon login, you will be redirected to your account dashboard. As shown in Figure 12-16, under the My Zaps tab, click on the Make a New Zap button to start the Zap creation process.

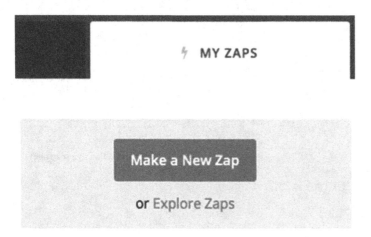

Figure 12-16. *My Zaps (list of all zaps)*

As shown in Figure 12-17, Step 1 requires you to choose a Trigger app and an Action app.

Figure 12-17. *Select Zap trigger and action*

Select Webhooks by Zapier from the Trigger app dropdown and select Catch Hook from the dropdown below it. This tells Zapier that whenever a certain URL is called, this Zap will be triggered. You will see the generated URL later. Figure 12-18 shows the trigger selection.

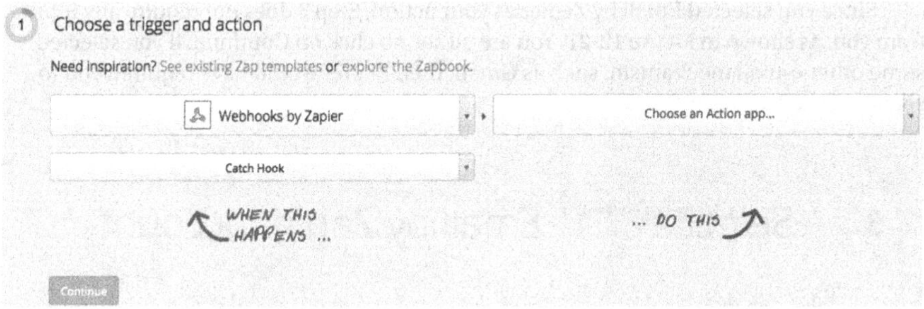

Figure 12-18. *Zap trigger*

You have to send out an e-mail when this task is called, so from Action app dropdown, select Email by Zapier and select Send Outbound Email from the dropdown below it, as shown in Figure 12-19.

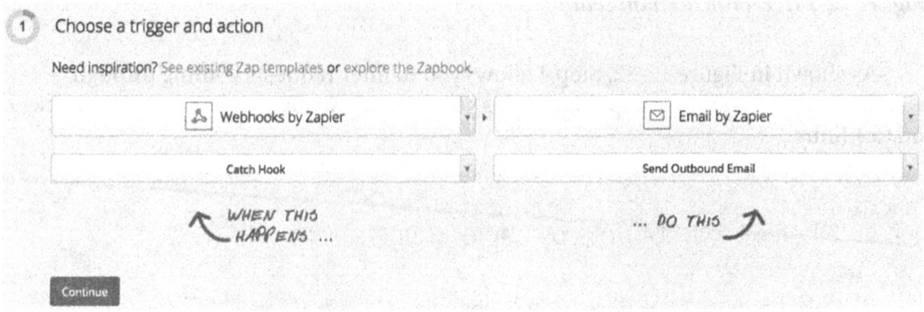

Figure 12-19. *Zap action*

In Step 2, Zapier will generate a custom webhook URL that Xively will call. Figure 12-20 shows the custom webhook URL generated by Zapier. Click Continue to proceed to the next step.

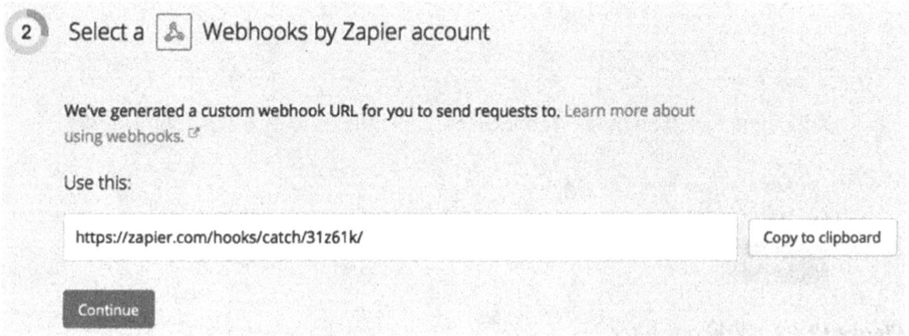

Figure 12-20. *Custom webhook URL*

265

Since you selected Email by Zapier as your action, Step 3 does not require any input from you, as shown in Figure 12-21. You are all set, so click on Continue. If you selected some other e-mail mechanism, such as Gmail, then Zapier would have required you to set up a Gmail account.

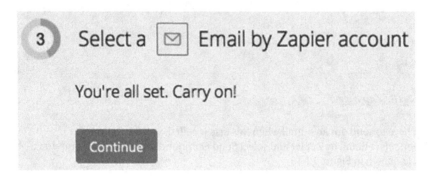

Figure 12-21. *E-mail account setup*

As shown in Figure 12-22, Step 4 allows you to filter requests coming through webhook. You can simply skip this step, as you want all Xively requests to come. Click on Continue.

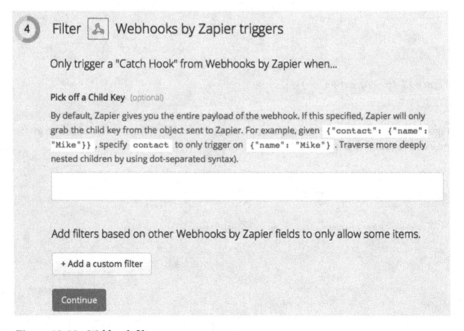

Figure 12-22. *Webhook filter*

In Step 5, you need to provide details about the e-mail alert, such as who it should go to, what should be the subject, and what should be the body text. When Xively calls the webhook URL, it will send some data in an HTTP POST request as well. You can use that data in Zapier wherever you see the Insert Fields option. Figure 12-23 shows the e-mail settings.

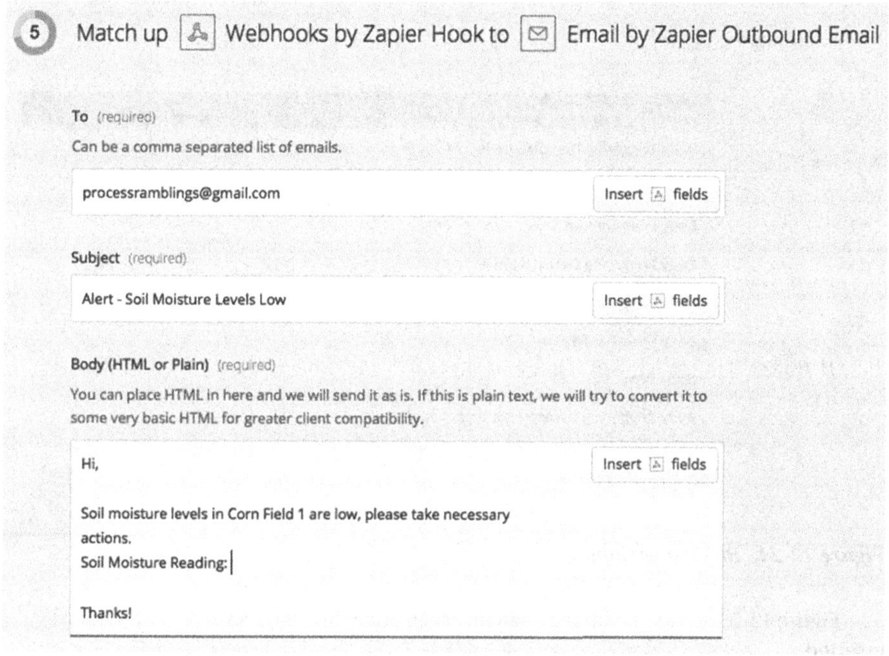

Figure 12-23. E-mail settings

For illustration purposes, this project uses the moisture sensor value and inserts it into the e-mail body. As shown in Figure 12-24, when you click on the Insert Fields button, it will show a list of all the variables that can be inserted. Initially, you might not see any data, so you can come back to this step after the Xively trigger has been set up and you have sent a couple of test requests. Zapier will automatically start showing a list of all the request variables.

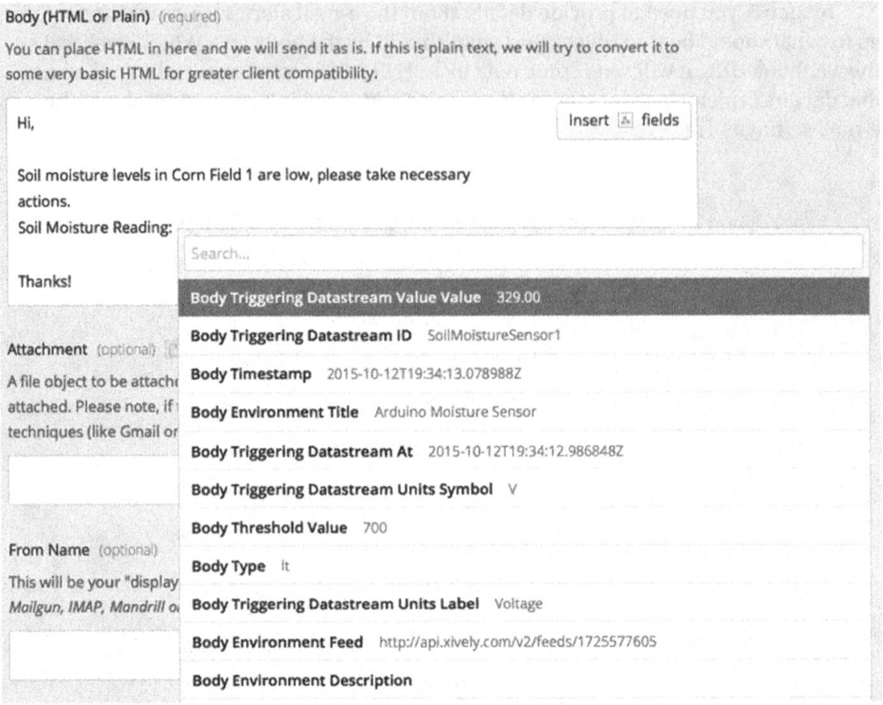

Figure 12-24. *Request variables*

Figure 12-25 shows the final e-mail message once the request variable has been inserted.

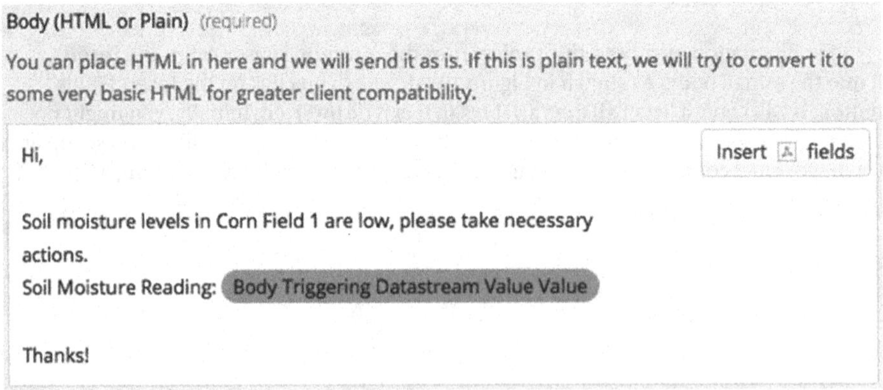

Figure 12-25. *E-mail body with request variable*

You can skip Step 6, and in Step 7 enter a name for Zap. Click Turn Zap On as shown in Figure 12-26.

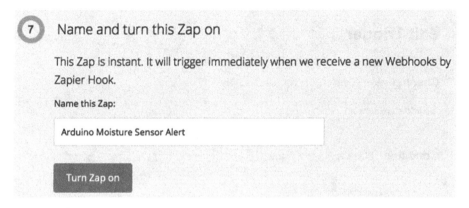

Figure 12-26. *Zap name and turn Zap on*

This completes the setup in Zapier. Now you just need to set up a trigger in Xively that will call the custom webhook URL generated by Zapier.

Xively Trigger

Log in to Xively and go to the Triggers section of device setup. Click on the Add Trigger button. As shown in Figure 12-27, select a condition when trigger should be fired; in this case it is IF `SoilMoistureSensor1 > 850` THEN CALL HTTP POST URL. In the HTTP POST URL field, paste the custom webhook URL that was generated by Zapier. Click Save Trigger to enable the trigger.

269

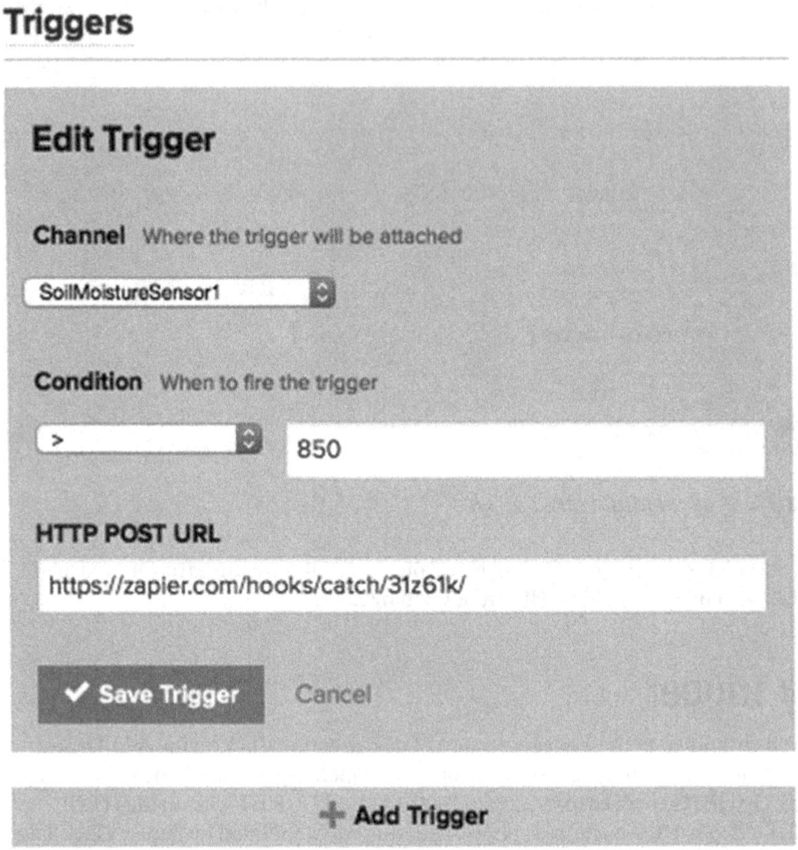

Triggers

Figure 12-27. *Xively trigger setup*

As shown in Figure 12-28, you can quickly test your trigger by clicking on Send Test Trigger. It calls the custom webhook URL that you provided in the HTTP POST URL field.

Triggers

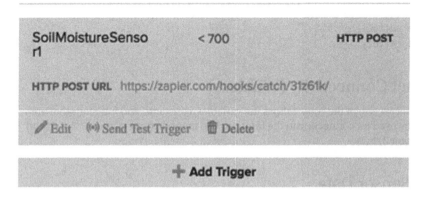

Figure 12-28. *Test trigger*

Code (Arduino)

Next you are going to write the code for connecting Arduino to the Internet using WiFi, reading soil moisture sensor data, and publishing it to a Xively channel.

Start your Arduino IDE and type the code provided here or download it from the site and open it. All the code goes into a single source file (*.ino), but in order to make it easy to understand and reuse, it has been divided into five sections.

- External libraries

- Internet connectivity (WiFi)

- Read sensor data

- Xively (publish)

- Standard functions

External Libraries

The first section of code, as provided in Listing 12-1, includes all the external libraries required to run the code. This sketch has multiple dependencies—for Internet connectivity you need to include the <WiFi.h> (assuming you are using a WiFi shield) and for Xively connectivity, you need to include <HttpClient.h> and <Xively.h>. You can download <Xively.h> from https://github.com/xively/xively_arduino.

271

Listing 12-1. Code for Including External Dependencies

```
#include <SPI.h>
#include <WiFi.h>
#include <HttpClient.h>;
#include <Xively.h>;
```

Internet Connectivity (Wireless)

The second section of the code defines the variables, constants, and functions that are going to be used for connecting to the Internet. Use the code from Listings 2-7, 2-8, and 2-9 (Chapter 2) here.

Read Sensor Data

The third section of the code is provided in Listing 12-2. It defines the variables, constants, and functions that are going to be used for reading the sensor data.

The readSensorData() function reads data from Analog Pin A0 and the result is between 0 and 1023. Higher values correspond to lower soil moisture levels.

Listing 12-2. Code for Reading Soil Moisture Sensor Value

```
int MOISTURE_SENSOR_PIN = A0;
float moistureSensorValue = 0.0;

void readSensorData()
{
  //Read Moisture Sensor Value
  moistureSensorValue = analogRead(MOISTURE_SENSOR_PIN);

  //Display Readings
  Serial.print("[INFO] Moisture Sensor Reading: ");
  Serial.println(moistureSensorValue);
}
```

Data Publish

The fourth section of the code defines the variables, constants, and functions that are going to be used for publishing sensor data to the Xively channel.

In order to communicate with Xively, you need to provide the Feed ID and API key that were generated after you completed device setup in Xively. Both of these keys are unique to you. You will also need to provide the exact channel name that you entered in Xively. If the API key or Feed ID are incorrect, your device will not be able to connect with your Xively account, and if the channel name is incorrect, the data will not show up in the correct graph on the Xively dashboard. All these values have been highlighted in the code (see Listing 12-3).

If you have multiple sensors and want to send data to Xively for all of them, you can simply set up multiple channels in Xively. In Arduino code you need to specify the channel name in a similar way that you defined moistureSensorChannel. All these channel names need to be passed to the datastreams array.

The XivelyFeed variable feed passes data for all the channels with a number that specifies how many datastreams are contained in the feed. In this case, there is only one datastream, so the value will be 1.

Next you define a XivelyClient variable using the WiFiClient. It will be used to actually create a connection and pass the feed.

All of these are one time setups and the repetitive code is inside the transmitData() function. The transmitData() function sets the latest moistureSensorValue in datastreams[0] and then sends the feed to Xively. If the status code returned from Xively in the ret variable is 200, that means your feed was successfully sent to Xively.

Listing 12-3. Code for Publishing Data to Xively

```
// API Key - required for data upload
char xivelyKey[] = "YOUR_API_KEY";

#define xivelyFeed FEED_ID // Feed ID

char moistureSensorChannel[] = "SoilMoistureSensor1"; //Channel Name

// Datastream/Channel IDs
XivelyDatastream datastreams[] =
{
  XivelyDatastream(moistureSensorChannel,
                   strlen(moistureSensorChannel),
                   DATASTREAM_FLOAT),
};

// Create Feed
XivelyFeed feed(xivelyFeed, datastreams, 1); // Number of Channels
                                             // in Datastream

XivelyClient xivelyclient(client);

void transmitData()
{
  //Set Xively Datastream
  datastreams[0].setFloat(moistureSensorValue);

  //Transmit Data to Xively
  Serial.println("[INFO] Transmitting Data to Xively");

  int ret = xivelyclient.put(feed, xivelyKey);

  Serial.print("[INFO] Xively Response (xivelyclient.put): ");
```

```
    Serial.println(ret);
    Serial.println("------------------------------------------------");
}
```

Standard Functions

The final code section is provided in Listing 12-4. It implements Arduino's standard setup() and loop() functions.

The setup() function initializes the serial port and connects to the Internet. The loop() function first reads the soil moisture sensor by calling readSensorData() and then transmits these values to Xively in a feed by calling transmitData(). For each iteration, you can add a delay depending on your requirements.

Listing 12-4. Code for Standard Arduino Functions

```
void setup()
{
  // Initialize serial port
  Serial.begin(9600);

  // Connect Arduino to internet
  connectToInternet();
}

void loop()
{
  readSensorData();

  transmitData();

  //Delay
  delay(6000);
}
```

Your Arduino code is now complete.

The Final Product

To test the application, verify and upload the Arduino code as discussed in Chapter 1. Either insert your soil moisture sensor in the dry soil or simply dip it in water as shown in Figure 12-29.

■ **Note**   Do not fully submerge the circuit or sensor in water or soil. Make sure the wiring does not get wet. For exact instructions about your soil moisture sensor, read the manufacturer's product specifications and directions.

Figure 12-29. *Final circuit with sensor submerged in water*

Once the code has been uploaded, open the Serial Monitor window. You will start seeing log messages similar to ones shown in Figure 12-30.

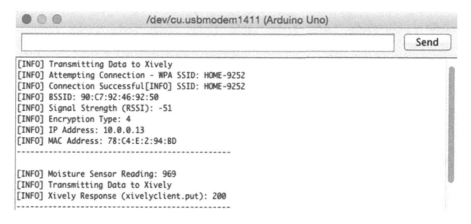

Figure 12-30. *Log messages from the soil moisture control*

275

As soon as you see the Xively response 200 in your serial logs, log in to the Xively dashboard and take a look at the Request Log section, as shown in Figure 12-31. The history of your sensor data feed will start showing up in this section.

Request Log   ❚❚ Pause

200	PUT	feed	19:31:41 UTC
200	PUT	feed	19:31:32 UTC
200	PUT	feed	19:31:23 UTC
200	PUT	feed	19:31:14 UTC
200	PUT	feed	19:30:44 UTC

Figure 12-31. Request log of the soil moisture sensor

Click on any of the requests and you will be able to see the exact request that was sent from the sensor to Xively (see Figure 12-32).

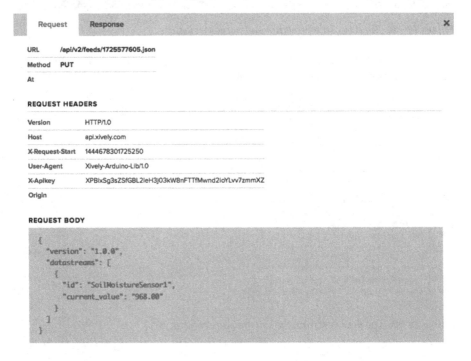

| Request | Response | ✕ |

URL	/api/v2/feeds/1725577605.json
Method	PUT
At	

REQUEST HEADERS

Version	HTTP/1.0
Host	api.xively.com
X-Request-Start	1444678301725250
User-Agent	Xively-Arduino-Lib/1.0
X-Apikey	XPBlxSg3sZSfGBL2leH3jO3kW8nFTTfMwnd2ioYLvv7zmmXZ
Origin	

REQUEST BODY

```
{
  "version": "1.0.0",
  "datastreams": [
    {
      "id": "SoilMoistureSensor1",
      "current_value": "968.00"
    }
  ]
}
```

Figure 12-32. Request details

Next take a look at the graph in the Channels section, as shown in Figure 12-33. Your sensor data will start populating a graph over a period of time.

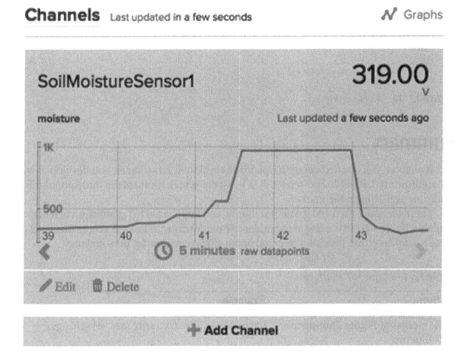

Figure 12-33. *Sensor data view*

Finally, ensure that your Xively trigger sends out an e-mail alert:

- If you were testing the moisture sensor using water, then take the sensor out. The reading should immediately go up, indicating that the moisture levels have dropped. Your Xively trigger will fire and Zapier will send out an e-mail alert.

- Similarly, if you are testing the moisture sensor using actual soil, take your sensor out of the wet soil. This will result in an e-mail alert as well.

Figure 12-34 shows an e-mail alert generated by Xively/Zapier.

Figure 12-34. Alert e-mail

Summary

In this chapter, you learned about IoT platforms and their advantages. You developed an IoT application that published sensor data to Xively, which is one of the more popular IoT platforms available on the market.

There are more than 100 small-, medium-, and large-scale IoT platforms currently available. Table 12-1 lists a few of the major IoT platforms with links to access them. All of these platforms either provide a free trial or cut-down versions for personal use.

Table 12-1. Major IoT Platforms

Platform	Example
IBM Internet of Things Foundation/ IBM Bluemix	`http://www.ibm.com/internet-of-things/`
Intel IoT	`https://software.intel.com/en-us/iot/home`
Microsoft Azure IoT	`https://www.azureiotsuite.com/`
Amazon AWS IoT	`https://aws.amazon.com/iot/`
Thingworx	`http://www.thingworx.com/`
Xively	`https://xively.com/`

There is a lot of material available that can help you determine which one is the best for your needs. IoT platforms are expediting the entry of so many people into the world of IoT. As IoT matures, these platforms are going to become more sophisticated and further simplify IoT application development.

Index

© Adeel Javed 2016
A. Javed, *Building Arduino Projects for the Internet of Things*,
DOI 10.1007/978-1-4842-1940-9

■ T, U, V

■ W

■ X, Y

Get the eBook for only $5!

Why limit yourself?

Now you can take the weightless companion with you wherever you go and access your content on your PC, phone, tablet, or reader.

Since you've purchased this print book, we're happy to offer you the eBook in all 3 formats for just $5.

Convenient and fully searchable, the PDF version enables you to easily find and copy code—or perform examples by quickly toggling between instructions and applications. The MOBI format is ideal for your Kindle, while the ePUB can be utilized on a variety of mobile devices.

To learn more, go to www.apress.com/companion or contact support@apress.com.

Printed in the United States
By Bookmasters